Preliminary Edition Notice

You have been selected to receive a copy of this book in the form of a preliminary edition. A preliminary edition is used in a classroom setting to test the overall value of a book's content and its effectiveness in a practical course prior to its formal publication on the national market.

As you use this text in your course, please share any and all feedback regarding the volume with your professor. Your comments on this text will allow the author to further develop the content of the book, so we can ensure it will be a useful and informative classroom tool for students in universities across the nation and around the globe. If you find the material is challenging to understand, or could be expanded to improve the usefulness of the text, it is important for us to know. If you have any suggestions for improving the material contained in the book or the way it is presented, we encourage you to share your thoughts.

Please note, preliminary editions are similar to review copies, which publishers distribute to select readers prior to publication in order to test a book's audience and elicit early feedback; therefore, you may find inconsistencies in formatting or design, or small textual errors within this volume. Design elements and the written text will undergo changes before this book goes to print and is distributed on the national market.

This text is not available in wide release on the market, as it is actively being prepared for formal publication. This may mean that new content is still being added to the author's manuscript, or that the content appears in a draft format.

If you would like to provide notes directly to the publisher, you may contact us by e-mailing studentreviews@cognella.com. Please include the book's title, author, and 7-digit SKU reference number (found below the barcode on the back cover of the book) in the body of your message.

The Business Communication Workbook

Skills and Strategies for the Working World

Preliminary Second Edition

Written and edited by Emily Carlson Goenner
St. Cloud State University

cognella®
SAN DIEGO

Bassim Hamadeh, CEO and Publisher
Carrie Baarns, Manager, Revisions and Author Care
Kaela Martin, Project Editor
Celeste Paed, Associate Production Editor
Jess Estrella, Senior Graphic Designer
Alexa Lucido, Licensing Manager
Natalie Piccotti, Director of Marketing
Kassie Graves, Senior Vice President, Editorial
Jamie Giganti, Director of Academic Publishing

3970 Sorrento Valley Blvd., Ste. 500, San Diego, CA 92121

Contents

1

Introduction

Why Study Business Communication?

Most students reading this text will be majoring in finance, accounting, marketing, management, or another business area. Many students wonder why business communication is a required or recommended course in the business program, and many feel uncomfortable with the topic. Perhaps they believe themselves to be bad writers or bad at English after negative experiences in high school. Perhaps they, like most Americans, are nervous or uncomfortable giving oral presentations. As you will read below, research consistently demonstrates that to be successful in business, people need to have effective communication skills.

Developing or improving communication skills is often key to getting a job and advancing in the position. People need to know how to present themselves in a professional business environment, how to share their ideas clearly and concisely in effective writing communications, and how to tell bosses, colleagues, and clients about projects, proposals, and developments.

In this book, you will learn a variety of skills to help you succeed in the workforce. This text will follow a consistent format for each section. First, there will be a short introduction to the topic, emphasizing the importance of the topic. Then, one or two articles about the topic, from outside sources, will provide detailed information, opinions, or ideas about the topic. Finally, the chapter will end with one or more Applying this Skill activities for students to complete. Depending on your instructor, you may be requested to complete an activity before class or during class. You will often work with other students in the class to apply information or practice concepts. In the text, these Applying This Skill activities will be clearly labeled, as will Learning Objectives, so you always understand the reason you are being asked to complete an assignment or activity. The text also includes Assignment headings; these assignments are to be completed outside of class.

If an instructor has requested you purchase this text for your business communications course, your instructor is dedicated to creating a classroom environment that may be unusual in many business schools. This text focuses on active learning techniques that you will apply in the classroom; this means you will be practicing and applying the skills you are learning, both individually and in small groups. Most likely, you will be involved in small group discussions, peer review of documents, group brainstorming, short competitions, and learning a portion of information and sharing it with others. Research and surveys of learners consistently reveal most students learn best and retain information most effectively if they practice and apply concepts during the course.

After successful completion of this course, you will be ready to present your best self to the work world, and you—and your company—will avoid embarrassing errors like the one below:

Figure 1.1 Dakotas Typo

Unit I

Foundations

- Chapter 2: Introductions
- Chapter 3: Elements of Written Communication
- Chapter 4: Peer Assessment and Review
- Chapter 5: Effective Writing
- Chapter 6: A Communication Miscellany

In Unit I: Foundations, you will learn some skills that will help you throughout this course and in the world of work. At every beginning, you have to meet and get to know people. So in this text you start with giving and making introductions. Then you will be introduced to the 5 Cs of communication, which are elements you will apply to written and interpersonal communication throughout the course. Next, you will learn how to provide both positive and constructive feedback to others and how to examine a document. You will review your writing skills and learn some stylistic characteristics of business writing that will help you create clear and concise documents throughout the course. Finally, you will evaluate some of your own communication skills and tendencies because understanding yourself is often the first step to successfully communicating with other people. As is true with many textbooks, this one builds upon the basics you learn in the first unit, so understanding these core concepts is vital to your success in the remainder of the course. In addition, a strong foundation is the first step to developing your effective business communication skills.

2

Introductions

Throughout your professional career, you will be introduced to and introduce other people. Each semester as you start new classes, you introduce yourself to the instructor and your fellow students. After college, you'll be new at a job, the new person on a team or at a meeting, or meeting new clients. You will have to introduce yourself and introduce other people, so learning skills to help you do so effectively will help your career.

> After completing this lesson, you will:
>
> o   Understand how to properly introduce yourself and someone else
> o   Know how to network

....

Reading 2.1

Master the Secrets of Networking

Brand You! To Land Your Dream Job

By Diane Huth

Now that you have joined several organizations, you have to show up and participate!

Most organizations have weekly or monthly luncheons, and a couple of evening networking socials throughout the year, in addition to workshops and -seminars. Some groups feature breakfast meetings, others evening dinners or cocktail events. Join organizations that fit into your lifestyle so it will be easy and convenient to attend the events. Attend whenever possible, and actively network with the others in the room.

How I Learned the Secret of Successful Networking

When I moved to San Antonio from Florida fifteen years ago, I knew nobody. I was a recently divorced single woman, and I didn't know a soul. I sat at home for a few months because I didn't know how to connect with other people. Then somebody from my homeowners' association said, "*Hey, there's a big party for a local charity this weekend; here's an invitation."* I decided I had to change my life as I was miserable and alone and lonely, so I made up my mind to go—by myself.

I sat in the car in my evening gown outside the event center, terrified to walk into a room full of hundreds of strangers by myself. I finally got up the nerve, walked in the door, stuck out my hand and said *"Hi, I'm Diane, and I'm a new Texan."* I repeated this -introduction all night long. I met dozens of people, and everyone was friendly and welcoming. I had a wonderful time and I danced until 1:30 in the morning. Then, just the next week, I ran into a couple of those same people at a restaurant, joined them at their table, and they weren't strangers any more. All of a sudden I had a wonderful group of friends. In the years since, it has snowballed until I have a huge personal and online network of friends and business colleagues. If I had not put aside my fear (terror is more like it) and walked into that room full of strangers and started introducing myself, my life would have taken a very different course. Yours will too when you master the art of networking.

How to Work the Room at a Networking Event

The goal at networking events is to network. So don't hang around or sit with your friends or sit at a table full of students from your school or colleagues from your office. Actively seek out new people you don't know, and ask to sit with them.

Force yourself out of your comfort zone and actively seek to meet new people. Shake hands, and say *"Hi, I'm Diane, and I'm brand new here,"* or *"Hi, I'm the PR Chair for this organization and I don't think I have met you before,"* or *"Hi, I belonged to this organization in Houston, but I just moved here and am looking forward to meeting other members like you."* Then, sit at a table of strangers. Always sit at a table with people you don't know, because at the end of the event, they're going to be your friends or at least acquaintances. How are you going to meet people if you don't sit with them and talk to them? You have to force yourself out of your comfort zone and actively reach out to new people.

Master the Art of Shaking Hands

Next you have to master the all-important hand shake. No wimpy finger shakes, ladies, and no crushing of fingers, guys. When you say your name, stick out your right hand, insert your hand securely into the other person's hand thumb-to-thumb and palm-to-palm. Firmly grasp the offered hand, look the person you are greeting in the eye, smile, shake hands 3 times, then release.

To be really sincere or intimate, use the two-hand shake. Look the person in the eye, and grasp the -offered hand firmly with your right hand, and then clasp the back side of the person's hand with your left hand, and shake. Release your left hand first, then release your right hand. I would recommend using this sparingly, as you don't want to be known as a groper, but it can be good for a very special person or relationship.

Wear Your Nametag on Your Right Shoulder

Nametags are essential for networking. Most organizations will have preprinted computer-generated stick-on nametags for networking events. Sometimes you will receive a blank adhesive nametag and a Sharpie pen to write your own name tag. Practice writing an attractive nametag, with your first name large and very visible, and your last name underneath a bit smaller. If you want to add your company name, it should be centered at the bottom in a smaller size printing.

Even better, you can invest $10 or $15 to create your own permanent nametag. If you currently don't have a job, list your profession instead of company—what you aspire to do. For example: Marketing,

Accounting, Human Resources, Writer-Editor, IT, Database Management, Auto Repairs, etc. Don't put your school name if you are still in school. And never put intern, job seeker, or unemployed on anything!

You wear your nametag on your RIGHT shoulder, just below your collarbone, about where you would put your hand to say the pledge of allegiance on the other shoulder. You want your name tag to be seen when you introduce yourself to someone. When you stick out your right hand to shake hands, your right shoulder will roll forward, and your name tag will be clearly visible. When you shake hands, your left shoulder rolls backwards and the person you are meeting can't see your nametag well if it is on the left shoulder.

Manage Giving and Receiving Business Cards

Presenting, accepting, and managing business cards is an art. I keep my business cards in the left pocket of my jacket, always within easy reach. You don't want to be fumbling in your purse or wallet for a card—that's awkward and distracting. When I meet someone I want to give a business card to, I dip my left hand into my left pocket and pull out a card while I am reaching out with my right hand to shake hands. Then I present my card so that it is facing the recipient and not upside down. At that point, the recipient feels obligated to return the gracious gesture, and he gives me one of his cards.

Take the offered card in both hands, read it, say the name, and thank the giver for the card. Then slip it into your RIGHT side pocket. In this way, you aren't fumbling through many cards to find one of yours, and you aren't giving away a card with a hand-written note on the back. Practice this before your next networking event so it comes to you naturally. Remember, your cards in your left pocket, and their cards in your right pocket.

Business card etiquette is very different in different countries and cultures, so study up on the cultural nuances before traveling overseas.

Learn My 3-Person Rule

I have a networking rule cast in stone: every time you go out to an event of any kind, you have to meet and really connect with 3 people. You can't leave until you have spoken one-on-one with 3 people, found out where they work, what they do, what their hobbies are, how long they've belonged to the association or have been attending their events. And you have to exchange business cards—that one with your photo, remember? Three new people should be your mantra.

So every time you network, you don't need to meet everybody. You just have to really meet and get to know just 3 people. It's not overwhelming when you focus on just 3 people. At the end of the year, you will know at least 36 new people well from just one group that meets monthly. Those people will introduce you to their friends to exponentially expand your network. Then all of a sudden you will walk into a room full of friends instead of strangers.

Introduce Yourself Memorably

Most people don't know how to introduce themselves. They say their name as if is just one word. *"Hi, I'm Barbarajacobson."* The person you are meeting can't understand what you just said. They hear *"Hi, I'm Barbara blah blah blah."* You need to put an auditory space between your first and last name so it can be heard, processed, understood and then hopefully remembered. You have to learn that you have a new middle name and it is SPACE. So when you introduce yourself, you say, *"Hi, I'm Barbara (space) Jacobson."* You need to practice it until it flows smoothly and naturally. There's a great TED Talk that demonstrates this: *Want to sound like a leader? Start by saying your name right*—by Laura Sicola of TEDxPenn.

Look for and try to create an auditory prompt so your name is easy to remember. If you have a name with another meaning, try using it as a memory prompt. My friend Brook Carey introduces herself by saying *"Hello, I'm Brook Carey. That's Brook like a babbling brook, and Carey like Drew Carey."* They will remember her name because she created a rich visual image in their mind, and a visual image is stronger than just an auditory message for creating memory. I have an unusual last name, so I introduce myself on the phone as *"Hi, I'm Diane Huth—that's H-U-T-H Huth."* In the past I tried to add, *"It's pronounced Huth—like Ruth."* That was memorable—but everyone remembered *Ruth* instead of *Diane* and called me *Ruth*, so that didn't work out so well. Your challenge is to come up with a clever way to help a stranger remember your name, and practice your introduction until it comes naturally.

It's Important to Remember THEIR Names

You must also remember and repeat the name of the person you just met. Repeat the new person's name at least three times in the first minute after an introduction to help remember his name. Your conversation might go, *"Hi, Steve, it's nice to meet you. Steve, what do you do for a living? Steve, I want to introduce you to my friend Mary. Mary, this is Steve, Steve, this is Mary."* At the end of this exchange, you will probably remember that his name is *"Steve."*

My Secret Name Recall Tip

Remembering someone's name is very important in creating likeability. But sometimes you do forget. Let me share my secret trip for recalling someone's name.

For several years, I headed up both a trade organization and a singles social group, and was on the podium presenting speakers and addressing the audience at events. Many people knew my name, but I didn't know or remember theirs. Like many people, I'm awful at remembering names in the first place, so it was a real challenge for me. I created this technique that will serve you well in your career.

When someone comes up to me and says *"Hi, -Diane, I haven't seen you in ages,"* I don't ask them who they are—that would be an insult. Instead I immediately shake hands and then introduce them to someone whose name I do know. The conversation might go like this: *"I'm great, thanks. I'd love to introduce you to my friend Bob."* Bob politely sticks out his hand and says *"Hi, I'm Bob Jones."* Then the new person introduces herself to Bob, saying, *"Hi, Bob, I'm Barbara Jacobson."* Aha! Now I know her name, and I can say *"Barbara, what have you been up to lately?"*

It's All About Them

When you're talking to people while you are networking, there is one golden rule: *"It's not about you, it's about them."* Being a good conversationalist doesn't mean that you talk in an enchanting or interesting manner about yourself. It means that you LISTEN to them talk about themselves! They don't care about you, quite frankly. They want to talk about themselves and you may have to prompt them to get started.

Ask them about themselves: *"How long have you belonged to this organization?" "What do you do for a living?" "How long have you worked for that company?" "That's an interesting last name—what is the origin?" "What are your biggest challenges in your job today?"* Your challenge is to get them talking about themselves, their company and their interests. As they talk, you nod and give them words or gestures and body language of encouragement or acknowledgement. They're going to think you're fascinating. Ask smart questions. Every time you ask smart questions and they answer, you should acknowledge and affirm what they say with a nod, a smile, an *"umhumm"* or a statement of interest.

My friend and mentor John Carter told me how he was hired right out of graduate school for a much sought--after job in account management with the J Walter
Thompson advertising agency in New York City—a plum of a job. He had an on-campus interview with a recruiter, just like twenty other students that day. When he sat down with the recruiter, he said, "*I know what an account executive does, and I know what a copywriter does, but I don't know what Human Resources does.*" The recruiter launched into an animated explanation of how important his job was and how business was changing and how they were the frontline for acquiring talent for the company and on and on. When the -half-hour interview was over, John had never talked about himself or the job or his qualifications. He left discouraged—expecting another polite rejection letter. The company extended a job offer to only one person from that campus recruiting trip. Yep, John got the job—only because he was a good listener and got the interviewer to talk about himself.

Another of my friends has not been able to find a job despite great talent and experience. I took her with me to a professional networking social, and all she did was talk about herself all night long. I was talking with somebody whom I wanted to have come and speak at a class, and every time I asked him a question, she interrupted talking about herself and how she felt about the topic. I redirected the questions to him again and again, saying, "*Brad, tell me about this,*" and every time he tried to answer, she jumped in talking about herself and her opinions and experiences. I finally had to drag her away and say, "*Shut up. It's not about you, it's about him. Let him talk about himself and don't interrupt or talk about yourself.*" She didn't know how to network effectively, and never really learned, which is why she still hasn't been able to land a job. So network wisely and effectively and listen much more than you talk.

Follow Up Immediately After a Networking Event

At the end of any event, go home and send your 3 special new contacts a quick email before you go to bed. Don't wait until tomorrow or you will never get around to it. It can be something simple like "*It was such a pleasure to meet you tonight at the AMA social. I'd like to stay in touch. Perhaps we can connect on LinkedIn.*" Immediately go to LinkedIn and send her an invitation. Then you can communicate and build on your relationship and set up that one-on-one meeting.

If you really are interested in the person or company, hand-write a thank you note with pen and -paper. Handwriting a thank you note is an almost -obsolete forgotten skill, but people respond to it, in part because they can't hit "delete" to make it go away. If you have bad handwriting, type the note nicely on a good linen paper or notecard stock, sign it and send it in the mail. The important thing is to reach out to the other person on paper, and insert or attach your business card (with your photo of course) as a tangible reminder of your meeting.

This connection really is very powerful. You can say, "*I enjoyed hearing about your company last night. It sounds like you have fascinating opportunities. Could we get together and have a cup of coffee next week to learn more about it? I'd love to work for a company like yours.*" It is that easy.

Master the Secret Art of Team Networking

One of the skills I have honed is that of Team Networking. My friend Marie is a very good graphic designer and we attend professional networking events together. When I meet someone new, I introduce them to -Marie with praise. "*It's a pleasure to meet you, John. I want to introduce you to my friend, Marie. She's the best graphic designer in town. She does all of my graphic design work, and I've worked with her for ten years. I think you need to know each other.*" Then -Marie says "*Oh, it's so easy to do great work for someone like -Diane. She is the most brilliant marketer I've ever met. She's introduced me to the most wonderful clients. I just love working with her.*"

So we each bragged about each other! I didn't brag about myself, and Marie didn't brag about herself, right? But we told John a great deal of favorable information about each other. In this way I can act modest because I bring my cheering squad with me, and we both look good. Plus it's much more fun to go networking with a friend—especially if you have complementary or non-competing skills and aren't both looking for the same job.

Networking No-Nos

Some topics should be avoided at networking events. You should never talk about religion or politics. And never, ever talk negatively about anybody, including nasty people that you've worked with before or people you hate. That's private. Discussing it will make you look petty. Don't ever bring negative topics or experiences into a professional social networking event, or interview for that matter. And don't gossip or reveal secrets about a former employer, even if you left unhappily. You will be seen as being disloyal. After all, if you will tell me confidential information about your former employer, I have to assume you would probably do the same if you end up working for my company.

TAKEAWAY—Networking is your secret weapon to landing a great job. People prefer to hire people they know. So your challenge is to effectively network and meet both the people who can refer you to a job, as well as your future employer, through industry and civic associations. Network your way to your dream job!

TO DO LIST:

- Practice shaking hands effectively and smiling, while introducing yourself memorably by saying your name slowly, with a space between your first and second name
- Practice your opening line—how you introduce yourself, and what memory-stimulating device you will use
- Practice exchanging business cards, keeping your cards in your left pocket and their cards in your right pocket
- Order a permanent name tag from your local trophy shop; make a note to always wear it on your right shoulder
- Find a friend with whom you can team network

Reading 2.2

Mind Your Business Manners

By Pamela Eyring

Manners Drive Success

In today's fiercely competitive business arena, understanding business etiquette and protocol intelligence gives training professionals the "edge" to cultivate new clients and ensures long-lasting, productive relationships with existing clients. Buyers of goods and services respond positively to business leaders who exude courtesy, a confident image, trust, and reliability. These skills are essential for business survival and success.

Etiquette and protocol intelligence positions you to build an effective team. It defines appropriate and inappropriate business behaviors between superiors and subordinates, co-workers, professional associates, and friends. This intelligence empowers you to create a productive environment that promotes problem solving and collaboration.

Thanks to the Internet and the globalization of business, your clients' level of sophistication and expectations of you are growing. You can't afford to get caught on sticky little details that hinder you from making a polished presentation and a polished impression. Learning about etiquette, practicing techniques, and putting them into action in a business setting will result in soft skills sure to improve your company's bottom line.

This edition of Infoline includes invaluable information on modern business etiquette. These strategies can be used by any one whether new to the business world or a seasoned veteran. You'll learn how to

- make a proper entrance at meetings and events
- execute proper introductions
- shake hands and greet international clients and associates
- navigate a business lunch
- close the deal after a business event.

Confidence In New Environs

The simple act of entering a meeting or reception is an opportunity for the smart business person. Why? Because people tend to keep an eye on the door, and it is your five seconds to make the best possible first impression.

Before the event, decide upon your agenda. Can your business benefit from this gathering? Are there new contacts you would like to make? Are there old relationships that might be improved? Visualize yourself meeting targeted colleagues and strangers, making introductions, and opening conversations so you are comfortable when you make your entrance. Then, follow these easy steps:

- Check your posture, stand tall, and look confident.
- Enter the room and move to the right.
- Pause so you can spot key people and allow others to see you.
- Avoid rushing to the bar or food tables.

Mingling

With your name tag firmly attached to your right lapel, enter the fray. Approach a group with a friendly smile, extend your hand and say, "Hello, I'm Jane Doe. May I join you?" Stating your name will prompt others to offer their names. Greet everyone in the group and offer a firm handshake. Remember that your body language can literally speak volumes in any setting.

Don't appear closed and unapproachable when you are part of a group. Ask yourself, "Would I like to be frozen out of this conversation?" That new person who would like to become part of your conversational group may be a potential client or someone whose acquaintance you will find valuable.

When you are mixing and mingling, respect others' social boundaries by not standing too close. Avoid gestures of affection that may be misunderstood. If someone is too affectionate with you, just step back to avoid further contact.

It is always a good idea to make yourself known to key people in your organization so they will know you are out front being supportive of your company.

If you own your business, be a role model to your employees by "working" the room with style. Be sure to introduce your employees to key people, too. For very important meetings, you might even prepare by strategizing with your staff about key contacts that may be helpful to your company.

Small Talk

Mastering the art of small talk will fuel your success in any business gathering. Small talk establishes a connection or defines a common denominator between two persons. Business people who can comfortably make polite conversation with anybody follow these rules:

- Read the newspaper every day so you are up to date on current events.
- Focus more on the other person and less on yourself.
- Allow people to finish their sentences. Interruptions are RUDE!
- Listen. Listen. Listen.
- Think before you speak. Pauses show you are thoughtful.
- Let your eyes show interest in the other person.
- Avoid talking about money, politics, religion, or health, and don't gossip.
- Avoid off-color jokes and controversial issues.
- Close a conversation before walking away. Say, "I enjoyed meeting you and hope we meet again."

Eye Contact

One of the most important ingredients of small talk is appropriate eye contact. Good eye contact should be made 40 to 60 percent of the time. Less than that and you slip into the s's—shifty, shy, or lacking self-confidence. If your eye contact exceeds 60 percent, the person with whom you are talking might feel over-examined or worry that you are focusing on his eyes because he has spinach in his teeth.

To make appropriate eye contact in a business setting, focus on a triangle on the other person's forehead. Directing your gaze on the upper part of the face creates a serious atmosphere and lets the other person know you mean business. If your gaze slips down between the other person's eye level and mouth, that indicates a social interaction that is definitely not professional. Do we need to mention what a lingering gaze that includes the mouth and other body parts communicates? Probably not.

Pay attention to what your eyebrows are doing. Lowering your eyebrows can be a sign of dislike, disagreement, uncertainty, or doubt. Raising your eyebrows shows surprise, excitement, or disbelief.

When making connections and meeting people, you will likely receive and hand out a number of business cards. For some tips, see the sidebar Exchanging Business Cards.

The Business of Introductions

A smooth, properly executed introduction sets the right tone for a business conversation or meeting. Simply put, it makes you look good. And, looking good helps you keep existing clients and engage new ones.

In mastering the business introduction, set aside some of the rules of etiquette that govern social introductions. For example, gender and age are not considerations in business situations. The name of the person of higher precedence or rank is always spoken first. The name of the person with lower precedence is always spoken last. Persons of greater authority receive or have presented to them persons of lower authority. For example:

- Chairman of the board, may I present new board member.
- National sales manager, may I present local sales associate.

Introducing Clients

When a client of your business is being introduced, the rules change. Clients receive, or have introduced to them, your colleagues and business associates. Why? Clients are more important than anyone in your organization. Without them, your business fails. The rule of "client first" holds true, even if the client is very junior and your colleague is very senior. For example:

- Matt Hopkins, I would like to introduce to you Ben Grossman, president of our company. Ben, Matt is our client from Chicago.
- Ms. Client, I'd like to introduce to you the members of our research team.

When introducing someone to members of a team, include each team member and treat each one as a valued asset. Use both the first name and surname, and speak slowly and clearly. Be mindful that overlooking someone may be viewed as a slight. Another option—especially if you are a little shaky on remembering names—is to invite team members to introduce themselves.

Exchange Business Cards

Think of your business card as a tiny billboard that advertises you to the world. Does it reflect the image you wish to convey? Is the print easy to read? Does it feel like something that deserves to be kept for future use? If you can answer a resounding "Yes!" to these questions, it is time to move on to the art and science of giving and receiving business cards.

Presenting Your Card

Keep your cards in a card case so they are pristine. When it is time to provide your contact details to a new colleague, present the card with your right hand or with both hands. Never offer a card with only your left hand. Present your card with the written side away from you so the receiver can read it easily.

If you are traveling to another culture and have been savvy enough to have your card printed in the language of that culture, present the card host-language side up. If you are in a group setting when presenting a business card, provide one for each person in the group so nobody feels left out.

Receiving a Card

Receive a business card with respect and look at it carefully. Don't stuff the card into your purse or pocket. Place it in an appropriate and respectful place. Fight off any impulse to write on a card you have just received.

If you are in a meeting and seated at a table, arrange newly received business cards in front of you so that each card corresponds to the position of the person from whom you received the card. Of course, if the occasion is a social one, this is not appropriate.

When you return to the office, file business cards away carefully and make notes about what follow-up is needed.

Elected and Appointed Officials

Officials—such as a mayor—have non-official persons introduced to them. Military, police, and fire department personnel who are in uniform receive or have other people introduced to them. A representative of a faith community, who is wearing clothing that denotes that position, should have other people introduced to them.

Mayor Williams, may I present Michael McNabb, principal of Oak Grove School.

Officer Hastings, may I present Mr. Kim, owner of a restaurant in your precinct.

Casual Introductions

You can introduce colleagues, friends, and peers in a casual way, keeping in mind that even casual introductions should be correctly done. If one person outranks the other, introduce her first. If the precedence of everyone is equal, introduce in the most convenient order. Use both given name and surname, even in a very casual setting.

Even though the use of first names is broadly accepted in the United States, providing only the given name makes you look sloppy or lazy. And, you don't want that!

Memory Lapses

Let's say you meet someone for the second or third time, but that person doesn't remember you. Never say something insensitive such as, "You don't remember me, do you?" Instead, rescue your new friend. Extend your hand, smile, and say your name. Help start the conversation by reminding the person of when and where you first met.

Everyone has recognized a face but forgotten the name. Don't blurt out, "I can't remember your name." Instead, simply say, "Please tell me your name again." You may also try extending your hand and introducing yourself, there is an excellent chance that your new friend will state his or her name in response.

Remembering Names

Remembering a person's name is a wonderful compliment, which is reason enough to work hard on improving this critical business skill. Stop telling yourself that you can't remember names. Have confidence in your abilities. Listen carefully when you are introduced, make eye contact with the person, and repeat the name in your head. Take the opportunity to use the new name in conversation.

Pronunciation

As our global economy brings us into contact with people from many other cultures, we'll encounter more names that are unfamiliar to us. If you are unsure about a pronunciation, just say, "I'm not sure how to pronounce your name correctly. Please tell me the correct way to say it." Never say anything that suggests the other person's name is odd or "too foreign." Keep in mind that different cultures have different rules for greetings. Always do your homework so that you can make a good impression!

Don't Point

Often, the introducer points first to one person and then the other. This is not a recommended practice. Clearly, they know who they are, so pointing is unnecessary. It is good manners to look at each person as you state his or her name. This focuses attention on the individual, makes him feel important, and makes you look confident and in control. What more could you ask for? A smooth, properly executed introduction sets the stage for success.

Handshakes

You are meeting a business prospect for the first time. This is the perfect opportunity to make a great impression through a firm, confident handshake. Handshaking is an important form of nonverbal communication. This interactive body language offers a peek into how the other person views the world, himself, or you. Understanding the messages and meanings of these brief encounters is beneficial to everyone.

Executing a Proper Handshake

The physical steps to a good handshake are simple:

- Extend your right hand while making eye contact.
- Make good web-to-web and palm-to-palm contact.
- Shake from the elbow, not the wrist or shoulder; two or three good pumps are all you need.
- Focus on the moment, and try to be the person who ends the shake.

Observe the other person during this process. Is he pulling away from you? Does she seem focused on you? Delighted to meet you? Bored? Once you begin to analyze these brief interactions, you'll draw a number of impressions that will help you understand how to interact with this person in business situations.

Send the Right Message

Begin by thinking positive thoughts. Relax. Take your mental preparation one step further by internalizing the message you want to send before you shake hands. Your message is the outcome you want to achieve during this meeting. Visualize that outcome. Do you want to get rid of this person? Do you want to add him to your list of clients? Make your message as clear and succinct as possible and imagine it flowing through your hand into his. It might sound like hocus-pocus to the uninitiated, but this approach does work.

Poorly Executed Handshakes

While good handshaking is a fairly simple process, there are lots of ways your shake can go south. Keep these tips in mind:

- Avoid using a bone crushing shake OR the limp fish shake. Some men think the latter is appropriate for women. It is not.
- Offer a dry hand. Hold your drink in your left hand so your right isn't cold or damp.
- Control clammy or sweaty hands by spraying with antiperspirant once a day. Avoid using too much hand moisturizer.
- Do not wear large rings on your right hand because they can interfere with executing a proper handshake.
- Avoid the two-handed shake in business settings. It can feel overbearing to the recipient.
- Do not use the glove handshake, which involves extending your hand horizontally as if you are—well—putting on a glove.

In the United States, extending your hand first shows confidence. But this is not always true in other cultures. For example, when you are meeting Western and Eastern Europeans, the ranking person should extend his or her hand first. In unfamiliar cultures, you can often pick up cues from those around you. Remember that the casual, back-slapping style of some Americans can be jarring. Choose a dignified approach over a more familiar or informal style.

To learn more, see the sidebar Understanding Handshake Types.

Understanding Handshake Types

You can tell a lot about people by the way they shake your hand. Review this sidebar to find out about some common handshake types and what they say about the people that use them.

The Pull-In shaker holds onto your hand and guides you in a direction. You could be pulled closer or directed toward a door or chair. This is a clever maneuver that means the shaker has accepted you and wants to place you somewhere. The shaker could be a little domineering or might just be from a culture with a small intimate space. Americans tend to have bigger social spaces or comfort zones around them than do people from many other cultures.

The Glove happens when the shaker extends his hand palm down so it is on top of the handshake. This form clearly says, "I'm in charge." This is often used by the conventional manager who operates by controlling subordinates.

The Finger Squeeze happens when the shaker avoids palm-to-palm contact and just grasps your fingers. It is designed to keep people at a distance and is uninviting. When too much pressure is applied, you know you are interacting with a modern incarnation of Neanderthal Man. Take care!

The Twister happens when someone grabs your hand and then twists it under. This person is saying, "We are coming into this even, but in the end, I'm going to be on top and you will be on the bottom." This is an aggressive handshake that often signals that the shaker has a hidden agenda.

The Fingertip Holder brings to mind a queen or duchess who avoids true interaction by providing a quick, limp, fingers-only dip into your extended hand. It coolly asks, "Do you know who I am?" This shake should have been retired at least a century ago. If you'll take a minute to remember televised shots of Princess Diana shaking hands, you'll recall that she offered a hearty, American-style handshake that successfully put people at ease. A great improvement on earlier royal styles of interaction!

The Water Pump occurs when somebody shakes your hand as if she or he is drawing water from a well. There are too many pumps that feel a bit too enthusiastic. This approach usually doesn't mean anything negative. It is just a bit too hearty for the professional person.

The Dreaded Limp Fish is cold, clammy, and indifferent. The shaker is a passive person with low self-esteem who has little or no interest in you. It can be draining, so end the shake fast and move on to somebody who can muster the energy and interest to give you a real handshake.

Greetings Around the World

Greeting styles vary from culture to culture. On the international scene, you'll find everything from the forthright all-American shake to the lingering Brazilian shake with air kisses to the Frenchman's cool, light, and brief shake. Prepare yourself to succeed in a new culture by learning about its etiquette and customs. Time invested in doing a little homework can pay big dividends later on.

Arab Countries

Men offer a light, lingering handshake that might include an embrace and a kiss on both cheeks if the person they are greeting is another male and a friend. Follow your host's lead. Handshaking is normal for Arab women who often travel to Western countries. For Western women, it is best to cover your heart with your right hand and let the Arab male make the first move to shake hands. It is also an appropriate gesture for both men and women to cover their hearts after shaking hands.

Bangladesh, Pakistan, and Taiwan

The Western handshake may be used in these countries with the grip being less firm than an American handshake. Avoid giving or receiving anything with your left hand, which is considered taboo.

China

People greet with a bow, nod, and a light, lingering handshake. Any of these gestures may be used. Wait for the Chinese to offer a hand, and always greet the senior person first.

France

The French offer a light, brief handshake with everyone, upon both greeting and departure.

Germany

Shake hands firmly and briefly with everyone upon arriving at and departing meetings. Don't leave your left hand in a pocket while shaking hands. Here, it is considered very rude.

Great Britain

A light handshake is standard in business, both in greeting and at departure. A man traditionally waits for a woman to offer her hand first.

Italy

The handshake is firm with good eye contact and may include a grasp of the arm with the other hand. Italian men wait for a woman to offer her hand first.

Japan

Expect a bow and light handshake. A light bow and nod of the head with eyes cast down is acceptable from Westerners. Western-educated Japanese people often shake hands and make eye contact.

Morocco

Men shake hands when greeting. The handshake is light and one might touch the heart after the handshake to express pleasure at seeing the other person. In a greeting between men and women, the woman must first extend her hand; if she does not, the man should bow in greeting.

Russia

Russians greet with a firm handshake. Never shake hands over a threshold as it is considered bad luck. Always step into the room before you shake hands.

South Korea

Here, men greet each other with a slight bow and a handshake. To show respect, support your right forearm with your left hand. Korean women generally don't shake hands after bowing. Western women may offer a handshake to Korean men, but should nod to Korean women. Wait for the senior person to offer his hand first. Maintain eye contact with people of the same authority level. Supporting your right forearm with your left hand is also used when offering money or credit cards to vendors in Korea.

Thailand

The traditional greeting is the "wai," which involves placing the palms of both hands together with the fingers held upward in front of one's face. The Western handshake will be used in most business meetings.

Turkey

Shake hands when being introduced to a Turkish man. Wait for a Turkish woman to extend her hand. Do not stand with your hands on your hips or in your pocket when greeting and talking with others.

A Dining Tutorial

Business professionals who can graciously host a business lunch or dinner will find themselves closer and closer to the head of the pack. Understanding the finer points of restaurant dining is an important step in impressing new clients and ensuring continued success with existing ones.

Planning

When planning a lunch or dinner, examine the reasons you should entertain targeted clients. Strategize with your employees to define goals for the event. Then, consider the taste and personality of your guest or guests. A quiet, old-school chairman of the board might be overwhelmed by a trendy hotspot filled with noise and activity, while a young business leader on his way up might bask in the hustle and bustle. Once you have selected just the right dining spot, visit it before your event so you can become familiar with the menu and meet the maitre d' or captain.

Invitations

When you invite your guests, be precise about the time, place, and where you will meet in the restaurant. Will you meet at the captain's stand? Should your guests ask to be taken to your table? Make your reservation and confirm it the day before your group arrives.

Paying

It is a good idea to handle payment with the captain while away from the dining table. Before the meal begins, the captain can stamp your credit card and add the customary tip. When a woman serves as host in a country other than the United States of America, the check should not be presented at the table. Why? In some cultures it is considered an affront for the woman to pay for the meal.

Dining Do's and Don'ts

Top Twelve Dining Do's	*Top Twelve Dining Don'ts*
1. Do try a little of everything served to you unless you are allergic to some foods.	1. Don't overload your plate at a buffet.
2. Do take small bites so you can comfortably converse with your guests.	2. Don't overload your fork when eating.
3. Do wait until you've swallowed food in your mouth before you take a sip of your beverage.	3. Don't spread your elbows when cutting meat.
4. Do take a quick sip of water if food is too hot.	4. Don't saw meat in a back and forth motion. Stroke the knife towards you.
5. Do remember solids (food) are on your left and beverages are on your right.	5. Don't chew with your mouth open or smack your lips.
6. Do leave your plate where it is when you are finished and position the knife, blade in, and fork, tines up, in the 10:20 position (as on the face of a clock) in the American style of eating. Utensils tips are at ten, handles are at four.	6. Don't mop your face with your napkin.
	7. Don't touch your face or head at the table.
	8. Don't reach across the table or another person to get something. Ask the person closest to the item to pass it to you.
7. Do look into, not over, the cup or glass when drinking.	9. Don't push your plate away from you when you are finished eating.
8. Do butter bread on the plate, never in the air.	10. Don't gesture with your utensils. Put them down on the side of your plate when not eating.
9. Do remember posture. Sit up straight and keep your arms, including elbows, off the table.	11. Don't talk about your personal food likes or dislikes when eating.
10. Do leave dropped silver on the floor. Ask the server to bring another piece.	

11. Do point out to your server bugs, stones, or hair in your food, but do so in a non-combative manner and try not to disturb the other diners. You'll get a replacement immediately. 12. Do remove an object such as bone or gristle from your mouth with your thumb and index finger and place it on the rim of your plate.	12. Don't eat your neighbor's bread or salad. A right-handed person reaches to the left across the dinner plate to eat salad.

Seating

Allow your guests to precede you when the captain takes you to the table. Take a seat with your back to the room so your guest or guests can look out into the room. To seat yourself, pull out your chair, step to the right of the chair, and enter the chair from the right side. When you rise to leave, you should also exit your chair from the right side.

At business meals, a woman should never expect a man to seat her. She seats herself. However, if a man offers to seat her, she accepts with a gracious "thank you."

If you are seated at the table when additional guests arrive, rise to greet the guests and remain standing until they are seated. Your guest of honor should be seated to your right.

Feel free to suggest menu items, and don't forget to offer bread and butter to guests before you help yourself. Allow your guests to order before you do. Be aware that the well-mannered guest will wait for the host to begin eating.

In addition to the basic rules of dining—critical things like chewing with your mouth closed—there are many do's and don'ts that should be mastered (see sidebar Dining Do's and Don'ts).

For more information on dealing with specific food items, see the sidebar Troublesome Foods.

Troublesome Foods

These are foods you are likely to encounter at a business lunch or dinner. They are also challenging to eat correctly. Read. Remember. Enjoy.

Bread: Break off only one bite-sized piece of your bread or roll at a time, then butter and eat it. Don't pull the roll in half. Do the buttering on your plate, never in midair.

Butter: When butter is passed, place a portion onto the butter plate with the butter server. If pats are used, pick them up with the serving fork provided and place on your plate. If a serving fork isn't provided, use your butter spreader.

Celery, Olives, Pickles, and Radishes: These foods are taken from the serving tray with the fingers and placed on the side of your dinner plate or bread plate. Celery and radishes may be dipped in salt and eaten with the fingers. Large olives with a pit are eaten in several bites. Discard the pit on the side of the plate. Small stuffed olives are eaten whole.

Fish: If the fish is soft and boneless, it is correct to use only the fish fork. When the fork is held in the right hand, the tines are up. If you are eating only with the fork, do not put the knife on your plate. When using only the fork, hold it in the right hand, the way a pencil is held, steadied between the forefinger and middle finger, except that the thumb is turned up rather than down. When you have finished, place the knife next to the fork on the plate in the 10:20 position. If tiny bones get in your mouth, remove them with your thumb and index finger and place them on the edge of your plate.

Pasta: For spaghetti, use a fork and separate a few strands. Hold the tip of the prongs against the plate and twirl the fork around to gather the strands onto it. Don't stir and don't use a spoon. Small-sized pasta, such as tortellini or penne, is eaten with a fork.

Water: Blot your mouth before taking a drink. Do not drink water while food is in the mouth, roll water around your mouth, or swallow loudly. Do not forcefully drain an entire glassful. Hold a tumbler-type glass near the bottom, a small stem glass by the stem, and large goblets at the bottom of the bowl.

Formal Place Setting

It is worthwhile to be prepared for a formal dinner. The diagram below helps you identify the various pieces of your place setting. This place setting is only for the most formal of events. If the dinner is less formal, you will see fewer pieces of silverware and be served fewer courses. For example, for a three-course menu you might only see a salad fork, dinner fork, salad knife, dinner knife, and a dessert fork or spoon. Remember, use your utensils in order from the outside in. Note, the below setting is European style, in which the salad is served after the dinner course.

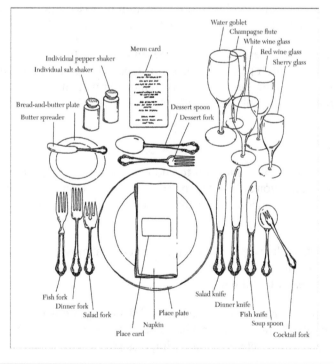

Electronic Etiquette

In just two decades, electronic communication has dramatically changed the way business people communicate. We have become more reliant on email and other informal means of communication, but we must make sure not to sacrifice courtesy for the sake of convenience.

Every email you send is an opportunity to remind the reader that you are a competent professional working hard to communicate clearly, properly, and in a timely manner. Carefully crafted emails can impress existing clients and result in new ones.

Email Etiquette Is Essential

What kind of dent do the hundreds of weekly emails you receive put in your day? Consider this: Cohesive Knowledge Solutions, a Connecticut-based company specializing in email management, reports that employees spend more than 40 percent of their workday on email. This statistic brings home the need to start improving your email etiquette and efficiency by adhering to the following rules:

- Email business associates only when you have something to say.
- Begin with a greeting and end with your name.
- Make emails clear and concise.
- Use proper structure to make emails more readable; bullet points can be useful for outlining important issues.
- Always put a detailed, relevant title in the subject box.
- Limit use of cc, or courtesy copy, and "Reply to all."
- Never send a chain email to anyone.

Once you've typed your email, proofread it to make sure you haven't made any grammatical or spelling errors. Read through the eyes of the receiver. Is the email clear? Does it represent you and your company in a positive light? Is there confidential information included that might be better addressed in a phone call or letter? Have you screamed at somebody by using all caps? This tactic is never good!

For especially important messages, try typing and editing the text in a Word document before cutting and pasting it into an email. If possible, ask a colleague to check your language for cohesiveness and to make sure there are no typographical errors. Finally, remember that once you hit the send button, you lose control of where your email goes. Think first; send second.

International Emails

International email requires additional attention to etiquette. Always address a person formally and use a title such as "Mr." or "Ms.," until you are invited to use a first name. Don't use all lower-case letters, idioms, jokes, slang, abbreviations, or emoticons. Help international readers by using dates and times familiar to them. For example:

- Use 10.01.03 instead of January 10, 2003. (Remember that most other countries put the day number first, followed by the month and year.)
- Use 1300 hours instead of 1:00 p.m.

To show respect for your international email recipients, try a greeting in their language. It is easy to secure phrasing from online dictionaries. Or, you can call the appropriate embassy for information about proper wording. These are the little details that truly impress potential clients!

Be Cautious!

It is never appropriate to send strongly worded, political emails that might come back to haunt you or your company. Sending jokes annoys people so use funny emails sparingly. Don't send anything that is obscene or vulgar. Remember, too, that you should not use your work email account to conduct personal business. Some companies track email use. While your boss doesn't need to know your shoe size, she will be even more unhappy to know you are spending part of the business day emailing about a shoe order.

See "Control That Email!," Infoline No. 250708, for more email tips.

PDAs and Cell Phones

All business telephones must be answered in a professional and pleasant manner. Instead of "yep" say, "Good morning. This is Ellen Hillman with Electronic Systems." When leaving a message, give clear information—name, company, phone number, and a convenient time to have the call returned to you.

Record a professional message on your voicemail. Avoid casual approaches such as, "Hey, Bob here. You know the drill." Try a respectful message such as, "Hello, you have reached Robert Williams. Please leave your name, number, a brief message, and a convenient time to return your call. Thank you." It is also a good practice to update your message daily with your particular hours and availability for the day. Return calls as soon as possible, certainly within 24 hours. If you absolutely, positively cannot return a call, ask your assistant to do so.

Silence Your Electronics

Commit to turning off all cell phones and personal digital assistants (PDAs) in training seminars, meetings, churches, restaurants, theaters, and concerts. Resist the urge to carry on a "conversation" by text messaging when you are in a business meeting. This is just as rude as talking to the person next to you when a speaker is making a presentation. Be respectful in teleconferences, too. Turn off cell phones, fax machines, pagers, and call waiting, which could interrupt while you are talking.

Old-Fashioned Communication

One of the best ways to show that you value your clients and good manners is to write a note after being treated to a business dinner, after securing a new account, or after meeting a new colleague. Note writing shows that you take valuable time from your day to select appropriate stationery and write a personal message. Consider using an attractive folded note with your business logo, your name, or your initials featured. Keep your message four to six sentence in length; begin with a formal salutation and close with your name. Be timely by writing your note within a few days of the event or meeting that you are referencing.

Sending Thank Yous

While you are selling yourself and your services to potential clients, you can distinguish yourself by exhibiting good manners and attention to detail throughout the process. When you meet a potential client, follow up with a handwritten note within 24 hours. Include another business card, just in case the one you presented at your initial meeting was abandoned in a coat pocket. If another colleague has orchestrated your meeting with a potential client, write that person a nice note, too.

It is acceptable to follow a meeting with a phone call to inquire about providing more information about your services by mail or computer, or arranging a time and place to meet. Think outside the box when trying to engage a new prospect. You might invite this person to attend part of a training series on a complimentary basis to get a first-hand look at what you can deliver. Or, you might suggest that they talk with one of your most trusted, long-term clients about the services you've provided over the years.

You are your business's best advertisement, but remember that every piece of paper you send to clients or potential clients suggests how you will do the job if hired. Notes should be clearly handwritten on paper that feels good to the touch. If you send an envelope with various materials inside, the envelope should be attractive but business-like. Materials inside should be carefully arranged and secured so the inside package will be impressive when removed. Show your attention to detail by using a stamp that fits with your business image.

Throughout the process of securing new clients, be polite without being aggressive. Never "bad mouth" your competition in an effort to promote yourself. That is a loutish approach at best. Simply move forward on the assumption that "no" never really means "no." It just means, "not at this time." Happy hunting!

Statement of Ownership, Management, and Circulation

1. PUBLICATION TITLE: Infoline
2. PUBLICATION NO. 8755-9269
3. FILING DATE: September 24, 2008
4. ISSUE FREQUENCY: Monthly
5. NO. OF ISSUES PUBLISHED ANNUALLY: 12
6. ANNUAL SUBSCRIPTION PRICE: $99.00 (ASTD members, $139.00 non-member)
7. COMPLETE MAILING ADDRESS OF KNOWN OFFICE OF PUBLICATION: 1640 King Street, Box 1443, Alexandria, VA 22313-1443
8. COMPLETE MAILING ADDRESS OF HEADQUARTERS OR GENERAL BUSINESS OFFICE OF PUBLISHER: 1640 King Street, Box 1443, Alexandria, VA 22313-1443
9. FULL NAMES AND COMPLETE MAILING ADDRESSES OF PUBLISHER, EDITOR, AND MANAGING EDITOR
PUBLISHER: American Society for Training & Development, 1640 King Street, Box 1443, Alexandria, VA 22313-1443
MANAGING EDITOR
10. OWNERS FULL NAME: American Society for Training & Development (ASTD) COMPLETE MAILING ADDRESS: 1640 King Street, Box 1443, Alexandria, VA 22313-1443
11. KNOWN BONDHOLDERS, MORTGAGEES, AND OTHER SECURITY HOLDERS OWNING OR HOLDING ONE PERCENT OR MORE OF TOTAL AMOUNT OF BONDS, MORTGAGES, OR OTHER SECURITIES: None
12. FOR COMPLETION BY NONPROFIT ORGANIZATIONS AUTHORIZED TO MAIL AT SPECIAL RATES. The purpose, function, and nonprofit status of this organization and the exempt status for federal income tax purposes has not changed during the preceding 12 months.
13. PUBLICATION NAME: Infoline
14. ISSUE DATE FOR CIRCULATION DATA BELOW: September 2008

15. EXTENT AND NATURE OF CIRCULATION			**Average No. Copies Each Issue During Preceding 12 Months**	**No. copies of Single Issue Published Nearest to Filing Date**
a. Total Number of Copies (Net press run)			2,894	3,000
b. Paid Circulation (By Mail and Outside the Mail)	(1)	Paid/Requested Outside-County Mail Subscriptions Stated on Form 3541. (Include advertiser's proof and exchange copies)	2,060	2,064

	(2)	Paid In-County Subscriptions (Include advertiser's proof and exchange copies)	0	0
	(3)	Sales Through Dealers and Carriers, Street Vendors, Counter Sales, and Other Non-USPS Paid Distribution	618	803
	(4)	Other Classes Mailed Through the USPS	0	0
c. Total Paid and/or Requested Circulation [Sum of 15b. (1), (2), (3), and (4)]			2,678	2,867
d. Free or Nominal Rate Distribution (By Mail and Outside the Mail)	(1)	Outside-County as Stated on Form 3541	0	0
	(2)	In-County as Stated on Form 3541	0	0
	(3)	Other Classes Mailed Through the USPS (e.g. First Class Mail)	10	10
	(4)	Distribution Outside the Mail (Carriers or other means)	140	60
e. Total Free or Nominal Rate Distribution (Sum of 15d (1), (2), (3) and (4)			150	70
f. Total Distribution (Sum of 15c. and 15e)			2,828	2,937
g. Copies not Distributed			66	63
h. Total (Sum of 15f. and 15g)			2.894	3,000
j. Percent Paid (15c divided by 15f times 100)			93%	97%
16. THIS STATEMENT OF OWNERSHIP WILL BE PRINTED IN THE NOVEMBER 2008 ISSUE OF THIS PUBLICATION				
17. I CERTIFY THAT ALL INFORMATION FURNISHED ABOVE IS TRUE AND COMPLETE: Cat Russo, Director, ASTD Press				

References & Resources

External Consultant

Mary Bosrock

President

International Education Systems

Articles

Brody, Marjorie. "Test Your Etiquette." T+D, February 2002, pp. 64–66.

Eyring, Pamela. "Broadening Global Awareness." T+D, July 2006, pp. 69–70.

Books

Bosrock, Mary Murray. Asian Business Customs & Manners. New York: Meadowbrook Press, 2007.

———. European Business Customs & Manners. Minnetonka, MN: Meadow-brook Press, 2006.

Brown, Robert, and Dorthea Johnson. Power of Handshaking. Herndon, VA: Capital Books, 2004.

Browne, Kelly. 101 Ways to Say Thank You. New York: Sterling, 2008.

Feinberg, Steven L., ed. Crane's Blue Book of Stationery. New York: Doubleday, 1989.

Forni, P. M. Choosing Civility. New York: St. Martin's Press, 2002.

Hickey, Robert. Honor & Respect: The Official Guide to Names, Titles, and Forms of Address. Columbia, SC: PSOW, 2008.

Johnson, Dorthea. Little Book of Etiquette. Philadelphia: Running Press, 1997.

Morrison, Terri, and Wayne A. Conaway. Kiss, Bow, or Shake Hands. 2nd ed. Avon, MA: Adams Media, 2006.

Peterson, Brooks. Cultural Intelligence. Yarmouth, ME: Intercultural Press, 2004.

Infolines

Brusino, Justin. "Control That Email!" No. 250708.

Websites

www.psow.com

Reading 2.3

ARE: Anchor, Reveal, Encourage

The Cure for "but I Never Know What to Say!"

By Carol Fleming

So there's a fellow standing next to me with available eyes and an open posture. Perhaps we've already smiled at each other, said hello, shaken hands, and introduced ourselves. Now we begin the kind of small talk you dread: from a cold start with a Them (as far as you know), with the goal of turning this stranger into an acquaintance. Here is where most people panic because they are unprepared to perform this act of human alchemy.

Luckily, there's an easy enough formula to walk you through this process: Anchor, Reveal, Encourage.

1. Anchor the conversation with a neutral topic from your shared reality.

2. Reveal something about yourself regarding that topic.

3. Encourage the other person to talk by asking them a question about that topic.

Designing ARE patterns is something you can do in advance (before you leave the house) so you don't have to be creative when you're the most uncomfortable. Take some time to review some possibilities: the occasion or aegis, the music, food, decorations, or the weather. Imagine in your own mind how you can build your opener:

(A) This seems to be a very large graduating class.

(R) I've been looking for my nephew, but I'm getting discouraged.

(E) Do you have a family member in there somewhere?

What you're actually saying in code is, "Hello! You seem like a nice person. I hope you'll like me. How about we talk for a while?" Would you feel more comfortable saying that? Your goal in small talk is to connect with another human being, to become known to them and they to you. The ARE sequence helps you use whatever you can in the present circumstance as your bridge to Us.

Anchor the Conversation

I am sometimes asked about having a good opening (i.e., anchoring) line.

Haven't we met somewhere before?

What's your sign?

Do you come here often?

A magic anchor, if such a thing existed, may help your insecurity, but canned openings are pretty obvious and irritating unless you're an exceptionally funny and clever person.

Before you leave the house, arm yourself with some probable topics to start chatting about at your event so you don't have to search for one on the spot. This will greatly increase your comfort. The easiest and safest place to start a conversation is with the aegis that brings you both together—the organization or theme that occasions the get-together, the host of the party, the chamber of commerce, the company-sponsored trip to a baseball game, Burning Man, an Easter Egg hunt, or a fashion show. Certainly, a comment on some aspect of the overarching occasion is appropriate for notice and comment, though I always recommend avoiding the negative, like "Whoever planned this event was really a pea brain."

A comment on the weather is always safe.

Hot enough for ya?

Isn't this a lovely day?

Will this rain never stop?

If you cringe when you hear these conversational anchors, it means you don't appreciate their friendly intent. They are conversational code for "Is it safe to talk with you? Will you reject me? Can we be friends?" If you are easily bored with these innocent exchanges and yearn to be more meaningful, I would also point out that you are assuming the other person is ready to join you on a more intense, substantive topic. This is not a wise assumption. In the initial phase of small talk, both parties are still deciding if they even want to talk with each other in the first place.

Now, maybe you're thinking, "What a rude jerk I have been! I've been sneering at all these well-meaning people because they did not approach me with an opening comment at the same level of my lofty intelligence!" Or something to that effect. Many of us need to dismount from our very high horses and learn to respond to the intent of friendly people who engage us in neutral, seemingly bland topics.

It pretty much doesn't matter what you are talking about; it's the fact that you've opened your mouth to engage someone else in what you hope will be a pleasant exchange. Don't take it too seriously. Simply look around and say something relatively pleasant or fun about anything that seems to be a shared experience for both of you. If you can comment on something that is beautiful or well done, certainly do so. You'll be setting the tone for pleasantry and comfort. With practice, you'll get better at picking anchoring topics that lend themselves to deeper conversational development. Or you can just stick to the weather.

Revealing Yourself

Speaking of our friend The Weather, it is actually the safest topic in the world to start a conversation: it is neutral, obvious, and part of everyone's shared reality. It affords a safe way to engage another person with no real personal intrusion.

The English are masters of the weather conversation. In Watching the English: The Hidden Rules of English Behavior, author Kate Fox summed it up this way: "The whole point of the weather discussion is to communicate, to agree, to have something in common; and shared moaning is just as effective in promoting sociable interaction and social bonding as shared optimism, shared speculation or shared stoicism.

"When we discuss the weather, we are invoking the one thing that we know we have in common with others. We are throwing a rope across the divide, asserting that, whatever our differences, we do share something. When it rains on me, it's going to rain on you too.

"The other person can expand on the topic to make it more personal and interesting. Or they can simply brush it off with the briefest of acknowledgements, thus avoiding engagement if they so choose."

MILO: Nice weather you folks are having.

NEAL: Yes, it is. The place to be today would be walking on the Embarcadero with my puppy. There'll probably be a lot of people out to enjoy the Bay view. Have you been down to the Embarcadero?

Do you see how Neal responded with free information? He revealed his thoughts related to the weather topic voluntarily, giving Milo the encouragement to continue the conversation, as well as new possible topics to explore. Milo's next statement could be "Where is the Embarcadero?" or "What kind of dog do you have?" or "Can you see the Golden Gate Bridge from there?"

This one thing, the revealing of information, is crucial to conversation development. I cannot stress enough the value of your providing additional information to allow a conversation to take a different direction. As the conversation progresses in this way or that, certainly you will discover a topic that you both really want to talk about.

We develop conversation by going beyond the simple anchoring opening and offering some information about ourselves before asking the other person to talk. In doing this you foster trust. It's also the kind thing to do, helping the other person get the conversation rolling by not playing hard to get. This is that attitude part that I hinted at previously, the attitude that covered your own uncomfortable feeling. You will soon meet Leo by way of illustration (Chapter 6).

However, you are always in control of how intimate you want to be and how fast you reveal details about yourself. If you want to keep everything out on the front porch, so to speak, you can keep all your references public. For example, a woman might comment, "What a lovely day. This should bring lots of people out to the opening of the arts center." This kind of observation is not at all personal for either of you. But she could also say, "What a lovely day! And with that breeze, it's perfect weather to take my sailboat out on the bay." Here she's revealed some interest in sailing and that she's in possession of a boat. This free information gives you the choice to get off of the weather topic and, possibly, on to the more personal one about sailing.

How many conversations have you murdered in their cribs by your lack of contribution of imagination and energy? Yes, you! Regardless of the number, I'm going to forgive you, because I'll bet you didn't know anything about revealing free information.

From Chat to Conversation

Here are three stories touting the value of free information. Carl never got the hang of it, Laura overflowed with it, and Marion had to be held down for extraction. Read on and tell me who you most identify with.

Carl

Carl was a self-effacing young man in the pharmaceutical industry whose career plans required that he leave the back room—his comfort zone—and represent his company in the business community. He knew this was an important promotion and he simply had to deal with the social demand, hence he began working with me. Carl needed to find people he could talk with to practice what he was learning in my office, but he was at a loss. Carl was a loner with a "don't bother me" posture. He avoided eye contact with other people. So where to start? He had to find a new someone to talk to. What he found was a someone willing to talk to him behind the dumpster of his apartment building.

A particularly gregarious homeless man greeted Carl one morning as he left the building. Carl walked on but immediately realized that someone had made a friendly overture to him. This was his big chance; part of his homework was to respond to all outreach to him. He turned back and returned the greeting. They managed to fashion an initial conversation and exchanged names. The next day was especially meaningful for Carl. As he left his apartment building, he heard a cheery "Hi, Carl!" from his friend behind the dumpster. Someone had called out his name. Carl felt a jolt of joy that surprised him. Someone had recognized him as an individual. Somebody had said, "There you are!" Carl could feel how hungry he was for validation and recognition, and that he had finally found the right path.

However, this association went no deeper. My guess was that both men experienced the social class barrier that prevented them from seeking other deeper mutual interests. They remained on the neutral small talk "chat" level—sometimes a ballgame, the weather, or traffic served as topic—for the duration of their acquaintance.

Carl and his dumpster friend had to be satisfied with occasional chat for the sake of sociability. It is completely possible, even probable, that they shared some other features of life that would have enriched their relationship. But no mention was made, so no connection was made.

Since Carl took a ride-share service to get to my office, I decided to use the resources available to him to try a different direction. I asked Carl to get in the front seat of the car and start a conversation with the driver. This was clearly not the habit of Carl, but this is how new habits get started. I asked him to tell me as much as he could about his driver during our appointment. The first driver was from Nepal. I asked, "Well, now, does he have a name? When and why did he come here? How did he get here? What surprised him? What does he miss from Nepal?"

Carl got the name and the make of the car and the Nepal part right. He had discovered that the driver liked driving with Lyft and that the traffic wasn't bad that day, but that was about it. I assured him he'd do better next time. Get curious about this person, I encouraged. Try to imagine his journey. Get out of your corner and mix it up with this guy. Pretend that you're going to have to introduce him as a speaker.

Come the next week and Carl's driver was from Yemen. "How in the world did you manage to get here?" Carl had asked. So he did better this second time, and even better with the following driver from Sudan. You can imagine poor Carl trying to penetrate Sudanese culture for a conversation. In the next stage of our work, Carl had to volunteer some information about himself to become an equal partner in the chat.

"So, what does Achmed know about you?" I asked him. "Could you say, 'Morocco! Wow. That's a long way away. I've never been there. Of course, I've never traveled abroad, if you don't count Canada.'" That was just a tiny bit Carl could have revealed about himself and it would have been a start. Achmed was followed by a driver named Eddie from Guam and then a Punjabi named Amar. Carl had never realized that he had access to the world in his rides and that he could plumb as much depth as he was interested in. That was the point, of course: to develop curiosity and an appreciation of other people. And these nice Lyft drivers were captive subjects of my speech client. Thank you, Lyft.

Laura

In this story, I was a speaker at a medical conference with my friend Janet, a physician in San Francisco. We were having dinner in a small restaurant when I saw Laura, a retired psychiatrist from the east coast whom I had just met during the conference. I invited her to our table and introduced her to Janet, and they proceeded with conversational exchange quite easily. Why? Because we were an Us. They were both female physicians attending the conference and they both knew me, so I could make a proper introduction. We all clearly belonged to the same tribe.

The topic of my probable knee surgery was mentioned, and Laura was reminded of a wonderful orthopedic surgeon she had gone to medical school with some thirty-five years ago, Lee Hong. As a matter of fact, they had been sweethearts. She hadn't seen him in many years and didn't know where he had gone. Then Janet piped in, "I'll tell you where! His office is two doors down from my nephrology clinic in San Francisco!"

Bingo! Then they really went to town on Lee Hong.

This story showcases the deliciousness of casual, aimless chat and how it can turn into a genuine conversation through the revealing of specific free and personal information.

One more story.

Carolyn

I was part of a team teaching a business development course at the University of California at Berkeley. Other than being brought together to teach this course, we were pretty much strangers who shared a car to Berkeley from San Francisco once a week. On one such trip, Carolyn, the woman who taught the accounting component, mentioned that she would not be with us the following week; she was going to visit her family.

ME: Where are they?

CAROLYN: Up north.

ME: Where up north?

CAROLYN: In Washington.

ME: Where in Washington?

CAROLYN: On the west coast.

ME: Where on the west coast?

CAROLYN: On an island in Puget Sound.

ME: Which island?

CAROLYN: Vashon Island.

ME: I went to grade school on Vashon Island.

CAROLYN: So did I! I was at Burton School.

ME: Me too!

We turned out to be first and second grade classmates. How cool is that? But the specific personal information that was so exciting did not come out freely, did it? Look how I had to chisel it out!

* * *

I'm hoping that you will not to have to dumpster dive for your social life. But wherever you find your new friends, know that you have the key for getting from chat to conversation: offer free, specific information. If you remember just one thing from your reading, let it be this. Always use specific proper nouns when you can—say "Washington," not "up north." Whatever reasons you offer as to why you don't do this do not impress me. Get me names and dates and I'll be interested. Try it out.

Encourage With Questions

On a trip to England in the mid-1980s, a friend and I had the privilege of spending a day on a cattle farm in Surrey with a retired World War II officer and his wife. He met us at the train, and we spent the morning touring his land and facilities. Thereafter, my friend and I sat in his Victorian parlor for a cup of tea with the wife. We beamed brightly at each other as an uncertain silence established itself. Then with the courage expected in a wife of a former British Gurkhas officer, our hostess remarked, "We haven't seen many Yanks down here for quite a while." After a long pause, she continued with a smile, "That Hitler was a bad sort, wasn't he?"

We had to agree with her, although I can't say the conversation went very far. I'll give her my Most Valiant Effort at Small Talk Award, but really we could have used some more encouraging questions on her part.

You can encourage the other person to talk with a question on the same topic you chose as your anchor and reveal. Just avoid yes or no questions. Even though simple yes or no questions can help open areas of conversation, the problem is that that the conversational partner may actually respond with just a yes or no. Then you're left having to come up with another question.

Many young people and some foreign-born citizens may not be forthcoming because they don't latch on to the intent of the question (i.e., to open a conversation). Instead, they respond as if the content of that particular question is all that matters (like my teaching colleague Carolyn in the story in the previous section). This is not fun. The better approach is the use of the open-ended question and the provocative question. Open-ended questions give the subject plenty of room to respond as he or she would like:

What did you think of the speaker?

How was the parking when you arrived?

When do people generally go skiing around here?

Where are the best women's boutiques in the city?

What kind of bait are you using?

Why did the jazz club fail?

What, why, where, and how questions are the tools of journalists—and of you too if you want to encourage a more complete response from a person. You'll probably end up with more free information for further conversation building.

JENNY: What did you think of the clown act with the balloon animals?

LUKE: To tell you the truth, my five-year-old was given a balloon kit for her birthday and she can make most of the animals that he did!

Now you have smart five-year-olds and maybe balloons as potential topics. Can you do anything with that?

JENNY: A balloon kit! I would have never have thought of that for little kids. I've got a four-year-old niece in Seattle who is super smart. I bet she'd love that. Where do you go to buy the right balloons for this?

Take a cue from Jenny. One of the most ingratiating responses you can make is a follow-up question because it demonstrates that you are interested enough to pursue the topic. This is one of those interview techniques that encourages the speaker and helps add dimension to the topic.

Making Your Passion Visible

Please indulge me. I want to tell you a story that begins with the repair of my red velvet slippers and ends with me listening to Dietrich Fischer-Dieskau late one night.

I went to pick up my shoes from the small shop in my neighborhood where you can get your shoes—or your vacuum cleaner—repaired. I would describe the shop as utilitarian, a place of serious repair. When the repair man disappeared to retrieve my slippers I noticed high on the wall a series of four fading posters all relating to Verdi opera performances.

When the man returned with my slippers, he said, "So, you are an opera lover!"

I then realized I had been humming "Celeste Aida" to myself (as one does).

ME: Looks like you're one yourself!

HIM: Yeah, I like it. I do. But what I really love is lieder, German lieder.

ME: Really? I went to a John Shirley-Quirk lieder concert and got to sit on the floor right in front of him—a sold-out concert in a small hall. He's wonderful, as I'm sure you know, but my most vivid memory was watching a stream of sweat coming down that man's face and ending in a drop on his eyelash that just stayed there. He's holding out this delicious pianissimo and the man does not blink! So disciplined!

HIM: Then you've got to have heard Fischer-Dieskau! He's "The Man" for lieder. Of course, Schubert is the necessary element here. Nobody sings Schubert like Dietrich Fischer-Dieskau! There is … I don't know what … just something in his voice that is so, so … I don't know what. It is wonderful.

ME: I'll want to hear that! But I did hear Marian Anderson sing "The Erl-King" when I was thirteen years old. I'm by myself, sitting in the front row, just because I got to the theater before anybody else. Long story short, she sang the child's part from the stage directly into my front-row face. It didn't take much of that before I started to sob—Anderson's storytelling!—and humiliate myself. I just didn't understand what was happening to me.

HIM: I know what you mean. I know what you mean!

This was our small talk, people! I know this is the kind of conversation that you want to have: genuine, mutual, and stimulating.

The repairman then reached across the counter, taking my hand and introducing himself, "I am Chang." "I am Carol," I responded. We are now friends. And that's why I listened to Dietrich Fischer-Dieskau on YouTube late that night—so I could hear what Chang had heard.

Now, suppose I had met him at the neighborhood block party, and suppose I had asked him, "What do you do?" He would have said, "I repair shoes and vacuum cleaners." We had been spared the tedious search for a topic because he had revealed his passion up on the wall and I had responded in a way that encouraged him to expound on it.

Pay attention to how this serendipitous conversation occurred. Chang had his passion on display—free information—above the vacuum cleaners and shoes. The moral of the story: Be thinking about what you'd love to talk about and how you could make that more easily apparent to a conversational partner.

What Do You Do?

The "What do you do?" question gets the prize for the most-often-used open-ended question to start a conversation, at least around these parts. In many circles, work is considered the only salient feature of another person. But there are quite a few people who consider the "What do you do?" question inappropriate, boring, rude, predictable, and intrusive.

Think twice before you poke this far into somebody's business. They may not want to be defined by their work. (This topic is especially disdained in Europe.) Here are some alternate questions for learning about people.

What do you like to do on weekends?

What do you recommend visitors do here?

Where would you take children for a great Saturday outing?

What kind of experience have you had with the local service clubs?

But let's say occupations do make their way into the conversation. Your partner just may have an interesting occupation that lends itself to conversation. Leil Lowndes' book How to Talk to Anybody About Anything gives you some excellent questions for unusual occupations that will ensure a thoughtful and informed exchange. But what if they say something that's not so readily engaging? Now it's your job to see if you can make them interesting by asking a thoughtful or provocative question.

What would be a provocative question for a shoe salesman? Probably not "How long have you sold shoes?" or "How did you get started in the shoe business?" While these aren't bad questions, they're just not especially interesting ones.

A good question is one that causes a person to think, to make a judgment.

You will make that person feel interesting, and that feels very nice indeed. Here are some possibilities:

Do you think men or women are harder to please?

What kinds of customers drive you nuts?

Where are most shoes made these days?

How do foreign-made shoes compare to American shoes in quality and price?

What can you tell me about the fashion trends for the next year?

What's the hottest sneaker for men?

Writer and tech entrepreneur Paul Ford suggested a particularly stimulating response to the "occupational reveal" in his Medium piece "How to Be Polite." In conversations with new acquaintances, Ford tries not to ask what they do for a living, but if it comes to that, he responds to their job description—whatever it is—with, "Wow. That sounds hard."

Think about it. Doesn't everybody think that their job is hard? And can you think of a better way to extend empathy?

* * *

Getting the Anchor, Reveal, Encourage sequence to come easy takes repeated practice. Practice means putting these sentences into your mouth and actually saying the words. The repetition will put them into your motor memory until they become automatic. I know this may feel a bit stupid to you, but we're dealing with sausage making here.

Practice it around the house. Don't quit when you are still fumbling awkwardly. Pick from an example in the book if you need to. Just keep changing a few words and try again.

(Anchor) Great day, huh?

(Reveal) I see they've put up some tents on the lawn out there; maybe they think some rain's coming.

(Encourage) What do you think?

This is all you need to do for starters. Practice will really pay off for you when you get out into the real world. You'll be glad you rehearsed.

Applying This Skill: Introductions

Since introductions are essential to starting relationships, you will practice introductions.

First, everyone will get up. . Introduce yourself to 3–4 people in the class. You must introduce yourself to at least two people on the other side of the classroom! You have to move around the room Practice some introduction skills, including:

- Shaking hands
- Saying your name clearly
- Asking for and sharing details
- Starting a conversation
- Establishing your presence in the class

Second, you will pair with another student. Now, you will do a more in-depth introduction; you'll need paper and pen to take notes. Find somewhere to sit as a pair. Ask each other some of the questions below; questions with an asterisk (*) are required. Take notes, and be prepared to introduce your partner to the class.

Questions:

- o Name*
- o Major*
- o Year in school*
- o Future goals
- o Interesting fact about you
- o Hobbies or interests
- o Something unique (travel, family, personal story, pets) or something completely boring*
- o Aspects of course you are concerned about*
- o Aspects of course you are looking forward to

Each person will stand up and introduce their partner to the class. Introductions are essential to building relationships and helping people connect. This exercise helps the class begin to build a welcoming, supportive community.

Figure 2.1 The Power of First impressions

3

Elements of Written Communication

In communications studies, you can learn about encoding and decoding, interference, and more, but for our purposes, you need to know, practically, the elements necessary for effective communication. The 5 Cs of communication provide an easy way to identify the major characteristics of effective communication. This will help you create and edit your written communications. After completing this lesson, you will:

- Understand the Cs of communication
- Be able to apply the Cs of communication to a written document

The 5 Cs of Communication

For our purposes, the 5Cs of communication mean your writing should be:

- Clear
- Concise
- Complete
- Consistent
- Considerate

The section below will explain, in detail, each aspect of communication.

Clear

Clear writing means communicating your message so the receiver understands easily. A clear message has a clear purpose, addresses the receiver's needs and questions, and is written using the following guidelines:

- Use short sentences: Readers may get lost or confused by long, convoluted sentences; one idea per sentence is best.
- Use concrete words: Concrete words refer to things we know through our senses; they are tangible qualities and characteristics. Abstract words refer to vague ideas or qualities and intangible characteristics.

  - Concrete: To succeed in this course, you must read the textbook, study hard, and attend class.
  - Abstract: To succeed in the course, you must work hard.
- Avoid clichés: Clichés are overused words and phrases that have a general meaning or have lost their meaning; using clichés can cause confusion, misunderstandings, and unclear writing and make you seem like a lazy, unoriginal writer. Common clichés include:

  - Every cloud has a silver lining.
  - It's raining cats and dogs.

- o   Get your ducks in a row.
- o   All over the map
- Use appropriate and accurate words: Tailor your message to the audience, and use appropriate terms (purview vs. area; pay vs. remunerate; cognizant vs. aware); use the correct version of commonly confused words (e.g., their, they're, there; affect, effect; whether, weather, etc.).
- Use appropriate facts and figures: Include details, figures, data, and statistics when they will increase the clarity of your message.
- Use visual enhancements to increase readability: Use bullet lists to itemize numerous tasks or points.

Concise

Concise writing presents a complete message as briefly as possible; use as few words as possible to get your message across clearly. Concise messages save companies time and money because no reader wants to wade through long blocks of text to find relevant information. State your point briefly and clearly. To improve conciseness, do the following:

- Avoid unnecessary repetition (e.g., completely finish, basic fundamentals, large in size).
- Avoid wordy phrases (e.g., first and foremost, in order to, point in time).
- Avoid circumlocutions (e.g., at this point in time vs. now; due to the fact that vs. because; in reference to vs. about).
- Avoid starting sentences with "it is" or "there are."

    - o   "There are two assignments due next week" versus "Two assignments are due next week."
- Unneeded modifiers (e.g., really, basically, actually)

- Weak phrases (e.g., seems like, might be)

    Aim to reduce the word count in your first draft by 10%–20%.

Complete

Complete writing means thinking of the needs of the audience. What does the audience need/want to know? What questions will the audience have? A complete message leaves the reader without any questions or need to continue a back-and-forth conversation.

    Remember the 5 Ws when writing, and answer as many of these questions as possible:

- Who
- What
- Where
- When
- Why

    Ensure the receiver has the information needed to take action. Include:

- Times and dates
- Order numbers
- Places

Consistent

Consistency covers both content and writing details. Failure to be consistent may, at worst, confuse your readers and, at best, show lack of attention to detail. Both show a lack of professionalism.

Consistency includes broad topics like products/services, general attitude toward customers and employers, and responsiveness to messages. Maintaining consistent messaging across areas of and among employees of a company is very important on a company-wide scale.

Ensuring consistency within your own messages is no less important. Plan and organize your document to ensure your reader understands the topic and purpose. Refer to people, places, topics, and so on with the same terms throughout the document. For example, use "customer" throughout rather than alternating between "customer" and "user." Clearly define different places, accounts, times, meetings, and so forth.

When writing, ensure consistency in the following ways:

- Format and style (e.g., document design, use of visual enhancements, spacing, etc.)
- Citations, references, and footnotes (e.g., use of MLA, APA, or other style guidelines)
- Grammar (e.g., comma use, capitalization, numbers)
- Spelling, including use of contractions (e.g., don't vs. do not)
- Abbreviations and acronyms (e.g., Avenue vs. Ave.)

Consistency in your messages will be developed through careful planning, editing, and proofreading.

Considerate

Writing with consideration means focusing on the reader's needs, problems, desires, and questions. It is a focus on "you" (the reader/receiver) versus a focus on "I" or "we" (the writer). As writers, we consider how readers will respond to our messages, anticipating their emotional reactions and potential questions/concerns.

Consideration is largely about the tone of your message. Who are you writing to? Is it a formal or informal audience? Does your writing target that audience?

- Use "you attitude" ("Your order will arrive in 3–5 days" vs. "We sent your order this morning").
- Write positively: Emphasize the positive, demonstrate benefits.
- Be tactful, thoughtful, and polite: Choose words carefully to be pleasant and respectful.
- Avoid discriminatory terms (e.g., manpower vs. workers/employees; server vs. waitress).

Writing with consideration will enhance goodwill, increase trust, and contribute to a positive business relationship.

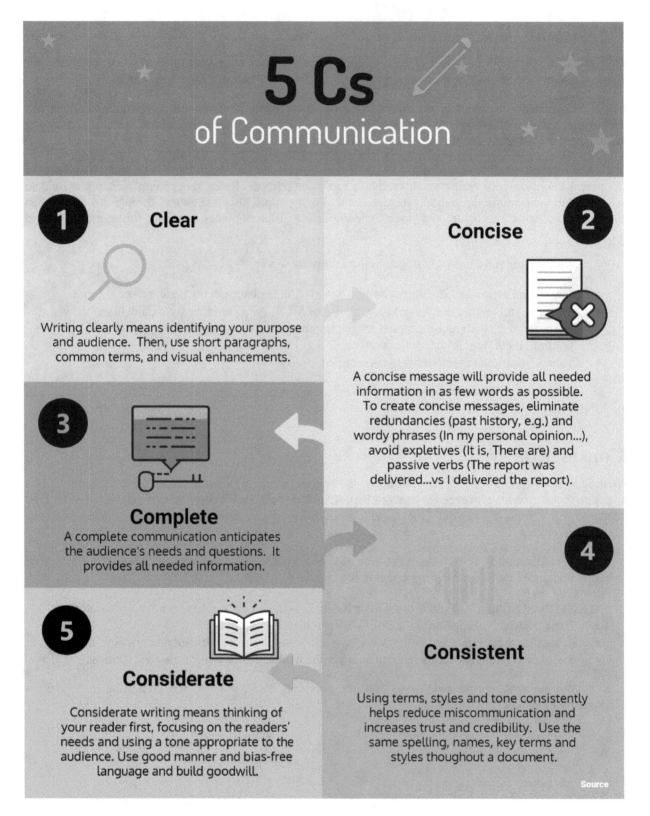

5 Cs
of Communication

1 Clear

Writing clearly means identifying your purpose and audience. Then, use short paragraphs, common terms, and visual enhancements.

2 Concise

A concise message will provide all needed information in as few words as possible. To create concise messages, eliminate redundancies (past history, e.g.) and wordy phrases (In my personal opinion...), avoid expletives (It is, There are) and passive verbs (The report was delivered...vs I delivered the report).

3 Complete

A complete communication anticipates the audience's needs and questions. It provides all needed information.

4 Consistent

Using terms, styles and tone consistently helps reduce miscommunication and increases trust and credibility. Use the same spelling, names, key terms and styles thoughout a document.

5 Considerate

Considerate writing means thinking of your reader first, focusing on the readers' needs and using a tone appropriate to the audience. Use good manner and bias-free language and build goodwill.

Source

Figure 3.1 5 Cs of Communication

Applying This Skill: 5 Cs of Communication Exercise

The class will be divided into five groups; each group will be assigned a "C" of communication. In order to develop an understanding of the 5 Cs of Communication, work as a group to apply your assigned "C" to the paragraph below. How does your assigned "C" apply to this paragraph? Is it used? Should it be applied? How?

Be prepared to explain your "C" and share your work with the class.

Someone called from the customer that we sent the big Shipment to, saying that they were having a problem with some of our product. The caller thought that there was probably going to be some more information heading our way pretty soon. They indicated that they were really concerned because this is not the first time this has happened. It might be fairly costly to them if something isn't done soon to take care of this problem. This might be a "no brainer" if the problem is the same as it was the last time we got on the "bad side" of this customer. We all know what a pain they can be when they don't get what they want. We have heard this song and dance before about them taking their business elsewhere. But we all know that the Customer is always right, and we will need to jump through any hoops they want us to in order to keep their business. If we don't hear something by the p.m., we will know the "ax" is going to fall on someone either here or in HQ.[1]

---

[1] Paragraph adapted from Peter R. Garber, *50 Communication Activities, Icebreakers and Exercises* (Amherst, MA: HRD Press, 2008).

4

Peer Assessment and Review

One of the most important skills needed in the workplace is the ability to communicate positive and negative feedback to others. Feedback is important for learning, insight, and growth. In your position, you will most likely have to give feedback to employees, peers, clients, and others. You may have to write performance reviews or give verbal feedback, either formally or informally.

One way to think of feedback is as a gift. You're helping the other person improve. Think of both giving and receiving feedback as a growth opportunity, but both giving and receiving feedback can be hard. When giving feedback, you may not feel qualified to make reliable judgments or provide insightful comments on another person's work or performance. You may be afraid to comment for a variety of reasons, including fear of hurting the other person's feelings and negative repercussions for you. Despite these fears, studies show students make judgments and comments similar to ones their professors would make. You are qualified to give feedback.

In this lesson, you will learn how to give feedback. You will think about positive and negative feedback in your life and then learn about the process of editing and revising written documents.

After completing this lesson, you will be able to:

- Deliver effective feedback
- Use the editing and revising process
- Identify common proofreader's marks

Feedback

Peer feedback activities help develop critical thinking and reflection skills, which employers sometimes say are lacking in new hires. Peer feedback helps develop sensitivity to how you say something and the impact of your words, and it helps you accept and respond to criticism. If you get multiple opinions, you may value the feedback more than if only one person makes a comment. Ultimately, everyone makes mistakes; learning to respond is important to developing resilience.

Positive Feedback

Think about how often you give positive feedback to coworkers, other students, friends, or family members. Do you give positive feedback daily? Weekly? Occasionally? Never? Think about in what situations you give positive feedback. Is it a work situation, when you praise a coworker? Do you find giving praise natural, or is it something you have to work at? If you rarely give positive feedback, why is that? What stops you from praising others?

Praise encourages people to keep doing a task. If your supervisor hands out minutes from a staff meeting and you mention how helpful that is to your project, your supervisor is likely to keep distributing meeting minutes. Praise increases confidence, performance, and motivation.

Critical Feedback

While positive feedback feels good, negative feedback can have an even bigger impact on a person's emotional state and job performance. Critical feedback may feel like a personal attack, unjustified or untrue. Think of a time when you received negative feedback. Was it hurtful or helpful? Why? What made it hurtful? Was it recent or a long time ago? A majority of adults report feeling extremely hurt when receiving negative feedback, which has lasting effects on relationships and job performance.

Is it possible to give feedback in useful, helpful, and less harsh ways? Of course! Most people will respond better to feedback that is valid, reliable, fair, and useful and when it is delivered as constructive criticism. Feedback is useful when it focuses on solutions or alternatives and when it is honest and tactful. Constructive, positive feedback can help build relationships and trust, improve job performance, and promote professional development. Completing the following readings and activities should help your class develop a common vocabulary for giving positive, constructive feedback.

Reading 4.1

Business Writing that Builds Relationships, Syntax Training

By Lynn Gaertner-Johnson

As a group, look at the list below.

Of the twenty tips below, ten should begin with the word "Don't"; ten should not. Cross out the word "Don't" if it doesn't belong at the beginning of the tip. If it does belong, circle it.

How could you rephrase these items?

1. Don't exaggerate.
2. Don't be cute or clever.
3. Don't make a sincere, positive comment before constructive comments.
4. Don't try to balance the positives and negatives.
5. Don't equate rudeness with straight talk.
6. Don't avoid the pronouns "you" and "your" in constructive comments.

7. Don't act dense.
8. Don't be specific.
9. Don't be a hit-and-run critic.
10. Don't avoid the word "but" after a compliment.
11. Don't provide suggestions or offer to provide them.

12. Don't copy other people on constructive feedback.
13. Don't be sure your correction is valid when you correct other people's work.
14. Don't assume someone else has a problem you can help to fix.
15. Don't comment if it is not your job to do so and you have not been asked or paid for an opinion.
16. Don't focus on the future.
17. Don't counterattack.
18. Don't put your feedback in context.
19. Don't give feedback when it is too late to incorporate.
20. Don't give constructive feedback privately.

Reading 4.2

Edit, Rewrite, and Refine

Follow the Three Stage Editing Process

By Jack Appleman

Pointer

Editing is a three-stage process that focuses separately on *message*, *organization*, and *mechanics*.

Follow the Three-Stage Editing Process

Editing can be divided into three major focus areas:

1. message
2. organization
3. mechanics.

In the three stages of editing, each area is addressed separately because it's impossible to pay close attention to all three at the same time. Let's look at the three stages.

Message

Editing should begin with the message because it makes no sense to waste time reorganizing or reviewing the mechanics of text that isn't conveying your points clearly.

To review the clarity of your message, ask yourself a few simple questions. These questions are similar to the ones you asked when you started writing the -document (Step 2: Know Where You're Taking Your Readers):

- Is the purpose or bottom line clear?
- Is the action required of the reader clear?
- Are the other important points clear?
- Is the tone appropriate for the message?
- Is the message written in a positive (rather than negative) way?

As you answer those questions, mark any text you're not satisfied with (for example, a confusing action step). On a paper copy, circle or highlight a group of words or sentences that may need revision. If you prefer editing only on a screen, use the highlighting feature or put that block of text in a different color.

Go through the entire document, marking places you may revise, before you begin revising. You may want to go through it two or three times. Then work on clarifying your message in each of the places you've marked.

Organization

All documents, even those with just a few paragraphs, need to be organized so that the reader can follow the text easily. The second stage of editing takes a hard look at how well you've imposed a logical order on the message you're trying to convey.

Here are some questions to ask yourself to determine if your document is properly organized:

- Is information separated into chunks that are easy to digest?
- Are those chunks arranged in a logical sequence?
- Does each paragraph contain just one basic idea so readers won't get confused?
- Are there transitions unifying sentences, paragraphs, and sections to help ideas in the document flow smoothly from start to finish?
- Is the structure reasonably similar throughout different sections?
- Could subheads before key sections make it -easier to read?

One method to separate and arrange your ideas is to read the document and list all the key points it conveys. In essence, you're re-outlining it. This is much easier when you're looking at text you've written than it is when you're staring at a blank page. The re-outlining process also will help identify any important concepts that you omitted. You can list them separately at the bottom of the page or on a separate sheet of paper and incorporate them as you reorganize the document. You'll also be able to spot repeated or similar ideas scattered throughout the document and then merge them into a single paragraph or section.

If you developed an initial outline before you started your first draft, compare that version to the re-outline to see if you omitted anything you initially intended to include.

During this stage, you may decide to change the order in which ideas are presented so they flow more logically from one to the next.

Consider adding subheads or a few words before each section (set in bold or italic, perhaps underlined) to pinpoint the key message that follows and to further separate each concept. (See Step 6 for more discussion of subheads.)

Good organization is a more subjective quality than are the message and proper mechanics. For example, the same information can be conveyed through shorter or longer paragraphs. And you can explain a multifaceted concept by using bullets to list the facets or by writing a few traditional paragraphs with no bulleted items.

When you get comfortable with your own method of organizing, you'll find that it not only promotes readability but also simplifies your writing process -because you can move text around into separate categories more confidently—and get the document done faster.

Mechanics

Most of the grunt work in editing comes in the third stage: reviewing the mechanics of your text. Mechanics form the micro level of the document, not the macro message or the mid-level organization. Mechanics are the weeds!

Editing for mechanics—spelling, punctuation, grammar, and word usage—may require you to be in a different frame of mind than you are when evaluating message clarity and organization. You need to scrutinize individual words or groups of words instead of the entire document. Here are some questions you need to ask:

- Spelling/typos

    o   Are any words misspelled?
    o   Are any homonyms (sound-alikes, such as there and their) used in place of the correct words?
    o   Are any words missing or out of place in a sentence?
    o   Have you placed apostrophes correctly?
    o   Are all proper names spelled correctly?

- Punctuation

    o   Do all of your sentences end with appropriate punctuation?
    o   Are all commas and periods placed inside quotation marks?
    o   Do commas separate all the items in a series?
    o   Do semicolons separate all the items in a comma-separated series?

- Grammar and syntax

    o   Do subjects and verbs agree in number?
    o   Do nouns and pronouns agree in number?
    o   Is text written in a consistent tense?
    o   Are sentences written in a parallel structure?
    o   Are bulleted or numbered lists written in a parallel structure?
    o   Are subheads written in a parallel structure?
    o   Does each introductory phrase directly relate to the noun that immediately follows it?
    o   Is everything written in complete sentences, where appropriate?
    o   Are there short, choppy sentences that can be combined for better flow?

- Word usage

    o Is there any stuffy language that can be -replaced with simpler words?
    o Are there any weak passive verbs or verb-nouns that can be replaced with more powerful active verbs?
    o Can you eliminate any redundant language?
    o Is there jargon or "business-speak" that can be simplified with more widely understood terminology?

You can start with the spelling/grammar-checking feature usually available with word-processing software. It helps catch obvious mistakes—but *don't* depend on it. The spelling-check feature won't catch homonyms you've used incorrectly (*here, hear; do, due; there, their, they're*); and if you've written *is* when you meant *in,* the software won't catch your mistake. As to the grammar-checking feature, sometimes the software's suggestions are just plain wrong.

Another way to find mistakes is to read your words aloud in a staccato, syllable-by-syllable rhythm so you actually can hear the errors. For example, when sounding out "Lu-pé out-lined four-teen work-flow -im-prove-ments is her re-port," you'll probably notice that "is" should be "in." Also try reading the text backward, forcing yourself to review one word at a time -instead of getting mesmerized by the flow of sentences and paragraphs.

Editing for mechanics can be handled in many ways. You can print out your document, write your revisions on the paper copy, and then key them into the electronic file. Or you can use the tracking/redlining feature of your word-processing program, which will enable you to keep your original version without interrupting the flow of the newer version. With time, you'll discover the system that works best for you.

Applying This Skill: Peer Review Exercise

Writing is a process and requires multiple revisions to ensure a polished product. Every writer needs an editor, often more than one. In this class, you will be asked to provide feedback on other students' work. To prepare you for that task, please read about the three-step approach below. Then edit the document below; the checklist appears on the following page. You will share and compare your review with a classmate.

Three-Step approach

1. Read first. Judge later. Read the piece all the way through without making marks or comments. Focus on what the writer is trying to say. Is the content clear?

2. Read again and edit. Read the piece again, highlighting sections for discussion and recording comments/questions. Mark grammatical errors or awkward wording.

3. Complete the checklist. Review the document with the related checklist.

Assess Your Document Here

Business Letter Format and Editing Checklist

□→ Sender's Address Here
Street Address Here
City, State, Zip Code

□→ Date Here

□→ Addressee's Name Here
Street Address
City, State, Zip Code

□→ Salutation Here:

□→ Introduction Paragraph: Open with the main idea (deductive approach). Include the reason for writing and an outline of information to follow in the document (outline statement).

□→Body Paragraph 1: Start with topic sentence. Include supporting information. Use specific details and in-text citations when appropriate.

□→Body Paragraph 2: Use basic body paragraph organization. Use visual enhancements and design elements as needed, including bullets, bold, italics, and subheadings. Remember and apply the 5 Cs of Communication.

□→Body Paragraph (if needed):

□→ Conclusion: Provide a sense of closure. Remind reader of main point; include action steps if needed. Include a forward-looking statement and include a contact statement (who reader should contact for more information).

□→Complementary Close,

□→ Signature Here

□→ Sender's Name

Sender's Title, if appropriate

□→ Enclosure Notation, if needed

Sample Letter for Peer Review

To: Professor Goenner, Herberger Business School,
Herberger Business School, Marketing & Business Law Department,
St. Cloud State University, 720 4th Avenue South, St. Cloud,
MN 56301

Hello Professor, my name is Gary Johnson. I am a student at St. Cloud State University. I graduated high school Albert Lea Minnesota in 2012. While attending there I also played hockey.

At St. Cloud State University I am currently pursuing a degree in accounting; I have completed my minor in mass communications. Upon coming to SCSU I didn't know what to study, so I decided on physics because I wanted to know how the world works. I always make the joke that this is the reason I am in accounting; I studied physics because I wanted to know what makes the world turn... I ended up in accounting because I discovered what actually makes the world turn. With in that journey I picked up a minor in mass communications because there was a short time that I thought I was going to major in it after changing from physics.

Currently I work at House of Pizza in Sartell as a delivery guy; I work there about 20 hrs a week. As I attend school I hope to build the skills to eventually become a CPA and work for a firm. I hope to work my way up the ranks and eventually become a partner at a firm. I don't individually do much volunteer work, but I am a member of Delta Sigma Pi and through that we have volunteered for things like Feed my Starving Children and Highway clean-up. Being a member of DSP has benefited me in many ways including networking and communication skills. Throughout school I have developed strong oral communication skills. I hope that it will play into my favor in the future working with different clients. I am assuming non face to face interactions will also be a huge part of the position I hope to attain. That is definitely a skill I hope to improve.

An excellent example of a professional in my hopeful field of choice is my second uncle Steve Johnson. I am uncertain the firm he worked for, but he has just recently retired as a CPA after 35 years of work. Last time I talked to him he mentioned that he himself graduated from SCSU decades ago. At the family reunion I talked to him at he said to me, "I haven't worked a day in my life for 35 years. I got paid to talk business with my friends." Although I had already decided my major before talking to him, hearing that only cemented my plan for the future.

Applying This Skill: Proofreading Symbol Matching

Proofreaders and editors use a standard set of marks when editing papers. While you're not required to use these marks, your instructor may. To ensure you understand the suggestions and comments made on your writing, complete the exercise below.

Match the symbol with its standard proofreading meaning.

1.	Insert period	_____	a. trans
2.	Insert	_____	b. 〫
3.	Insert comma	_____	c. ≡
4.	Awkward construction	_____	d.
5.	Insert apostrophe	_____	e.
6.	Delete	_____	f. 𝒴
7.	Comma splice	_____	g. agr
8.	Referent unclear	_____	h. sp
9.	Wrong word	_____	i. w
10.	Paragraph	_____	j. awk
11.	Capitalize	_____	k. ∧
12.	Lower case	_____	l. cs
13.	Informal or inaccurate vocabulary	_____	m. ....
14.	Spell out	_____	n. ww
15.	Transpose	_____	o. /
16.	stet (let original stand)	_____	p. ?
17.	Spelling error	_____	q.
18.	Wordy	_____	r. ••
19.	What?	_____	s. tr
20.	Align	_____	t. ¶
21.	Agreement error	_____	u. ⧕
22.	Need transition	_____	v. ref
23.	Space	_____	w. v

5

Effective Writing

Every time you share a written document, you are representing yourself and the company. While most people will excuse one typographical or proofreading error in a document, multiple errors look bad, both for you and your company. Poor written communication can cause confusion and reduced efficiency, lower employee morale, and reduce creativity. Errors in policy, for example, can hamper business efforts, while mistakes in marketing materials may affect customer–client relationships. Errors make you appear unprofessional and sloppy, with a lack of attention to detail. Customers or clients may wonder if you will treat them with the same lack of concern. So the details of writing and proofreading are important.

After completing this lesson, you will be able to:

- Write clearly and concisely

- Use professional, unbiased, positive language

- Use active voice and parallelism

Do you believe a comma cost one company $10 million? Or that a typo and one missing letter ruined a company?

Reading 5.1

The $10 Million Comma

How one law that was missing a comma cost a company $10 million.

By Mignon Fogarty

People have such strong opinions about the Oxford comma that in 2013 the satire site The Onion published an article titled "4 Copy Editors Killed in Ongoing AP Style, Chicago Manual Gang Violence," which ended by lamenting an innocent bystander who committed suicide after being "caught up in a long-winded dispute over use of the serial, or Oxford, comma."

But that little comma before the *and* in a series like *red*, *white*, and *blue* is no joke for contract lawyers. Last week, news broke that the Oakhurst Dairy in the state of Maine would have to pay its milk-truck drivers approximately $10 million because of a missing serial comma in Maine's overtime law.

In this class action case, the two sides were arguing about the duties employees do for which they *don't* get overtime pay. This is the ambiguous sentence that -describes the exemptions:

The canning, processing, preserving, freezing, drying, marketing, storing, packing for shipment or distribution of:

1. Agricultural produce;
2. Meat and fish products; and
3. Perishable good.

The drivers do distribute perishable goods—milk—but the important part is that there is no comma after the word *shipment* in the phrase *packing for shipment* or *distribution,* therefore the drivers argued that the word *distribution* is modifying packing and isn't a separate thing that makes them exempt.

In other words, the drivers said, "We don't package milk" so we aren't exempt from overtime pay, and the dairy said, "Wait a minute, you distribute perishable goods, so you are exempt." And this all rests on how you interpret the final part without a serial comma: *packing for shipment* or *distribution of ... perishable goods.*

Complicating matters is that Maine Legislative Drafting Manual tells lawmakers not to use serial commas—an outrage if you ask me because as the court decision pointed out, the addition of a serial comma would have made the meaning absolutely clear: it would have clearly marked *distribution* as a separate activity.

Instead, lawmakers left it out.

The Maine Manual actually warns lawmakers about sentences just like the one in question—where a list item is modified, and it says that instead of trying to solve the problem with a comma, they should rewrite the entire sentence so they don't need one.

But they didn't, which left the dairy and the drivers with an ambiguous sentence. Worth $10 million.

An earlier court ruled in favor of the dairy, but now the United States Court of Appeals for the First Circuit has overturned that ruling in favor of the drivers. Circuit Judge David J. Barron wrote the opinion, which is more pleasant to read than most court documents I've seen, opening "For want of a comma, we have this case."

There's a long section in the middle about whether the words *shipment* and *distribution* are synonyms, and then we get to a grammatical argument: that each of the words that describes an exempt activity—*canning, processing, preserving,* and so on—are gerunds, but *shipment* and *distribution* are both nouns.

Ah ha!" said the drivers. This means *shipment* and *distribution* both serve the same function, and it's a function that is different from the gerunds, also known as the exempt activities. They argue that if distribution of perishable goods were an exempt activity, it would have been called distributing perishable goods. And the court agreed. Boom. $10 million.

This isn't the first time a court case has hinged on a comma either. Back in 2006, a Canadian company lost a million-dollar case that came down to a comma before a modifying phrase.

As the Maine Legislative Drafting Manual noted, "Commas are probably the most misused and misunderstood punctuation marks in legal drafting and, perhaps, the English language. Use them thoughtfully and sparingly," and I would add "use them with extreme caution when modifying phrases are involved and millions of dollars could be at stake."

Below, you will find more articles about the cost of bad writing and the principles of professional writing. Following the articles, a series of exercises will help you develop and polish your writing skills. After completing this lesson, you will be able to:

- Evaluate and assess your current writing abilities
- Demonstrate the ability to write concisely and clearly
- Select vocabulary appropriate for the situation
- Use pronouns, numbers and parallelism
- Distinguish between and use active and passive voice

....

How a Missing 'S' Killed a 134-Year-Old Company

Court rules in Taylor & Sons' favor

By Kate Seamons

There are bad typos and there are *bad typos*. This story is a case of the latter. Taylor & Sons is a Welsh engineering firm founded in 1875; on Feb. 20, 2009, Companies House, the UK agency that incorporates and dissolves limited companies, listed it as being "wound up," essentially in liquidation. Except it wasn't: Taylor & Son was the company having issues. Even though the error was rectified on Feb. 23, Taylor & Sons says that the erroneous info had already been sold to credit reference agencies. Customers spotted the notice, didn't catch the missing S, and started abandoning the firm, which at the time boasted 250 employees. Among the customers who fled: Tata Steel, which had been paying the firm about $600,000 a month, per the BBC.

The *Telegraph* reports that owner Philip Davison-Sebry said that within three weeks' time, all 3,000 of its suppliers had contacted the company about terminating orders or canceling credit. The company went into administration within two months of the typo, the business having been damaged "so as to become of no real value," he says. And so Davison-Sebry sued Companies House. In a ruling Monday, a High Court judge agreed with Davison-Sebry, noting that Companies House was obligated to take reasonable care when recording such "winding ups" to verify that the correct company was being named. And while Companies House argued that the three-day lifespan of the error was too short to cause the Taylor & Sons' failure, the judge disagreed. Davison-Sebry sued for roughly $13.3 million; the BBC reports the preliminary ruling didn't address damages.

....

Reading 5.3

Fundamentals of Professional Writing

By Janet Mizrahi

Whether you are a student about to step into the world of work or a more seasoned employee with years of experience, you must be able to communicate effectively to advance your career. Employers consistently rank good communication skills—speaking with customers and colleagues, presenting information, and writing—in the top tier of desired skills for both new hires and current employees. The ability to concisely and accurately convey meaning to different people is a prerequisite in today's fast-paced world.

Writing like a professional—whether the document is printed or on the screen—is best taken on as a process, with careful attention paid to detail. This chapter will describe how to break down all writing tasks into a series of steps to streamline the process as well as describe the characteristics that all professional writing should embody.

Writing as a Process

Many people think that good writing flows out of the brain, into the fingers, and onto the page or screen. Nothing could be further from the truth. Professional writers know that writing, like any acquired skill, requires patience and persistence. Whatever we are composing—whether an e-mail message or a proposal for a new business—the key to writing well is to consider writing a process rather than a one shot deal. Your prose will be better and will take you less time to compose if you look at writing as a series of tasks. For those who suffer from writer's block or who shudder at the thought of writing, I can promise that if you break down writing into several component parts, the result will be better and you will feel less anxious.

The task of writing can be broken down to three separate steps, for which I've developed an acronym: **AWE**, short for assess, write, and edit. These three steps should be completed for every piece of writing that will be seen by another person. The only writing that doesn't require this process is personal writing.

Step 1: Assess

Before you ever put your fingers on the keyboard or put pen to paper, begin by assessing the writing situation and define your **audience and purpose**. I advise making this step formal: Write down your answers.

Knowing the audience—your reader—is imperative for successful writing. Writers need to be very clear about the end user because the language and style we use depends upon who will read what we write.

In essence, we have to psych out the reader to accomplish our writing goal. We cannot do that unless we analyze the reader accurately.

Define the characteristics of your reader as is shown in Table 5.3.1:

Table 5.3.1 **Audience profile template**

Audience characteristic	Rationale
Age	Writing for children differs from writing for adults or teens. Your tone, word choice, and medium may differ greatly depending on the age of the reader.
Gender	Writing for an all-male audience will differ from writing for an all-female audience. Likewise, if the audience is mixed, you may make different language choices than you do for a homogeneous group.
Language proficiency	The reader's knowledge of English will affect your word choice, sentence length, and other stylistic elements.
Education level	You may be writing for an audience with a 10th grade reading level or one comprised of college graduates. Each audience will have different expectations and needs, both of which you as the writer must be aware.
Attitude toward writer or organization	You must know if the audience is skeptical, frightened, pleased, or hostile toward you, the topic, or the organization. Anticipate your audience's reaction so you can write in a way that will support the document's purpose.
Knowledge of the topic	A document may be geared to people who are experts in a field or who know nothing about it. Even within an organization, several different audiences will exist. You may emphasize different aspects of a topic depending upon the readers' knowledge level.
Audience action	What do you want your audience to do after reading? Click a link for more information? Call to take advantage now? You must have a clear vision of your goal in communicating for your writing to be effective.

Begin the audience analysis portion of the first stage of the writing process (assessing) by completing an audience profile template, using the criteria mentioned in Table 5.3.1.

The next part of assessing the writing situation is defining your **purpose**. The reason or purpose for writing in the professional world falls into three basic categories: informing, persuading, or requesting. Informative writing is a large category that includes generalized information, instructions, notifications, warnings, or clarifications. Persuasive writing makes an impression, influences decisions, gains acceptance, sells, or recommends. Requests are written to gain information or rights and to stimulate action.

Unless you define the desired outcome of the written task, you cannot possibly achieve that task's objective. Are you writing an e-mail in response to a customer complaint? Are you using social media to generate traffic to a website selling nutritional supplements? You must be clear about what you want your words to accomplish before you write.

Sometimes you do not have all the information on hand that you need to write your document. Once you have defined for whom you are writing and what you want to accomplish, continue your analysis of the writing situation by gathering the information to produce the document. Sometimes that will entail conducting **research**. Sometimes you may just need to download information from your experience. Either way, have your information on hand *before* you begin to write. Nothing is more frustrating than being on a deadline to compose a writing job and realizing that you do not have the information you need.

Once you have the information, **organize** it. For shorter pieces, think about the organizational structure you need to follow to attain your writing purpose. We will discuss these writing strategies in greater detail in Section 2. For longer pieces, begin by creating categories of information. From these sections, draft an **outline** with headings.

This assessing portion of the writing process will make the actual writing much easier. Why? It is always easier to begin writing if you have something on the page rather than nothing.

Step 2: Write

Enter the second step of the writing process—writing a draft—knowing that it is not the last step. A draft by definition is not final. Its purpose is to transfer the information you have gathered onto the page. For short documents such as routine e-mails, consider composing offline. (It's too tempting to write and hit send without carefully going over your draft!) Begin by including the information you've gathered, making sure you include each point. For longer documents, use your outline. Write section by section, point by point. If you have trouble with one section, move to another.

Your goal at this stage of the writing process for both short and longer documents is to put something down on paper (or the screen) that you will revise later. It's a waste of your valuable time to labor over any individual word or sentence as you write your draft; the word or sentence may be eliminated by the final version. If you cannot think of the precise word you need, leave a blank and return later to fill it in. If you are having difficulty wording a sentence smoothly, leave a bracketed space or perhaps type a few words as a reminder of the gist of what you want to say. The important point to remember is that a first draft is one of several stabs you'll take at this work.

If you write using information you have taken from other sources, avoid using someone else's words or ideas without attributing them. **Plagiarism** occurs when you use or closely imitate the ideas or language of another author without permission. Even if you paraphrase through rewording, you should still cite the source to avoid plagiarizing. With the abundance of material available to us with a few keystrokes, it's tempting to cut and paste and call it a day. But you leave yourself and your organization open to criminal liability for copyright infringement laws if you use words, images, or any other copyrighted material. Besides, you will never learn to express yourself if you use others' words.

Before you move to the next step, I advise printing your draft. But don't read it immediately. Let it marinate. It's too hard to edit our own copy immediately after we've written it. We need to let some time pass before we return to a draft so that we can be more objective when we edit.

Step 3: Edit

I saw a great T-shirt at a meeting for the Society for Technical Writers. On the front was the word *write* in bold type. Following that was line after line of the word *edit*. The final boldface word at the end of the last line was *publish*. Of course, the idea is that writing requires more editing than writing.

Editing is a multistepped process and begins by looking at the overall effectiveness of the piece. As you read your draft, return to your audience and purpose analysis and ask yourself if the content meets the needs of the audience while it accomplishes your purpose in writing. Does the document provide all the information readers will need to do what you want? Does it make sense? Is it well organized? If not, go back and make changes.

Once you are certain that the content is correct and complete, it's time for **paragraph and sentence level editing**. This is where you'll need a good style guide (see discussion of Writing Tools), unless you are one of the few who have perfect recall of all grammatical rules. Begin by examining the effectiveness of each paragraph. By definition, a paragraph is a group of sentences about one topic; the topic is generally stated in the first sentence of a paragraph and is called a topic sentence. Good paragraphs have **unity**, which means they stay on topic, so first check each paragraph for unity. Make sure your paragraphs aren't too long. Long paragraphs scare readers off.

Next check your paragraphs for **cohesion**, meaning that each sentence leads logically to the next. A common writing error is to jump from one idea to the next without providing a logical connection between those two ideas. Unless each idea expressed in a sentence logically segues to the next, your reader will not be able to follow. Writers link ideas several ways:

1. Using transitional words and phrases. Transitions are broken down into types: adding information, contrasting information, comparing information, illustrating a point, and showing time.
2. Using pronouns that refer back to a specific noun.
3. Repeating keywords to remind a reader of a central idea.

Table 5.3.2 illustrates the types of transitions writers use to compose cohesive sentences and paragraphs.

Table 5.3.2 **Types of transitions**

Type of transition	Words or phrases used
Additive—used to augment an idea	additionally, again, also, and, in addition, moreover, thus
Contrast—used to show how ideas differ	although, but, conversely, however, instead, on the other hand, yet
Comparison—used to link similar ideas	likewise, similarly
Time—used to show a sequence	after, finally, first, in the meantime, later, next, second, soon

Once all paragraphs are edited, examine each sentence. Now is the time to nitpick grammar and stylistic elements. Pay special attention to egregious errors such as:

1. Subject and verb agreement

2. Comma splices
3. Sentence fragments
4. Run-on sentences
5. Dangling modifiers

Find every pronoun to make sure it agrees with its antecedent and that the noun to which it refers is clear. Make sure you have written numbers in the correct way, using numerals and spelling out numbers appropriately. Stay in the same verb tense.

Also beware of dangling modifiers, phrases that confuse readers by saying something other than what is meant. They often appear in an introductory phrase at the beginning of a sentence but omit a word that would clarify meaning in the second part of the sentence. Look at the following sentence:

After finishing the copy, the website was difficult to understand.

The website did not finish the copy; therefore the meaning is obscure. Perhaps the sentence should have read:

After finishing the copy, the writer found that the website was difficult to understand.

As you edit, take some time to **read** your document **aloud** and make marks next to areas that require editing. This is the single best way to improve your writing. Professional writing should sound natural. If you find yourself stumbling as you read your copy, the chances are good that you have a problem; your ears will not allow you to pass over stylistic elements that your eye will just ignore. Listen for frequent repetition of the same word, for short, choppy sentences, and for sentences that begin with the same word or phrase. Make sure your sentences have variety in length, aiming for a good mix of short, medium, and longer sentences. Note whether you have started too many sentences with *there is, there are, this is,* or *it is.* Overuse of this wordy construction is a red alert for any professional writer to rewrite. Finally, make sure you have used words according to their actual definition, called the denotation. (Use the Avoiding Wordiness Checklist at the end of this chapter to help you edit for conciseness.)

The final element of the editing portion of the writing process is **proofreading**. Proofreading includes editing your copy for spelling, capitalization, punctuation, and typos. Begin by double-checking the correct spelling of names. Then make sure you've correctly used words that are commonly mistaken (i.e., affect and effect, complimentary and complementary). If you have included a phone number or a URL in the content, determine both are correct by phoning or checking the link.

A warning about using your word processor's spell check function: Spell check is far from fail proof. Just the omission of one letter (say the last *s* in *possess*) can change the word's meaning, and the program won't pick that up. *Posses* is a word (the plural of posse) but it isn't the word you meant to use. Additionally, a spellchecker won't find names spelled incorrectly or words not in its dictionary.

Proofreading for punctuation is critical. Proper use of commas makes a huge difference in a document's readability. Be especially on the lookout for inserting commas after introductory phrases and between two independent clauses joined by a coordinate conjunction. Likewise, tossing in a comma or semicolon haphazardly or omitting a comma or semicolon are common writing errors that affect readability. Both can affect flow and meaning. Consider how the comma alters these two sentences:

That, I'm afraid, has not been the case.

That I'm afraid has not been the case.

The first sentence refers to a previous statement and conveys the meaning that an earlier statement is untrue. The second means that the individual claims to be unafraid.

Capitalization is another part of the proofreading stage. Use your style guide to know when to capitalize nouns and titles and be consistent. Next examine the appearance of what you've written. Remember that copy must not only be well written; it must look attractive on the page or screen to maximize readability. You may find the Editing and Proofreading Checklist at the end of this chapter a helpful tool to guide you through this portion of the writing process.

[...]

Professional Writing Characteristics

Writing for the world of work has certain characteristics that form the underpinning of anything you write, from an e-mail to your boss, to a resume for a new job, to a proposal for new business. Integrate the following elements into your work.

Accuracy

One of the best ways we can illustrate to our readers that we are professionals and experts is through accuracy. Inaccuracies show a carelessness that few professionals or organizations can afford in a competitive, global marketplace. Attention to accuracy is therefore paramount to professionals.

Active Voice

To enliven your prose, avoid using passive voice construction when you can. Passive voice makes the object of an action the subject of a sentence, as the following example illustrates:

Passive voice   *The e-mail was written by me.*

Active voice   *I wrote the website.*

However, if you wish to obscure the person committing an action, you *should* use passive voice. You do so by avoiding naming the actor, as is illustrated below:

Passive voice   *The students were given poor grades.*

Active voice   *The professor gave the students poor grades.*

If you have trouble identifying your own use of *passive* voice, you can adjust the Grammar Tools in Microsoft Word's Preferences, which when activated, will point out passive voice construction. If you are using passive voice purposefully because you want to sound objective, great. But if you have used passive voice unintentionally, change it.

Avoiding Gender, Racial, or Age Bias

English doesn't make biases easy to avoid. The best way to stay away from the he or she conundrum is to use the plural of a word. To avoid racial or age biases, beware of stereotypes when composing. Even if you feel the reference is complimentary, those to whom you refer may find that reference offensive.

Clarity

If a reader has to reread to understand anything you write, you have not done your job. Every sentence you write that another person will see should be easy to read. Clarity comes from using words the audience will recognize and using them correctly. Stay away from jargon or SAT-prep vocabulary. One way to check your work for clarity is to give your draft to someone who knows nothing about what you are writing. If that reader can understand the document, it is probably clear.

Conciseness

Busy professionals are impatient and expect brevity. No one wants to wade through wordy prose to get to a point. As mentioned earlier, the Avoiding Wordiness Checklist at the end of this chapter contains some tips to make your writing more concise.

Conversational Prose with Smooth Flow

The rhythm of any prose needs to be conversational and natural. The best way to achieve good flow is to read your document aloud and keep amending until you are able to read without hesitation. Use simple, plain language in sentences that are not complex or convoluted. Make sure your punctuation does not *impede* your reader by adding unnecessary halts or by avoiding pauses that will aid understanding.

To make your prose more conversational, you can also use contractions when appropriate. Instead of *they will*, use *they'll*. You can also begin your sentences with *and* or *but*, which many English teachers taught as an inviolable rule. Sometimes beginning a sentence with a conjunction gives prose just the right rhythm to create that highly desired conversational tone.

Correctness

Poor grammar and words used incorrectly make both the writer and the organization appear ignorant and sloppy. To hone your grammatical skills, work with a grammar guide next to you. (The use of writing tools is discussed later in this chapter.) Consult the guide when you are unsure about any writing issue. Make use of your word processor's grammar and spell check, but do not rely on them solely. Another way to work on grammar issues is to create a *never again* table (see Table 5.3.3). This is a three-column table (see the following sample) that lists a grammatical error, the rule that governs the problem, and a mnemonic device to remember the solution. When you keep a list of grammatical errors and refer to it as you compose, you will eventually learn to correct the problem. Keep adding and erasing errors until you no longer need to consult the chart.

Table 5.3.3 **Never again table**

Grammar problem	Rule	Mnemonic device
Its versus It's	It's **always** = it is	The dog bites its tail because it's plagued with fleas.
Effect versus affect	Effect = noun Affect = verb	Ibuprofen adversely affects my stomach, but the medicine's effect cures my headache.

Parallelism

Good writing often uses a device called parallelism, or parallel structure. Writers use parallelism instinctually because it appeals to our natural desire for symmetry. Parallelism matches nouns with nouns, verbs with verbs, and phrases with phrases: "For *faster* action, *less* stomach upset, and *more* for your money, use XX." Readers expect parallelism, especially in sets of two or three items, and in bulleted and enumerated lists. Using parallel phrasing correctly is key to writing in the workplace.

Positive Voice

Positive voice uses affirmative words to make a point. For example, instead of saying, "We are out of green T-shirts," we would emphasize the positive and say, "Order any size of our orange and gray T-shirts." Avoid downbeat words or words than can convey a negative connotation and rephrase in a positive way. Instead of, "No coupons will be honored after April 30," say, "Coupons will be honored through April 30."

Reliance on Strong Nouns and Verbs

Good writing uses nouns and verbs to do the heavy work and saves adverbs and adjectives for rare occasions. Instead of "Our brightly-colored, twinkling lights will be reminders of the happiest, most memorable times you and your family will ever enjoy," say, "Our dazzling lights will twinkle their way into your family's memories." Replace "Our auto policies are competitive," with "Our auto policies beat the competition's." Avoid using the most boring and overused verb in the English language: to be. Check for overuse of *is*, *are*, *were*, and *was* and see if you can eliminate them by using a stronger, more specific verb. We can't entirely avoid adverbs or adjectives or *to be*, but we can be mindful of how often we use them.

Sentence Variety

Sentence variety is linked to conversational prose and has two elements. The first is sentence beginnings. As you edit, look at the way your sentences begin. Do three in a row begin with *The*? Do two sentences within two paragraphs begin with *There are*? Avoid writing sentences that begin with the same word or phrase. The second way to attain sentence variety is to vary sentence length. Short, choppy sentences make prose annoyingly staccato. Natural-sounding prose combines short, medium, and longer sentences.

One way to check your sentence length is to look at how the periods line up. If you see a vertical or slanted line of periods, you need to alter some of the sentence lengths. This can be accomplished in several ways. Join two sentences whose content is closely linked by embedding the gist of one sentence into another. Combine two sentences with a coordinate conjunction to create a complex sentence. Or try an alternate sentence beginning such as an introductory phrase, which will add sentence variety.

Simple Words

Avoid jargon. Always, always, always choose the simpler, more recognizable word over the longer, more showy one. Instead of *rhinovirus* say *a cold*. Opt for *e-mail* over *electronic message*. In *utilize* versus *use*, *use* wins! (Also notice how the number of words your reader has to wade through goes down with simpler words.)

Shorter Paragraphs

Long paragraphs are appropriate for essays, but they have no place in professional documents. Big blocks of type scare readers away. The longest paragraph should be no more than six to eight lines. Always be aware of how a paragraph appears on a page (or a screen) and take pity on your audience—don't make your reader slog through dense prose.

Style: Formal versus Informal

Writers must wear different hats and adjust their writing style—sometimes called voice or tone—to the task at hand. In professional writing, we always aim for a natural style, as mentioned earlier. However, we must sometimes be even more specific about the style we choose.

Table 5.3.4 Formal and informal writing styles

	Formal style	Informal style
Types of documents	Letters Long reports Research Proposals	Most communication within the organization including e-mail, IM, memos, text messages Routine messages to outside audiences Informal reports
Characteristics	No personal pronouns (I, we) No contractions Objective voice or use of passive voice No figurative language or clichés No editorializing Limited use of adjectives No exclamation points Longer sentences Some technical language	Use of personal pronouns Use of contractions Shorter sentences, easily recognizable words Limited use of warm, inoffensive humor

Choosing to use an informal or formal writing style depends on the audience and the document's purpose. There is no clear-cut way to determine when to use each style; sometimes, an e-mail may require formality. Most of the time, however, e-mails are informal. To determine which style fits your needs, understand that informal writing allows the writer and reader to connect on a more personal level. It can convey warmth. Formal writing, on the other hand, produces the impression of objectivity and professionalism.

Some genres, however, have generally accepted styles. Use Table 5.3.4 to help guide you in choosing which style best suits your task.

Writing Tools

Just as a doctor wouldn't enter an examination room without a stethoscope or a carpenter wouldn't pull up to a job site without a hammer, no writer can be without the tools of the trade: a good dictionary, thesaurus, and style guide.

Many excellent writing reference books are on the market, both in electronic and print format. I use both. Although I often visit www.dictionary.com when I compose, I also rely on my hard copy dictionary. Dictionaries in book format allow us to browse, and sometimes the writer will happen upon a word or meaning, which doesn't happen when you use Dictionary.com. The same goes for the thesaurus. I find the thesaurus built into Microsoft Word to be very weak. As a writer, I need to make the most out of the bounteous English language. A hard cover thesaurus is worth its weight in gold as far as I'm concerned. I use *Roget's 21st Century Thesaurus* edited by Barbara Ann Kipfer, PhD. I particularly like that it's organized like a dictionary.

Many good style guides are likewise available. For a grammar guide, I use Diana Hacker's *A Writer's Reference*, 7th edition, but many excellent grammar reference books are available.

Many good grammar websites can also be useful. The Grammar Book (http://www.grammarbook.com/) and the Purdue Online Writing Lab (https://owl.english.purdue.edu/) are handy and reliable websites to look up any grammar issues you may have.

The important thing to remember is to keep your tools nearby as you compose. The more you use these references, the less you'll need them. You will internalize the rules of writing as you use them.

Conclusion

Writing well on the job is key to career success. By breaking down writing into stages called the writing process, your end product is more likely to accomplish its ultimate purpose. When composing on the job, effective writers integrate many elements that will distinguish their work as professional, well-edited, and clear. Whether you choose hard copy or digital, use writing tools including a dictionary, thesaurus, and grammar guide to create professional documents. Doing so will help you excel in the workplace.

Avoiding Wordiness Checklist

Wordy phrase and example	Solution	✓
Avoid beginning a sentence with *There are* or *It is.* *There are four points that should be considered.* *It is clear that cashmere is warmer.*	Begin sentences with the true subject. *Consider these four points* or *Four points should be considered.* *Cashmere is clearly warmer.*	
Avoid beginning sentences with *That* or *This.* *Choosing teams should be done carefully. This is because a good mix will generate better results.*	Connect to previous sentence. *Choosing teams should be done carefully because a good mix will generate better results.*	
Use *active voice* rather than passive. *Rain forests are being destroyed by uncontrolled logging.*	Passive voice depletes prose of vitality and can almost always be rewritten in active voice. *Uncontrolled logging is destroying rain forests.*	
Omit *that* or *which* whenever possible.	Unless that or which is required for clarity, omit it.	

The water heater that you install will last 15–20 years.	*The water heater you install will last 15–20 years.*	
Avoid prepositional phrase modifiers. *The committee of financial leaders meets every Tuesday.*	Replace with one-word modifiers. *The financial leaders committee meets every Tuesday.*	
Avoid *be* verbs. *New Orleans is one of the most vibrant cities in the United States.*	Replace with a strong verb. *New Orleans vibrates with activity like no other U.S. city.*	
Tighten closely related sentences of explanation. *When hanging wallpaper, three factors need to be considered. The factors are X, X, and X.*	Join closely related sentences of explanation with a colon to avoid repetitions. *When hanging wallpaper, consider three factors: X, X, and X.*	
Tighten closely related sentences. *MRIs are used to diagnose many ailments. MRIs create an image of organs and soft tissues to diagnose.*	Omit repetitious phrasing in second sentence. *MRIs diagnose many ailments by creating images of organs and soft tissues.*	
Tighten verb phrases with auxiliary + ing verbs *Management was holding a staff meeting.*	Replace is/are/was/were/have + verb with a one-word verb. *Management held a staff meeting.*	
Avoid using *there is/are* within a sentence. *When creating a mail list, there are many pitfalls.*	Find an active verb to replace *there is/are*. *When creating a mail list, many pitfalls exist.*	
Remove redundancies. *An anonymous stranger may be dangerous.*	Know the true meaning of a word. *Strangers may be dangerous.*	

Editing and Proofreading Checklist

Check your draft for the following	✓
Document content is tailored to meet the needs of the audience and attains writing purpose	
Copy is edited for conciseness	
Body paragraphs have unity and cohesion and are shortened for visual appeal	
Transitions in and between paragraphs adequately link ideas	

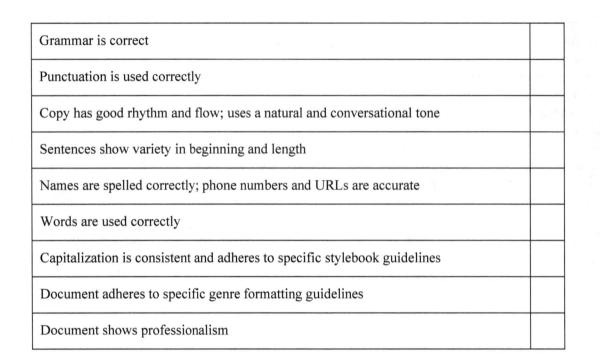

Grammar is correct	
Punctuation is used correctly	
Copy has good rhythm and flow; uses a natural and conversational tone	
Sentences show variety in beginning and length	
Names are spelled correctly; phone numbers and URLs are accurate	
Words are used correctly	
Capitalization is consistent and adheres to specific stylebook guidelines	
Document adheres to specific genre formatting guidelines	
Document shows professionalism	

Applying this Skill: Audience Analysis, Foods with Moods

Assume you work for a young company that is expanding quickly. Foods with Moods is an organization that sells ugly or mis-sized produce direct to consumers. Foods with Moods (FM) is growing rapidly as consumers become more and more accustomed to mail-order groceries. FM its has two basic ideals that drive its company: reducing food deserts in urban areas and reducing food waste.

Since FM has been growing so quickly, you are facing problems sourcing some of your basic products, like apples and spinach. You just learned from your product supplier that you will not have apples or spinach to send in orders for the next two weeks.

As the communications director, you must relay the message about the missing product to a variety of people in your organization. A series of audiences is listed below; as assigned, determine which medium and message you would send to each audience.

- New customers who are expecting apples and spinach in their orders

- Shipping company that needs to adjust its delivery schedule and cost estimates because of smaller orders

- Warehouse manager who may need fewer employees to package boxes for the next two weeks

- Finance director who needs to expect lower revenue for the next two weeks

- Social media manager who posts about available products

Applying This Skill: Conciseness and Clarity

Revise the following sentences to improve the conciseness and clarity.

1. One thing that can be said to have greatly improved the presentation was the extra week of rehearsal.

2. The office manager was good at organizing. She also managed the schedule good and helped people with a friendly smile.

3. There are many executives who have not made any progress about the art of writing.

4. There is one supervisor who is of the opinion that this policy will prove destructive to the morale of employees.

5. The thing that prevented the committee from meeting was the stormy weather.

6. The snow was falling in such a way as to cover up the level parking lot, until soon nothing was visible to our eyes except for a thick blanket of dense snowfall.

7. This particular article is about things that can be done to help you along the way with salary negotiations.

8. As a result of the fact that he had never learned the basic fundamentals of grammar, he found writing difficult to such an extent that he had to withdraw from the course.

9. The following report touches on the process we took to complete our report along with an individual breakdown of each team member's contribution toward the project.

10. The supervisor was annoyed by the fact that we arrived late instead of on time.

11. It is recommended that all pages in the document be numbered correctly in the right order.

12. Attempts were made unsuccessfully by the division staff to assess the project.

Applying This Skill: Pronoun Use

Pronouns are words that replace nouns, such as "he," "she," "it," "they," and "us." Using the correct pronouns ensures your writing is clear and understandable. Rewrite the following sentences to correct the pronoun errors.

1. The three most common devices are email, cell phone, and instant messages. They would all be lost without email.

2. I would like to transfer you to another branch location if they have internship openings.

3. When a member joins a gym, they discover the many benefits of exercise.

4. Our sales team will work with a client to ensure the products meet their needs.

5. The company is promoting their new product.

6. It is convenient to use text messaging to contact clients.

7. I tell students that when they are trying to save money, you should buy used textbooks.

Reading 5.4

Bad Writing Costs Businesses Billions

It's not just a chore to wade through the badly written memos, emails, and other lousy business communication—this inefficiency costs us insane amounts of money.

By Josh Bernoff

There is a fundamental inefficiency at the heart of American business. It is right in front of all of our faces, and yet we fail to recognize it.

It's the fuzzy, terrible writing we slog through every day at work. And it's costing American businesses nearly $400 billion every year.

Think about it. You start your day wading through first-draft emails from colleagues who fail to come to the point. You consume reports that don't make clear what's happening or what your management should do about it. The websites, marketing materials, and press releases from your suppliers are filled with jargon and meaningless superlatives. This problem is as common as rust, and just as welcome; in my survey of businesspeople who write at work, 81 percent agreed with the statement: "Poorly written material wastes a lot of my time."

Poor writing creates a drag on everything you do. It functions like a tax, sapping your profits, and I can quantify it. American workers spend 22 percent of their work time reading; higher compensated workers read more. According to my analysis, America is spending 6 percent of total wages on time wasted attempting to get meaning out of poorly written material. Every company, every manager, every professional pays this tax, which consumes $396 billion of our national income. That's more than half of what we pay for Medicare—but the poor writing tax pays for nothing but waste.

We're so immersed in this stuff that we hardly notice it any more. I'm talking about job descriptions like this one, from a health care company:

"The Area Vice President, Enterprise Customers will develop and manage a sustainable strategic relationship that transforms the current commercial model by creating joint value that results in the ongoing reduction of costs, continuous process improvement, growth and profitability for both partners with the ability to export key learnings."

How much time did the HR department and the job candidates waste trying to figure that out?

How about the lede from ++ Samsung's recent statement ++ about its smartphones?

[https://news.samsung.com/global/statement-on-galaxy-note7]

"Samsung is committed to producing the highest quality products and we take every incident report from our valued customers very seriously. In response to recently reported cases of the new Galaxy Note7, we conducted a thorough investigation and found a battery cell issue."

Battery cell issue? The phones are catching on fire—but you'd never know it from the company's statement, which mentions only "incidents." *Say what you mean.*

Of all the serious problems in the American workplace, this one is the most solvable. And we can solve it one company, one culture, one worker at a time.

The first step is to adopt what I call "The Iron Imperative" in everything you write: *treat the reader's time as more valuable than your own.* To embrace it means that every time you send an email or write a document, you must take a moment to structure it for maximum readability and meaning. We are lazy; we'd rather save our own time than someone else's. But writers who adopt The Iron Imperative stand out in the workplace for clarity and efficiency, and are more likely to get ahead. Workplace cultures that adopt it will reduce their poor writing tax.

Recognize that everybody reads on a screen now—either a smartphone or a computer screen. That reduces attention spans and concentration, which in turn demands a radical rethink of the way you communicate in writing. In this environment, brevity must become a core value. Regardless of what you write, the title or subject line and the first two sentences must carry the payload. Unlike Samsung in its press release, you must never bury the lede.

People use jargon to impress other people—but for each person you impress, many others are just confused. Clear, plain language communicates better, is easier to consume, and is more likely to get its point across to more people.

A primary cause of incoherent writing is committee speak—documents that become a pastiche of -contradictory comments inserted based on management reviewers. In my survey, only 32 percent of writers thought that their process for collecting and combining feedback worked well. Along with clarity, brevity, and plain language, a disciplined and coherent review process goes a long way toward improving the quality of the documents we're struggling to get meaning from.

It's not that hard to embrace clear, pointed, and direct writing that doesn't waste the reader's time. Commit to do that, and to eliminate the poor writing tax at your company. You'll get ahead. And you'll make American business a little more efficient while you're at it.

Applying This Skill: Parallelism

Rewrite the following sentences to make them parallel.

1. If you want to succeed in this course, you must listen carefully, read the material, attend class and be participating.

2. At my last job, I:

- Participated in meetings
- Strengthened interpersonal skills
- Lead and participated in teams

3. The job requires applicants to have:

- Basic knowledge of marketing
- Knowledge of different cultures
- Completed international business courses
- Speaking, reading and listening fluently in Spanish and English

4. A bullet list on a resume:

- Worked with a team to sell concessions
- Independently maintained cash drawer
- Problem solve in a fast-paced environment

5. A bullet list on a resume:

- Achieved financial goals planning fundraising
- Attending events
- Collectively created best solution to complex situations

6. The company must either increase sales or it will be necessary to reduce expenses.

7. A bullet list on a resume:

- I had the role of secretary where I'd take meeting minutes
- Required time management
- Voluntarily does community service

Applying This Skill: Numbers

Rewrite the following sentences to have them correctly use numbers.

1. 2013 was a very productive year for the company.

2. We sold eight units this week but were aiming to sell 11 by the 1st of the month.

3. The meeting is scheduled for December 1st, but we need to change it to December 10th.

4. Please review the company's two new client files by October 15th.

5. By September 1st, 2014, the website should be live.

6. The last outbreak of smallpox occurred in the late seventy's.

7. Can you meet for lunch at 12:00 noon?

Applying This Skill: Active and Passive Verbs

Active verb sentences clearly identify who is doing an action in a sentence. In passive verb sentences, who or what does the action of the sentence is implied, unknown, or comes after the verb in the sentence. Passive verbs are often used when a writer wants to deflect blame or criticism or when the action of the sentence is more important than the doer/actor.

Confused? Consider these examples:

o The report was requested.
o My boss requested the report.

Which sentence has the passive verb? The first sentence's verb ("was requested") is passive. The sentence does not identify who requested the report. The second sentence clearly states who did the action—the requesting—which leaves no room for confusion or conjecture.

For most people, determining whether a verb is active or passive is very difficult at first. The easiest way to determine if a verb is active or passive is to ask the following:

o What is the verb (the action word)?
o Who/what is doing the action (verb)?

▪ If you know who is acting = active verb
▪ If you're unsure who is acting = passive verb

Here is how to use these questions to identify active and passive verbs.

The sentence is: Companies expect accounting positions to increase in the next ten years.

1.   What is the verb? Expect

2.   Who/what is expecting? Companies

3.   The actor is clearly named before the verb, so this sentence is active.

The sentence is: The report was left on the desk.

1.   What is the verb? Left or was left

2.   Who/what left the report? We don't know.

3.   Who performed the action in this sentence is unknown; therefore, this sentence is passive.

4.   Fixed: Susie left the report on the desk.

The sentence is: Several students were failed because of poor writing.

1.   What is the verb? Failed, were failed

2.   Who failed the students? We don't know. Did the professor fail the students? Did the assessment team fail the students? This sentence is passive.

3.   Fixed: The professor failed several students because of poor writing.

Sometimes, a sentence includes who or what did the action of the verb, but it is after the verb, which generally makes for wordy sentences.

For example: Several students were failed by the department because of poor writing.

1.   What is the verb? Failed, were failed

2.   Who failed the students? The department did. We know who did the action, but it appears after the verb. This sentence is passive.

3.   Fixed: The department failed several students because of poor writing.

Identify whether the sentences below have an active or a passive verb. Rewrite the sentence using the opposite verb form.

1.   The interview was conducted by Jane, who is the recruiter at the company.

2.   I assigned each team member a different task.

3.   All of our employees are encouraged to read the employee handbook to understand the company's expectations.

4. You may add more detail to your resume to make it stronger.

5. People from other cultures can offer insights Americans may not have considered.

6. A dress code needs to be established for this company.

7. I'm sorry I cannot fulfill your request.

Applying This Skill: Word Choice

Rewrite the following sentences using different word choice.

Consideration is one of the 5 Cs of communication that relates to the tone and choice of words an author uses.

Positive Versus Negative Wording

Negative: We cannot process your order because your payment information is not correct.

Positive:

Negative: We do not answer phone calls after 3:00 p.m. on Fridays.

Positive:

Writer Centered (You) Versus Reader Centered

Writer: We shipped the order this morning with a 3- to 5-day delivery.

Reader:

Writer: We are pleased to award you a scholarship.

Reader:

General Versus Specific

General: The class was good.

Specific:

General: Please complete the forms as soon as possible.

Specific:

Gender Biased Versus Gender Neutral

Biased: Each person must complete his homework on time.

Neutral:

Biased: Foreman

Neutral:

Biased: The best man for the job.

Neutral:

Clichés Versus Direct/Clear

Cliché: Don't throw the baby out with the bathwater.

Direct:

Cliché: It's all black and white.

Direct:

Old-Fashioned Wording Versus Clear Phrasing

Outdated: As per your request, please find the enclosed form.

Clear:

Outdated: I refer to your application of the 24th last month regarding your suitability for the post of sales clerk.

Clear:

Formal Versus Informal

Formal: terminate   utilize   remunerate   appeal

Informal:

Applying This Skill: Word Choice 2

Revise the following sentence to remove wordiness, to use the correct form of who/that, and to improve word choice.

1. I don't have any contacts that are in my field of study.

2. I would like to land an internship this spring.

3. Down the road, I see myself in a management position.

4. I am fairly strong when it comes to oral communication and I feel like my job really helps a lot with that because I use it every time I am talking to customers.

5. One business professional in my field that could be interviewed is James Joe, my manager.

6. I am a nontraditional student that has recently returned to college after taking a break.

7. It is strong verbal skills that I have developed by explaining a process or concept to a person and by talking them through it.

8. I intend to begin looking for references that can assist me in my job search.

9. The reason why I chose to interview this person is because she is my manager.

10. The money was used to pay off student loans deemed uncollectable by the banks who funded them.

Applying This Skill: Improving Your Writing

Section 1: Conciseness

Rewrite the sentences below to improve conciseness and word choice.

1. Going into depth on the issue, the author states that people should designate times of their week to be with family and friends to reduce the work overload stress that comes with having work-capable devises 24/7.

2. The article talks about many things in regards to potential hidden fees associated with 401(k) plans. Some of these things include the fact that businesses hire people to manage these accounts.

3. When diving deeper into my group members, I definitely agree texting was the quickest and most efficient way to contacting each other and we have had absolutely zero issues so far.

Section 2: Slanguage

Rewrite the sentences below to eliminate popular millennial slang words and clichés.

1. We all talked about what to do to stay on the same page and stay on top of things.

2. Now that we've figured out our strategic game plan, we can get the ball rolling and start rebuilding the company from the ground up.

3. Dude, I really screwed up when I sent that email.

4. Hey, it was awesome to meet you—you're really cool. I think I'd be a pro at the stuff you mentioned about the internship.

Section 3: Commonly Confused Words

Circle the correct term in the sentences below.

1. We will consider all candidates whose applications are complete (**e.g.,/i.e.,** include a resume, letters of recommendation, and writing samples).

2. The problem was resolved **anyway/anyways** when the IT staff rebooted the system.

3. Many customers were **affected/effected** by the data breach.

4. The interview as **alright/all right**, but the candidate's writing samples failed to impress the hiring committee.

5. The **amount/number** of people at the alumni event was more than expected.

6. Jiawei works hard and wants to be a **part/apart** of the team.

Section 4: Multiple Verbs and Wordiness

Rewrite the sentences below to use shorter verb (action words) forms.

1. I told her about what my roles were and I proceeded to tell her about a situation.

2. The heads of each department should sit down with one another and get a realistic idea of their needs.

3. I worked to figure out what I am interested in professionally.

4. I came to the conclusion that the reason Wells Fargo was a good choice was because I have always wanted to guide people into making good decisions about their finances.

5. This experience that I have gained will help me to be able to develop and hold the team accountable right away at your company to make sure that the goals that have been set are being fulfilled.

Applying This Skill: Subject-Verb Agreement and Wordiness

Section 1: Subject-Verb Agreement

Rewrite the sentences below to make the subjects and verbs agree. Fix other errors as needed.

1. A company can have work culture and activities that bonds and creates for a better work environment.

2. Disadvantages from working at home is a big trust in your employees when it comes to accountability but can also be hard to communicate when working on a project with other employees.

3. Daniel covers the consequences that happens for when unethical behavior is displayed in the workplace.

4. Jude informed the class about the time management Tips. He said that setting boundaries on our time and workload can be one effective way to do that and taking breaks are important to recharge and refresh the mind.

5. Some ways to achieve this is showing recognition, respect, acknowledgment, value, encouragement, empowerment, and celebration to employees

Section 2: Wordiness

Edit the paragraphs below to reduce wordiness. Cross out words and/or rewrite sentences and fix other errors as needed.

1. Approximately 43% of people sick days are due to stress. Professionals spend $43.7 billion on depression annually. To help employees that may be at risk, reach out and ask if help is needed. Be sure to be proactive and supportive of people who are going through a run time. Mental health days are good for employees and the company because someone should take a day for a break and try to recover than to have them stay at work being unproductive and feeling unhappy.

1. Research is the most significant advantage you can give yourself. When researching, find what your market value is. Be prepared to make a counteroffer and understand how to make a compelling counteroffer. Also, understand that in some cases the salary isn't the only thing you can negotiate.

2. The first type of plan to make you ready for retirement is having health insurance. Having health insurance or a Health Savings Account (HSA) can over the bigger medical cost that might be associated with getting to an older age. Another plan would be having life insurance if you pass then the cost of everything is covered and providing for your loved ones. Stocks, such as penny or blue chip stocks, are another popular options for earning money for retirement.

3. Malia proceeded with talking about balancing friendships in the workplace.

Section 3: Faulty Parallelism and Clarity

Edit the sentences below to ensure parallel construction and increase clarity. Fix other errors as needed.

1. The purpose of this was to eliminate mistakes and not adding to your workload over time.

2. Mark spoke a lot about how much your job can ask of you, creating time for you and your own interests helps to separate your work and life.

3. One presentation was revolved around how to manage work and life and being able to balance those two together.

4. He gave several tips on how to improve your time management and practicing it.

5. Things you can do to ensure this is trying to stay proactive, staying supportive for others, and to communicate how you're feeling.

Applying This Skill: Positive and Negative Language

Rephrase the sentences below to make them more positive.

1. Why don't you answer the phone?

2. The copy machine is out of paper.

3. I'm sorry to hear you are unhappy with the team's performance.

4. You're late.

5. The meeting has been cancelled.

6. I quit.

7. John did not send the letter.

8. That was a bad decision.

9. Productivity is down this quarter.

10. Lei doesn't know much about cyber-security.

6

A Communication Miscellany

A large portion of effective communication is being aware of one's self; this includes styles, tendencies, assumptions, and biases. Once we are aware of the way we tend to communicate, we can more easily adapt our communication to the needs of our audience and, hopefully, reduce miscommunication that can cause distress and cost companies money. Each topic in this chapter may be an entire course in itself; the information here is meant to introduce you to the topic, and hopefully, you will continue exploring the subjects on your own.

In this chapter, you will explore a variety of aspects of communication, focusing on how you communicate. After completing this lesson, you will be able to:

- Identify your communication style and evaluate your soft skills
- Understand emotional intelligence in business communication
- Know your personal communication apprehension score
- Understand your listening skills
- Understand your leadership skills
- Evaluate your conflict management style
- Understand cross-cultural business communication
- Evaluate your ethical framework
- Be aware of nonverbal communication
- Understand business etiquette

Communication Styles and Soft Skills

People's communication skills vary widely, obviously. You will find some people easy to communicate with; you may just "click" and easily understand each other. With other people, you may argue, frustrate each other, and rarely easily understand each other. Some of these differences are due to communication styles. Understanding your own and other people's preferred communication style can help you communicate more effectively.

People usually lump together a variety of social skills as "soft skills." These skills include communication, emotional intelligence, leadership, and more. They are skills that are hard to quantify but highly valued in most, if not all, workplaces. Part of developing your soft skills is understanding your current skills and working to enhance your strengths and improve upon your weaknesses.

Take the online assessment: Activity--Communication Style self-assessment

Reading 6.1

Soft Skills

By Michael Edmondson

Objective: To evaluate your non-cognitive or soft skills that are critical to personal and professional development.

Directions: For each of the following soft skills, ask yourself "How frequently have I practiced this trait during the last month?"

Never (0); Rarely (1); Sometimes (3); Often (4); Always (5)

1. Comprehension: When introduced to a new project or task, a student is able to comprehend and analyze information and expectations provided by the teacher and ask the right questions to complete the task beyond expectations and on time.

2. Independent learning: A student takes the personal initiative to seek out and make use of new resources and inspirations to include them in learning independently beyond the classroom.

3. Problem solving: A student routinely solves problems and works toward answering questions.

4. Progressive learning: The student is able to apply principles, facts, and feedback to improve upon what they are responsible for having learned.

5. Process: A student understands, enjoys, and respects the process by which work is completed.

6. Initiative/Motivation: A student exhibits a love, drives for what he or she does, and seeks opportunities to continue and expand his or her personal growth.

7. Self-evaluation: A student takes a critical eye to the details of his or her work, carefully checking assignment requirements prior to presenting his or her finished product.

8. Improvement: A student continually works to improve his or her knowledge, skills, and craft.

9. Professionalism: A student conducts himself or herself in a professional manner, presenting his or her work in its best light.

10. Respects opinions: A student understands the value of other's opinions and insights.

11. Verbal interaction: A student uses professional, nonabusive, socially appropriate, and grammatically correct language when interacting with coworkers, clients, and service providers, both in person and online communication.

12. Express concepts: A student effectively expresses his or her process, thoughts, ideas, and solutions verbally.

13. Participation: A student contributes to the creative collective by joining in activities, discussions, and critiques. A student is attentive while others are speaking (lectures, presentations, and critiques) and enthusiastically and actively participates in class discussion or activities.

14. In-class conduct: A student maintains thoughtful and professional conduct when interacting with coworkers, clients, and service providers. A student follows stated rules of classroom conduct as defined in syllabus and student handbook—including appropriate use of lab facilities, cell phone, or computer when prohibited (i.e., during lecture and demonstrations) and uses class time appropriately.

15. Preparation: A student demonstrates the ability to manage time, supplies, and resources, and comes to each class prepared to accomplish requirements of scheduled activities in order to deliver the job on time and meet job expectations.

16. Out of class work: A student is expected to spend at least the minimum required hours outside of class for each credit hour doing homework or computer time to accomplish course objectives. The student understands that to exceed expectations often requires much more time and energy than the minimum time requirements.

17. Meeting deadlines: A student meets intermediate and final deadlines throughout the process of a job, as established by the client's needs.

18. Time management: A student plans the workload of a job wisely to manage all stages of the job and to allow proper attention to details in the process. A student worker demonstrates the ability to prioritize school work or other demands in order to successfully manage his or her time to accomplish learning objectives.

19. Attendance: A student understands how missing work affects one's ability to complete a job well and on time and communicates necessary lapses in attendance.

20. Responsibility: A student takes responsibility for his or her actions or in-actions rather than making excuses.

Scores:

- 80 to 100: You practice soft skills frequently and have a good sense of what they are. Moving forward you will need to maintain this high level of practice. Please note that anyone rarely scores over 90 as it is very difficult to practice so many soft skills at a high level of frequency.
- 60 to 79: You practice some soft skills frequently and could certainly increase your practice of others. Make a decision to increase the level in which you practice some soft skills and be sure to work on those you seldom use.
- 40 to 59: You seldom practice most soft skills and there is plenty of room for you to grow both personally and professional. Remember, this is not about strengths and weaknesses but instead, about the frequency in which you practice each soft skill. Now that you have increased your self-awareness you can make a commitment moving forward to identify those soft skills you would like to practice more often.

Next Steps

1. Which two or three soft skills can you rely on during the next month?

2. Which two or three soft skills would you like to practice more often during the next month?

···

Active Listening

Listening is a skill you know you should develop, but it is hard to actually *hear* what other people are saying. Listening with intent, interest, and attention is a skill that takes time and effort to develop. Effective listeners make excellent coworkers and leaders.

···

Reading 6.2

Using Active Listening

By Elizabeth Dickinson

> *Being listened to is so much like being loved that most people can't tell the difference.*
>
> —Unknown

> *We have two ears and one mouth so we can listen twice as much as we speak.*
>
> —Epictetus, former slave and Greek philosopher

The Importance of Presence in Active Listening

While there are specific techniques I will share to use active listening, those techniques are built on demonstrating an accepting presence and attitude, and treating someone else as the expert in their own life. Active listening is the active part in demonstrating unconditional positive regard.

What Active Listening Creates

Active listening to someone else may be the greatest gift you can offer another person. A large part of this is because active listening creates a safe emotional space. In Maslow's hierarchy of needs, safety is the second most basic need, immediately after food, water, shelter, and warmth.

We often interpret safety to mean physical safety. However, emotional safety is just as important to being—and feeling—secure, stable, and free from fear (the components of both physical and emotional safety).

Consistent active listening in relationships is also a buffer against times when there are the inevitable misunderstandings or disappointments. A history of consistent active listening in relationships or organizations promotes trust. The biggest gift of trust is that it offers protection when there are unintended miscommunications or when something is mishandled unknowingly.

Essentially, if a person feels listened to by another person (or organization), it will encourage him or her to give you or that organization the benefit of the doubt in unfamiliar or mishandled situations.

Active listening creates a sense of safety because feeling heard is a basic human need. According to mediation training centers, good listening can transform relationships, alleviate the need for decision-making, resolve conflicts, and solve problems.

However, simply listening without using active listening skills isn't always enough to make a person feel heard. If the other person hasn't felt heard, it's often a sign that person doing the listening is too passive or disengaged.

Even if one person is listening intently, using active listening skills can promote a deeper connection between people, and help the person listened to "hear themselves think," which helps them discover and/or commit to solutions.

Sometimes people who demonstrate unconditional acceptance of others are also naturally good listeners. However, there are specific and easy skills to learn which demonstrate *active* listening.

What is Active Listening?

Active listening is:

- The conscious effort to hear
- The creation of a respectful space
- The placing of full attention on the speaker
- The communication of active availability
- The reflecting back of what is said
- The withholding of judgment and rebuttals (at least while the speaker is talking!)
- The understanding (or at least the effort to understand) not just what is said, but what is meant

Let's unpack each aspect of active listening.

Make a Conscious Effort to Hear

Active listening is a conscious choice. Just as you eliminate distractions in order to focus on yourself or tasks, active listening to others requires the same degree of focus. Ask your coachee to do the same.

- Let others know you are not to be disturbed except in an emergency.
- If you are trying to listen, that's all you should be doing. No multi-tasking!
- Turn off or mute all electronic devices-phones, tablets, and computers.

New research indicates that simply having a cell phone visible between people who are talking tends to encourage more shallow conversations. Anticipating possible interruptions from a phone can take both people out of a deeper conversation.

Create a Respectful Space

Creating a respectful space involves creating a welcoming external and internal ambience. If I am coaching a client in my office, I tidy it up to eliminate other physical distractions for both of us.

This symbolically and literally "creates space" in my mind and in my office for my client.

If you are pressed for time, even clearing a small space on your desk signals to your mind that you have prepared space for something new/important to be created when you meet with another person.

Place Full Attention on the Speaker

Just as you clear physical space for your coachee, you also create and maintain open space in your mind and heart.

Give them your undivided attention throughout the time you are together. Don't allow your mind to wander off their needs. If your mind starts to wander, it's ok to ask the other person to repeat what they just said because you want to make sure you heard it correctly.

If you have planned and scheduled an important conversation with someone, prepare yourself physically so you can focus on it.

Leave yourself enough time beforehand for a bathroom break, make sure you're not thirsty or hungry, and take three deep inhalations and exhalations before you meet with others. Deep breathing calms both body and mind.

Communicate Active Availability

Use your physical presence to adopt an open, undefended body position. Consider uncrossing your arms and legs.

Open body positions communicate a sense that you are either open to your coachee's needs or are in harmony with their emotions.

You may even want to mirror their body position to create rapport. Studies show that people tend to feel more rapport after about 45 minutes and are likely to start mirroring each other's body positions.

The neuroscientist Vilayanur Ramachandran, author of The Tell-Tale Brain posits that mirror neurons in our brains underlie empathy and allow us to imitate other people, resulting in closer relationships.

Reflect Back What Is Said

This is the heart of *active* listening.

Reflecting back a client's own words is what allows a client to "hear themselves think" and to become aware of their thoughts in a different way. I usually notice an increased alertness, attention, and focus from my clients when I reflect their words back to them. As clients relax more deeply their breathing changes, their shoulders lower, and so on.

For some clients the attention and active listening from a coach may be the only time where they really get to "hear" what they're thinking.

The two main ways of reflecting are repeating exactly what was said or paraphrasing. The main benefit of repeating exactly what was said is that it shows respect for the client. It also means you're far less likely to misinterpret those words ☺

Paraphrasing or providing a summary of what's been said is useful when there is limited time or if you need to understand what's been said in a different way, or to make sense of it.

Withhold Judgment and Avoid Rebutting

Judging or formulating opinions about another person's behavior (even if it is not shared) takes a coach out of the moment and removes attention from what a client is saying.

You already know that the learning and behavioral change parts of the brain are less likely to activate if you judge or provide an answer for your coachee.

Additionally, the judgment may be flawed. Social psychologists Mark Leary and Rowland Miller have found that judgments of people who begin to predict behavior of others halfway through the others' self-description were less accurate than people who waited until the end.

Finally, remember what I wrote in earlier regarding judgment and self-judgment. Simply being judged raises cortisol levels and makes your coachee's brain less creative and able to think of long-term solutions.

Understand What Is Meant, Not Just What Is Said

Words may convey only a fraction of meaning. For some people voice tone, facial expression, gestures, and eye movement reveal significant parts of conversation. When you're coaching someone, it's important to pick up the signals when, for instance, "I'm fine" really means "I'm not fine."

If you get an uneasy sense that someone is not telling you the truth about how they're feeling or a sense that someone is putting on a good face/doing the socially acceptable thing of trying to appear like they're feeling better than they are, you need to pay attention to your senses.

Communicating that information back to the person without making them defensive or feeling overly confronted is an art.

One way to do this is to make a gentle observation about their physicality without interpreting or reading a specific emotion into their behavior.

For instance, "You've said you're fine. I also notice your eyes look moist, and your voice lowered when you said it." Unless you know a person really well or are especially intuitive and empathic, it can be wise to avoid saying, "You seem sad or you sound angry" because (a) it may be inaccurate and sound judgmental and/or (b) because it can be overly confronting for some people.

Simply making an observation about their physicality will be perfectly accurate and allows them space to interpret their body reaction for you.

If you already have a truly trusting relationship with the other person, then you may be able to accurately intuit the emotion and name it to the other person without that person feeling judged.

But if you don't have a trusting relationship or if you're unsure, it's always safer and more respectful to name the physical reaction (a statement of fact) and not interpret the emotion or feeling behind it.

Listening Under Duress: How Active Listening Can Defuse Highly Emotional Situations

If you're in a situation where emotions are escalating or have escalated, active listening can act as water on fire.

Many differences or opinion or arguments escalate simply because one or more people start to feel like the other people aren't listening or understanding their point of view. Voices get louder, arguments get more emphatic, and stress levels rise.

Often the sense of not being heard contributes to a sense of desperation.

If one person simply starts reflecting back what the other person says, using their exact words, it helps the other person know that they're not crazy and that they have been heard.

In extremely emotional escalations, it may be useful to repeat back EXACTLY what they've just said. And it's always a good idea to avoid manipulating the other person's words so you can prove they're wrong or show how smart you are.

If you're the person doing the reflecting, it doesn't mean that you agree with their perception, analysis, feelings, or words. Repeating or reflecting another person's words back also does not mean you're somehow losing the argument (no matter how it feels!)

"I heard you say that x, y and z happened and that you felt x."

Try it next time you feel an argument escalating. It's the closest thing you can get to a magic bullet.

Here's what's happened when I've used it outside of coaching when something has triggered me.

The person suddenly focuses on me. They start to really "see" me.

They either relax, stop talking, or interrupt with an emphatic "yes!"

If you can master active listening and use it routinely, all your relationships have the potential to improve.

Questions to Consider

What part of active listening is generally easy for you to do?

When is it more difficult?

What can you do to make it easier to use active listening?

When will you commit to doing it?

....

Take the online assessment: Think you know everything about Listening? Take this 9-quesiton quick to test your knowledge

Leadership

One of the soft skills highly prized by employers is leadership. Leaders may be quiet or loud, bold or gentle, but their guidance and direction is useful in most workplaces. Developing and honing your personal leadership skills is an important part of creating your personal brand.

Conflict Management

Conflict is unavoidable. Handled effectively, conflict may lead to new ideas, improved communication, and other benefits. Handled ineffectively, conflict may lead to unhappy employees, lost productivity and revenue, and, ultimately, loss of employees. Knowing how to manage conflict is one of the soft skills that will help you in your career.

....

Reading 6.3

Managing Conflict

By Beth Bratkovic

"Where all think alike, no one thinks very much."

—Walter Lippmann

Conflict can create emotions of excitement, sadness, fear, anger, or joy. When approached in a constructive way, it can create and enhance ideas, opportunities, growth, relationships, and business outcomes. But handled incorrectly, conflict can be costly. According to one study, "Conflict is inevitable—85 percent of employees experience conflict to some degree (typically around 2.8 hours per week).... Conflict is costly—at least $359 billion in paid hours this year"[2]

The more differing perspectives that are represented in the resolution of a business issue or problem, the higher probability for an excellent outcome—or at least the best solution possible. But at the same time, the more perspectives differ, the higher the likelihood for conflict. The trick is balancing the need for better, stronger ideas and practices with people's need for comfort and safety.

Conflict Styles

Some individuals are hard wired for conflict; they are the competitors. We know them as athletes, sales teams, competitors in some way, shape, or form. They enjoy conflict; in fact, many thrive on it. This group needs guidance in managing conflict.

Then there are those who avoid conflict and want nothing to do with it. They may focus on accommodating others so no one gets uncomfortable. Conflict makes their skin crawl (literally, in some cases; there are those who break out in rashes from the stress conflict causes them), their stomachs hurt, their heads ache. They consider conflict a categorically bad thing, which can cause them to keep their creative ideas, differing perspectives, and input to themselves to avoid offending others. This group needs new skills, language, and filters to help them manage conflict in constructive and productive ways that are comfortable for them.

Finally, there is a third group who are the collaborators and compromisers. These individuals are always looking for a win/win situation or a middle ground in which everyone is accommodated. Most people consider themselves to be in this group, but that is not really the case.

All of the above styles are appropriate in certain situations. Issues arise, however, when we rely on one specific style for every situation. This can result in ineffective outcomes such as injured relationships, lack of creativity, recurring conflicts, unmet needs (for both the individual and the organization), bad decisions, and so forth.

There are many tools one can use to manage conflict more productively. This article will focus on language to define the main styles of dealing with conflict, how perceptions affect conflict, and strategies for understanding intent and slowing down knee-jerk reactions.

Ways of Dealing With Conflict

There are five preferred styles for dealing with conflict, as measured with the Thomas-Kilmann Conflict Mode Instrument, which is influenced largely by the management grid developed by Robert R. Blake and Jane Mouton.[3] This model uses axes to identify an individual's preferred style: focus on issue and focus on relationship. A competitor will have a high focus on the issue and a low focus on the relationship, while an

---

[2] "Workplace Conflict and How Businesses Can Harness It to Thrive," CPP Global Human Capital report, July 2008, available at https://www.cpp.com/Pdfs/CPP_Global_Human_Capital_Report_Workplace_Conflict.pdf.
[3] Kenneth W. Thomas and Ralph H. Kilmann, *Thomas-Kilmann Conflict Mode Instrument* (Tuxedo. New York: Xicom, 1974), and Robert R. Blake and Jane Mouton. *The Managerial Grid: The Key to Leadership Excellence.* (Houston, Texas: Gulf Publishing Co., 1964).

avoider will have a low focus on the issue and a low focus on the relationship. An accommodator will have a high focus on the relationship and a low focus on the issue; a compromiser, a midlevel focus on the relationship and a mid-level focus on the issue; and a collaborator, a high focus on both the issue and relationship.

These words provide a filter you can use to start assessing yourself and others when dealing with conflict. If you lean toward avoiding or accommodating, are you dealing with a competitor who will ensure a win/lose situation as the end result? If you are a competitor, are you leaving differing perspectives on the table so that you can "win" or "be right," while perhaps negatively affecting the health of the relationship or the effectiveness of solutions that are presented? Are you collaborating to the point of being seen as wishy washy and wasting the time of others? Or are you comfortable with all five styles, approaching each situation based on what is likely to work best in a given situation?

The key to using this tool is understanding each of the styles and adjusting your individual style as needed, Maintain flexibility and adaptability based on the situation and the style of the person or people with whom you are dealing. Gaining a clearer understanding of what drives another person's behavior—whether that person is focused on relationship, issue, both, or neither—will help you have a more effective, constructive conversation.

Personal Conflict Metaphor

The way we view things is really only a reflection of our beliefs about ourselves, and not necessarily an objective picture of what's really happening. In fact, as TV's Dr. Phil says, "There is no reality—only perception."

The phrase "perception is reality" has become an adage, and the concept is useful when considering your own personal perception of conflict, how it is described or played out in your mind. If you had to define conflict as a personal metaphor, what would your metaphor be? Do you see conflict as a boxing match? A bridge? A puzzle? A storm? How would your metaphor play out in your mind? Your conflict metaphor, whether it is positive or negative, shapes the way you approach conflict.

Your perception is your reality, and you have the ability to adjust it. Once your conflict metaphor is defined, ask yourself if this is how you want conflict to function in your life. Is this what you want as your reality? Then accept, alter, or abandon this metaphor.

Know Your Intent

When walking into a tough situation or discussion, you need to understand your intent. Ask yourself, "What do I want to achieve in this conversation?" Just establishing this focus provides a framework you can use to determine whether a conversation has been successful. Did your outcome equal the intent? Were you effective?

Consider the number of conversations you have in a day and how many of those actually result in the desired outcome. Focusing on your intent provides a different filter for dialogue: Is it more important to achieve the outcome you have identified or to say what you might want to say, even if it is at odds with your intent? Think about how different your behavior will be when your dialogue is less about language and more about behavioral changes or outcomes.

Slow Down Knee-jerk Reactions

Many people find that when they are driving fast and passing people on the highway, it is because they are good drivers. But when other people drive fast and pass us, it's because they are crazy. It makes sense to ask ourselves why we believe these things. Why am I good driver when it's convenient for me, and others are crazy? Introspection helps us understand how and why we act in a certain way. The fight or flight instinct is just that: instinct. Learning how to manage this behavior becomes a significant tool when approaching conflict.

The fight or flight response adapted as a means of survival; life was hard for our early ancestors, and the ones who lived were the ones who figured out when to fight and when to run. Circumstances have changed greatly for most of us, but we still have the same knee-jerk reactions. The way this plays out in tense situations, when we are stressed or anxious, can cause a destructive form of conflict—we tend to shut down or be overly aggressive. But we have another option—managing our knee-jerk, fight or flight reactions.

The most common tool is the "count to ten" rule. A variation on this is something you might remember from the television show "The Honeymooners," in which Ralph Kramden used the saying, "Pins and needles, needles and pins, a happy man is a man that grins." The idea is to give yourself a moment to breathe deep and manage the fight or flight instinct. Having a clear understanding of your physiological responses as they are occurring is extremely helpful when slowing down knee-jerk reactions. Try to notice when you are getting stressed by acknowledging your body's signals. Then you can identify your reactions and apply methods for managing them.

Conclusions

We are in control of our approach to conflict: indeed, most people change their approach to conflict over their lifetime.[4] But adjusting the way we deal with conflict—changing our behavior—is not easy to do. We behave in certain ways because those behaviors have somehow worked for us in the past. Trying something different is nerve racking and difficult because it requires us to take risks, but such changes can enhance our effectiveness at work and, in general, in our relationships with others.

This article provides some actions you can take to change your style and competence when dealing with conflict. Identify your preferred style of dealing with conflict—determine whether you a competitor, collaborator, compromiser, avoider, or accommodator, and then challenge yourself to adapt your style to the situation. Analyze your personal conflict metaphor, practice identifying your intent prior to conversations, and slow down your knee-jerk reactions. These steps will help you to manage conflict in a way that improves your effectiveness at work and in every area of life.

Emotional Intelligence

Emotional intelligence is being aware of one's own and other people's emotions and being able to handle those emotions and relationships empathetically. High emotional intelligence is often correlated to professional success.

---

[4] CPP Global Human Capital report.

Reading 6.4

Improving Emotional Intelligence

By Golnaz Sadri

Executive Summary

Most people are familiar with the old IQ tests that measure a person's intelligence quotient. But these days, scholars and practitioners are paying additional attention to how a person's emotional intelligence affects performance. Luckily, organizations have many options to increase their workforce's emotional intelligence.

Most of us are familiar with the use of intelligence tests for predicting behaviors such as educational achievement and job performance. Intelligence tests are standardized instruments designed to measure IQ (intelligence quotient). Recently, the concept of emotional intelligence has generated interest, with some authors suggesting that emotional intelligence (EI) may be more important than intellectual intelligence in determining success in jobs with a heavy interpersonal component such as management, sales and leadership.

EI relates to four dimensions of skills and behaviors: a person's ability to understand his or her own behavior, a person's ability to regulate his or her own behavior, a person's ability to understand other people's behavior and a person's ability to regulate other people's behavior. This article reviews the literature on the concept of EI and makes some recommendations about how to develop the EI of managers and leaders. The article is divided into four sections: the first section examines the two most cited models of EI; the second section reviews research evidence linking EI with management performance; the third section looks at whether EI responds to training; and the fourth section gives suggestions for developing EI.

EI Models

J.D. Mayer, P. Salovey and D.R. Caruso in *Psychological Inquiry* define emotional intelligence as "the capacity to reason about emotions, and of emotions to enhance thinking. It includes the abilities to accurately perceive emotions, to access and generate emotions so as to assist thought, to understand emotions and emotional knowledge, and to reflectively regulate emotions so as to promote emotional and intellectual growth."

Their model for EI, which has been widely accepted by the academic community, consists of four levels of emotional abilities. The most basic level is the ability to perceive emotion and includes skills such as recognizing facial expressions in others and interpreting what those expressions mean. The second level is the ability to use emotion to facilitate thought and includes skills such as weighing conflicting emotions against each other to determine how one should react. The third level, understanding emotion, involves labeling emotions and understanding the relationships associated with shifts in emotion. The fourth level is the ability to manage emotion within oneself and others. This can include, for example, calming down after becoming angry or being able to alleviate the anxiety of another person. This model is measured through the Mayer-Salovey-Caruso Emotional Intelligence Test (MSCEIT), a self-report measure.

In his book *Emotional Intelligence,* Daniel Goleman defines EI as "abilities such as being able to motivate oneself and persist in the face of frustrations; to control impulse and delay gratification; to regulate one's moods and keep distress from swamping the ability to think; to empathize and to hope." Goleman's model has gained more attention from the nonacademic community.

This model of EI consists of five skill areas, three of which relate to personal competence and two of which relate to social competence. The personal competencies include self-awareness (awareness of one's inner feelings, preferences, capabilities and intuitions); self-regulation (the ability to manage one's inner feelings, impulses and capabilities); and motivation (the ability to direct one's emotions toward goal attainment). The social competencies include empathy (the ability to be aware of the feelings, needs and concerns of others); and social skills (the ability to direct the behavior of others toward goal attainment). Two measurement tools are based on Goleman's model: the Emotional Competency Inventory (ECI) and the Emotional and Social Competency Inventory (ESCI).

EI and Management Performance

A number of authors and researchers argue that EI is important for effective management and leadership and that EI shows a relationship with performance beyond intellectual ability and personality factors. There is evidence that managers high in EI are able to perceive, evaluate, anticipate and manage emotions in a way that enables them to work with and motivate their subordinates. Research has shown that a manager's or team leader's EI helps motivate the team and builds supportive relationships among team members.

R.K. Cooper in *Training and Development* identifies a number of high profile business leaders who demonstrate what he refers to as the "four cornerstones" of EI: emotional literacy, emotional fitness, emotional depth and emotional alchemy. A study of 350 university students participating in 108 teams found that teams consisting of members higher in EI performed better than teams with members lower in EI. This study found that EI affected the type of conflict strategies adopted. Those higher in EI were more likely to use collaboration when resolving conflicts at the individual and team level.

In a study comparing 51 high potential managers with 51 regular managers, the EI subscales of assertiveness, independence, optimism, flexibility and social responsibility separated the high potential managers from managers performing at an average level. Another study found that employees were more creative when their team leaders possessed self-control against criticism and were more empathetic.

There is a relationship between EI and transformational leadership. In one study, managers with higher self-reported ratings of EI were rated as more transformational by their subordinates. Subordinates rated managers with higher self-reported ratings of EI as showing more idealized influence, inspirational motivation and individualized consideration.

The studies described here show that EI relates to managerial effectiveness. In a study of 40 managers participating in a leadership development center, M. Higgs and P. Aitken in the *Journal of Managerial Psychology* found EI to be related to a number of aspects of leadership, and they suggest that EI is likely to prove a good predictor of leadership potential. As such, assessment centers and other selection procedures targeted at selecting effective managers and leaders will benefit by including EI as one of the selection criteria.

Self-reported measures of EI can be used to determine the level of a person's EI. In addition, observation of participant behavior in the various interpersonal and group activities included as part of an assessment center is a valuable source of information about someone's EI.

Training. It Works

Evidence shows that a person's EI can be improved through training and development. For example, American Express financial advisors developed an emotional competence training program in the early 1990s. The study compared the performance of financial advisors who worked under managers that received emotional competence training against those who worked under managers that did not receive the training. P. Smith at the Consortium for Research on Emotional Intelligence in Organizations reports that advisors who worked for a trained manager were able to grow their businesses at a rate of 18.1 percent over 15 months. This compares favorably to the 16.2 percent growth rate for advisors who worked under a manager who did not benefit from EI training.

R. Kelley and J. Caplan in *Harvard Business Review* describe a study at Bell Labs where nine nonintellectual strategies that differentiated star performers from average performers were identified. The nine strategies included: taking initiative, networking, self-management, teamwork effectiveness, leadership, followership, perspective, show-and-tell and organizational savvy. Bell Labs developed a program that focused on teaching these skills to engineering employees. Kelley and Caplan note that at the time their article was written, 600 engineers had participated in this program, which led to an increase in worker productivity (about 25 percent after one year) and an improved organizational climate.

K.S. Groves, M.P. McEnrue and W. Shen in the *Journal of Management Development* found that a group of 135 employed business students who underwent an 11-week EI training program showed significant gains in EI, while a control group showed no pre-test, post-test differences. These studies show that people are able to develop their EI, and much of the executive coaching currently being performed by organizations focuses on developing people's interpersonal and social skills.

A Plethora of Choices

Management development programs are popular and cost organizations billions of dollars annually. Such programs take a variety of approaches. S.J. Allen and N.S. Hartman in *S.A.M. Advanced Management Journal* identify 27 approaches to training managers and leaders: group reflection, individual reflection, service learning, outdoor management development, low ropes course, team building, fellowships, sabbaticals, developmental relationships, networking with senior executives, degree programs, self-paced learning, classroom-based learning, e-learning, executive coaching, instruments, assessment centers, 360 degree feedback, just-in-time training, developmental assignments, simulations, games, personal development plans, action learning, job enrichment, job enlargement and job rotation. A number of these approaches can help organizations develop their employees' EI.

Self-awareness is developed by getting participants to look at themselves. Of the activities identified by Allen and Hartman, those most pertinent to developing self-awareness include individual reflection, group reflection, executive coaching, instruments, simulations, personal development plans, low ropes course, team building, fellowships, sabbaticals, assessment centers, developmental assignments, simulations, job enrichment and job enlargement.

Individual reflection focuses on a person's goals, past experiences and personal mission and is captured through activities like keeping a journal of work activities, challenges and responses. Group reflection typically occurs after a team building activity. Participants discuss the pattern of events during the exercise and identify strategies for improvement. Executive coaching is an individualized method of learning where a coach works with a client in a one-to-one relationship to assist in accomplishing behavioral improvements back at the workplace.

Instruments are a popular vehicle for raising self-awareness. A combination of self-reports and 360 degree instruments is used often as part of management development programs. A number of measurement tools have been developed to measure EI, including the Social Competency Inventory and the Mayer-Salovey-Caruso Emotional Intelligence Test mentioned earlier. But EI training programs will increase their benefits by including any measures that help raise awareness about different dimensions of the self. While the specific instrument used may vary, it is important to pay particular attention to the psychometric properties of each instrument to ensure that the measure adopted is reliable, valid and will strengthen a training and development program.

Simulations can focus on a number of aspects of behavior, such as communication or conflict resolution. Such exercises provide employees the opportunity to practice these skills in a nonthreatening environment and then reflect on how effectively they handled the situation and whether they would change their approach to similar situations in the future. Low ropes courses typically are outdoor activities that present participants with developmental scenarios, providing opportunities after completion to reflect on how well participants handled the challenges presented to them.

Fellowships require participants to engage in a focused project and can help managers identify and refine their particular interests and passions. Sabbaticals, like fellowships, provide participants with time to focus on projects of particular interest to them and help redefine and develop a person's interests, skills and priorities. Assessment centers involve participants in a variety of activities, including group activities, paired simulations and role playing exercises, and trained observers give participants feedback about their strengths and weaknesses. Feedback of this nature can be a valuable vehicle for developing self-awareness. Finally, job enrichment (adding tasks of greater responsibility to a person's job) and job enlargement (adding tasks of equal difficulty to a person's job) can help develop self-awareness when, after several weeks, the job incumbent reflects on the experience and on how well she is doing.

Self-regulation requires that a person observe his behavior and make changes where necessary. Of the activities identified by Allen and Hartman, those most likely to enhance self-regulation include self-paced learning, executive coaching, 360 degree feedback, developmental assignments, games, personal development plans and action learning.

Self-paced learning is an individualized form of learning in which the participant completes a book, workbook or recorded material at her own pace. Having a coach work with a client on a one-to-one basis to raise awareness of how the client's behavior affects the workplace is a useful tool in developing self-regulation. Feedback, both self-generated as well as 360 degree, assists with self-regulation because it identifies the strengths and pitfalls of the individual's particular style and identifies next steps in managing behavior. Feedback from others helps develop self-regulation if measurements are taken twice or more, particularly if the manager is given opportunities in the interim to change his behavior.

Developmental assignments are structured so that they challenge individuals and provide them an opportunity to learn. Personal development plans involve the individual in developing and taking responsibility for her training and development. This might include looking at behaviors or asking people to reconnect with their inner values, talents and passions. To develop self-regulation, a person sets behavior-oriented goals and then monitors progress toward these goals.

Awareness of others can be developed through group reflection, service learning, team building, developmental relationships, networking with senior executives, classroom-based training and job rotation.

Group reflection typically involves a team simulation exercise, ranging from simple paper and pencil activities to more elaborate outdoor training, paired with group reflection at the completion of the team simulation. These drills help build awareness of others and how one's behavior affects the group. One simple way to generate feedback is through a round-robin exercise where each group member asks the other group members for feedback on specific aspects of her behavior. Think of having the group answer questions like this: Do you see me as a person who dominates the group discussion?

Service learning involves engagement in activities that target individual and community needs. This is a very good way to raise awareness about other people with diverse backgrounds and needs. The focus of team building is to facilitate cooperation among team members and helps team members set goals and priorities, examine the way they conduct their work and how they interact. Developmental relationships aim to provide individuals with the support they need to meet their developmental needs. Managers can help raise their awareness of others by taking on the senior role in the developmental relationship. Networking with senior executives provides exposure to other people and can help managers understand different work styles and preferences.

Classroom-based training typically lasts from three to five days and also can assist in raising awareness of others. For this, training content should be geared toward relevant topics, such as the differences between individuals. Finally, job rotation and cross-training can increase awareness of other people's jobs, skill sets and challenges.

Regulating the behavior of others relies on collaborative goal-setting and using effective social skills to motivate and guide subordinates toward goal accomplishment. Of the activities identified by Allen and Hartman, those that contribute best to developing skills at regulating others are outdoor management development, low ropes courses, team building, developmental relationships, action learning and group simulations.

Outdoor management development simulations get managers to examine the strengths and weaknesses of their current approach to leading others. Similar benefits accrue from low ropes courses, after which managers are asked to examine and reflect on their leadership.

Team building involves members working cooperatively to analyze the task aspect of their work as well as the interpersonal processes occurring within the group. These activities help managers develop skills to motivate and guide others. Developmental relationships may be formal or informal, but they help provide the target individual with information, support and challenges. Again, these relationships can help managers develop skills at regulating the work of others if the manager takes on the senior role in the developmental relationship. Action learning engages participants in concrete experience and subsequent reflection on that experience with the objective of developing ways to overcome potential challenges existing within the workplace. Group simulations mirror the ways managers work with others and can help develop their skills at managing and working with people.

Picking and Choosing

Organizations that aim to develop the EI of their managers should not attempt to improve all four EI competencies—self-awareness, self-regulation, awareness of others and regulation of others—in the same training program. Instead, focus on developing one or more as stand-alone competencies and provide training to participants who lack the requisite skills on an as-needed basis.

For example, the top training priority for one manager might be developing self-awareness, for another it may be improving self-regulation, for a third, developing awareness of others, while for a fourth, the initial focus for training might be developing skills for motivating and regulating others. The level of priority will depend on an organization's assessment of each manager's EI prior to the training program.

Apprehension

The majority of people face fear or apprehension in communication at some point in their lives. Whether introducing oneself to a new group or speaking in front of a large group, public speaking is a common fear. Knowing your personal level of anxiety may help you to conquer your fear to help you succeed in your career.

Take the online assessment: Personal Report of communication apprehension

Ethics

Many fields and organizations have ethical codes of conduct to help guide your actions as you work in your field. However, you may face ethical dilemmas, large or small, during your career. Knowing your ethical stance will help prepare you to face decisions with ethical components.

Ethical behavior is essential in today's business world,but understanding how to make ethical decisions may be challenging. Some fields, like accounting and law, have well-defined ethical codes to help and guide practitioners. Other fields rely on people's own ethical codes to ensure ethical behavior and decision making.

Ethics is, at its most simple, decisions between right and wrong. Ethical decisions may include whether or not to cheat on a test or take credit for another person's work. Other ethical decisions may involve plagiarism, stealing ideas or accounts, or misrepresenting information, like expense reports or profits, to name a few. People may make decisions based on their personal sense of right and wrong, moral and religious beliefs, virtues, rights, duty, fairness, and justice.

The stories of unethical—and often illegal—behavior are everywhere. The media is full of stories of business managers or officers who place profits above all else, trade on insider secrets, and justify illegal or immoral behavior. Unethical business behavior damages the trust between companies, clients, consumers, and corporations—and often results in legal action.

Companies want employees who will act ethically, so being aware of ethical issues and your personal ethical values is important to your career. Will your employer be able to trust you to act in the best interests of the company? Will you protect and enhance the company's reputation? Having a clear framework though which to make ethical decisions will help you act ethically and thus present yourself as a trustworthy employee.

Take the online assessment: Are you ethical-ish? Take this ethics quiz and find out

A Model of Ethical Decision Making

Decisions that require ethical consideration are ones in which a problem or situation has several possible solutions, none of which may be ideal. The solution that seems obvious to you may be in opposition to the obvious solution to your coworkers or manager. One way to make complex ethical decisions is to follow the five-step framework described here:

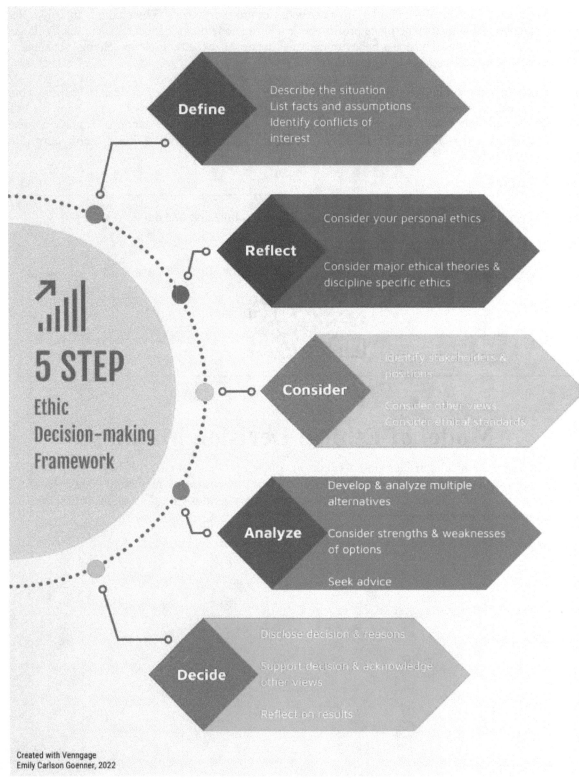

Figure 6.1 5 Step Decision-making Framework

Step 1: Define

The best way to deal with any problem or task is to clearly define the situation. What is at stake? What are facts? What are opinions or assumptions? Who is affected by the situation? Who may have differing opinions or see differing results? When facing a problem, describe the situation, listing facts, assumptions, options, and conflicts.

Step 2: Reflect

People involved in the situation may have very strong feelings about a solution. Many people react instinctively and/or emotionally to situations without examining the reasons for their reactions or opinions. Clearly stating your personal ethics will help you see why you are responding the way you are.

Step 3: Consider

Viewing different perspectives is important to making an ethical decision. Identify who will be affected by this decision or situation. Talk with people who have different opinions and ideas. Consider other people's views and opinions. Does your field have guiding ethical principles? If so, consult them. Step 4: Analyze

The problem or situation may have one solution that is very obvious to you, but in any complex situation there are multiple alternatives. What are other options? How might those options work? Is a combination of options possible? To help analyze a situation, you may ask some of the following questions:

- Who would be harmed by this decision? (The Harm Test)
- Is this option legal? If not, eliminate it from consideration. (The Legality Test)
- How have similar situations been handled in the past? (The Precedence Test)
- Would I be comfortable with my decision if this decision was on the front page of a newspaper? (The Publicity Test)
- If I were challenged on this decision, could I provide a reasonable explanation for how and why I made it? (The Defensibility Test)
- How would my mom react to my decision? (The Mom Test)
- If I were adversely affected by this decision, how would I feel about it? Would I feel it was a fair and just decision? (The Golden Rule Test)
- What do my professional ethics suggest is the best option? (The Professional Ethics Test)
- Ask a few trusted colleagues what they think of the different alternatives. (The Colleagues Test)

Talking to others and asking for advice is often useful when analyzing a situation and evaluating solutions.

Step 5: Decide

Select an option or solution. Be prepared to explain why you selected this option. Acknowledge that not everyone may agree with you, and be prepared to explain and support your decision. Be open to change and reevaluation based on results.

Reading 6.5

The Real-World Impact of Workplace Ethics

By Paul Falcone

March 1, 2022

COVID-19 has forced many ethical considerations to the forefront of HR. Whether confronting issues related to vaccinations, masking, employee retention or mental health, making decisions based on ethics is a daily chore for many HR professionals. Here are four considerations worth contemplating as you prepare to address your next ethical dilemma.

The Ends Do Not Justify the Means

The first ethical rule to consider is a twist on Machiavelli's famous saying, "The ends justify the means," meaning that no matter what needs to be said or done, nothing is more important than the end result. Clearly, the opposite should be true in corporate America: The ends should never justify the means.

"This pithy saying is well-known in corporate ethics and code of conduct circles, primarily to address shortcuts that accountants and finance professionals could potentially take to justify a certain outcome in the financial records: a big no-no per the Sarbanes-Oxley Act of 2002," said Steven Mintz, ethicist and professor emeritus at California State University, San Luis Obispo, and author of Beyond Happiness and Meaning: Transforming Your Life Through Ethical Behavior (Ethics Sage LLC, 2019). "The act holds accountants and finance professionals responsible for financial statements and internal controls. In fact, knowingly manipulating financial statements violates the integrity principle of ethical behavior and could result in a summary dismissal of employment if done knowingly and with an intent to unduly in influence or manipulate financial results."

Essentially, how an organization achieves its goals is just as important as the goals themselves. This should be an easy ethical rule to follow.

The Need for Transparency

Transparency also plays a role in ethical decision-making. Senior executives have an obligation of full transparency when striving to keep their workers safe from harm, particularly during the COVID-19 pandemic.

"Understand that decisions made both individually and organizationally have real-world impact on your employees and their families and, as such, are worthy considerations in a time marked by the extremes of outright panic and virus apathy," Mintz said. "Make no mistake, however, that workers and their families remain concerned, if not downright scared, of further virus mutations that may come their way, potentially combining the worst of the alpha, delta and omicron variants."

Transparency is critical no matter what issues a company faces, said Richard Shell, a professor of legal studies, business ethics and management at the University of Pennsylvania's Wharton School of Business.

"Workplace cultures that promote ethics revolve around transparency; every values-based organization relies on practices that emphasize disclosure and review to resolve ethical challenges," said Shell, author of The Conscience Code: Lead with Your Values, Advance Your Career (HarperCollins Leadership, 2021). "Ethical quandaries are solved as a team sport in healthy workplace cultures."

For example, he explained, if corporate leaders opt not to disclose positive coronavirus cases where employees were active at work during the contamination stage, positive asymptomatic workers could potentially transmit the virus to family members. The leadership's logic? "Let's not worry anyone." And on a potentially more deliberate level, "What they don't know won't hurt them," Shell said.

Such lapses in ethical decision-making could have a tremendous impact not only on employees' health, but also on their decision to seek employment elsewhere. After all, think of the message that employees may be hearing: "We want you here at work, but we're not going out of our way to make it safe for you to be here, despite a global pandemic that has killed millions worldwide."

One of the clearest reasons why workers have left and continue to leave companies is due to the mishandling of the pandemic, Shell said, and this example rises to the top of the list as a significant moral transgression for not appearing to care about employees' health and well-being.

Environmental Sustainability and Corporate Social Responsibility

What about the moral needs of your workforce? How can you address their problems, wants and needs? Millennials and members of Generation Z currently make up about half of the U.S. workforce, and their numbers are growing exponentially. They are the most studied generational cohorts in world history, and we know what they want: diversity, equity and inclusion; corporate social responsibility; career and professional development; and trust in senior leadership.

What exactly is your organization doing to help the local community? How has your company stepped up to the demands of the day and helped employees live safer lives? Have you developed incentives to promulgate behaviors that help employees and their families? Have you educated people to the degree necessary to help them make informed decisions? Equally important, have you shared wisdom and attempted to calm the room and drown out so much of the noise coming at your workers from so many different sources—cable TV, the Internet, social media and the like? If so, have you highlighted and publicized your efforts so your workers and key stakeholders understand your core values and your attempts at making their lives safer? If not, there might have been a missed opportunity to demonstrate your moral and ethical leadership that may now be worth readdressing.

Ethics and the Future of Work

We're on the precipice of what may be the most important chapter of our lifetimes as we re-enter the workplace and begin resuming normal activities post-pandemic. Opportunities to reshape our culture and norms have never been more prevalent, all surrounding the fundamental question of what will work look and feel like once we fully return?

"We know that workers want a greater sense of work/life equilibrium; that caregivers need greater support; that gender parity needs to be addressed, both in terms of compensation and promotional opportunities; and that wellness issues deserve greater resources," Shell said. "In the context of a pandemic, time is required to consider the impact of choices on people's lives—whether considering individual versus company/societal rights, or risks from vaccines versus risks from viruses—yet time is the one resource that pandemics don't allow.

"It's this compressed disruption that leaves us building the plane while flying it, balancing conflicting messages from scientists and politicians. That, in turn, creates polarized responses ranging from rage to apathy that leave us disengaged. However you feel about the current state of pandemic affairs, one thing's for sure: COVID has raised the stakes for all of us to make ethical thinking and discussions a high priority."

Some ethical best practices worth considering:

- Err on the side of overcommunicating and come from transparency.
- Make known to your key stakeholders your efforts at addressing the pandemic and your organization's role in bettering the local community.
- Remember the golden rule: What you want for yourself, give to another.

Such moral lessons will find a welcome home among your employees, and the practical benefits of employee retention and engagement will help you weather this storm and any others that come your way.

Applying this Skill: Ethical Mini-Cases

Read one or more of the following mini-cases and discuss possible solutions based on the five-step ethical framework.

Mini-Case 1: Posting on Social Media

Last summer, James, a marketing student at a 4-year college, missed work at this internship. After the second absence, the human resources manager emailed James a warning, saying the company required employees to provide notice if they would not work on a particular day and that if a similar incident occurred, James would be fired.

On July 5th, after a long weekend with his friends, James failed to show up for work and was subsequently fired. James posted to Instagram, "ABC Company sucks, man, I was just hangin' with my bros." The post included a photo of James and three friends at a party.

Six months later, James is close to graduating with his marketing degree and looking forward to starting his career. At an interview with a prominent firm, James was surprised when the interviewer said, "I'm sorry. We saw your social media feed and you are not right for this position." James thought the interview went well and had no idea the company looked at his social media accounts.

Should the company deny James the job because of his social media posts? Be prepared to share your answers with the class.

Apply the five-step ethical framework and discuss the following:

- Did James act ethically when posting on Instagram?
- It monitoring potential employees' personal social media accounts an invasion of privacy?
- Is monitoring potential employees' personal social media accounts ethical?

Mini-Case 2: Should Employers Check Your Social Media?

Most employers participate in some type of employee monitoring. Employers can see the emails you write, the websites you visit, and everything you write in Slack, Google Workplace, and Microsoft Teams. During the COVID-19 pandemic, some companies moved to using productivity monitors or "bossware" that can allow an employer access to your attendance, your screen, and even your facial expressions. As an employee, there's little you can do about monitoring on company-owned devices.

However, some companies also monitor employees' activity on personal social media accounts. A company's goal is to protect itself from negative publicity or breaches in privacy. But employees generally do not want their bosses looking at their personal social media pages. Questions can arise about employers' right to discipline or even fire employees for posts or comments made on personal social media accounts.

What do you think? Be prepared to share your answers with the class.

Apply the five-step ethical framework and discuss the following:

- Is monitoring employees' personal social media accounts ethical?
- Is monitoring employees' personal social media accounts an invasion of privacy?
- Does employee monitoring improve performance?
- How does monitoring affect employee–management relationships?

Mini-Case 3: A Cell Fire

Several years ago, a well-known cell phone manufacturer faced problems when its newly released cellphone, aimed at being an iPhone rival, began catching on fire. Consumers called for a recall of the product.

In response, the company issued a statement saying they were "committed to producing the highest quality products and we take every incident report from our valued customers very seriously. ... We conducted a thorough investigation and found a battery cell issue." The company's statement failed to mention the phones started on fire.[5]

Was the company's press release ethical? Be prepared to share your answers with the class.

Apply the five-step ethical framework and discuss the following:

- Is it ethical for a company to avoid mentioning problems with a product?
- How should the company have addressed the problem?

---

[5] Samsung Newsroom, "Samsung Will Replace Current Note7 with New One," September 2, 2016, https://news.samsung.com/global/statement-on-galaxy-note7.

Mini-Case 4: Natural-Hair, Where?

Asya applied for a customer service representative position with a large management company. She was excited to accept the resulting job offer until the company told her she had to change her hairstyle. "We require a neat appearance," the human resource manager told Asya. "You'll need to straighten or relax your hair. We must project a professional appearance."

Asya had recently had her naturally textured hair braided. She had friends who had their hair straightened ever few weeks to conform with some people's ideas of "professional" but Asya was not prepared to change her hairstyle.

What should Asya do? Be prepared to share your answers with the class.

Apply the five-step ethical framework and discuss the following:

- Was it ethical for the company to ask Asya to change her hairstyle?
- How should the company have addressed the idea of professional appearance?
- How should Asya respond to the company?

Mini-Case 5: Leaving Early

Erin, a junior programmer, works next to Denise, a senior programmer. For the last six months, Denise has been battling breast cancer and has been missing a significant amount of work. At first, Erin and the other staff members were happy to pick up some of Denise's workload as she went through chemotherapy.

Now, Denise has finished chemo and has returned to the office full time. She excitedly tells everyone in the office how well she is doing and how happy she is to be finished with her treatment. But Denise still leaves the office every day about two hours before everyone else and is not getting her work completed. At first Erin was happy to help Denise, but she is starting to feel taken advantage of. Why is Denise leaving early if she's feeling good? Erin feels resentful at having to do part of Denise's job and wishes she could leave early every day. She is considering telling her supervisor about Denise's behavior.

What should Erin do? Be prepared to share your answers with the class.

Apply the five-step ethical framework and discuss the following:

- Has Denise done anything wrong? Is her behavior ethical?
- With whom does Erin have an ethical conflict?

Diversity and Cross-Cultural Communication

The world we live in is more and more diverse. In a single company, you may meet people from different generations, genders, ethnicities, countries, and cultures. Being aware of the variety of differences is important today; gone are the days when we could assume "everyone is like me." Being able to work with a wide variety of people is a valuable skill in today's business climate. Companies continue to expand internationally and promote diversity and inclusion efforts in the United States. Your ability to recognize and work with diverse people from a range of backgrounds will enhance your career.

The Essentials of Cultural Intelligence

By David C. Thomas and Kerr C. Inkson

The twenty-first-century world is increasingly global, and relating effectively to others who are culturally different has become a daily necessity. This globalization is being fueled by dramatic economic shifts in many countries and by advances in communications technology. We may not travel the world, but the world has come to us. We have to deal daily with international issues and transactions, and with people from other countries and cultures.

Despite rapid modernization, culture is slow to change. For the foreseeable future, cultural differences will remain a key factor in interpersonal interactions. And we have long known that in the organizations where we spend most of our time—both those we work in and those we are customers of—interacting effectively with others is the most important part of our lives. In an increasingly competitive world, individuals who do not keep their skills up to date run the risk of losing out. Organizations that do not develop these skills in their employees risk falling behind their competitors.

In this book, we have introduced what we believe to be a key competency for the twenty-first century: cultural intelligence. Cultural intelligence, the capability to deal effectively with people from different cultural backgrounds, is a multifaceted competency consisting of cultural knowledge, the practice of mindfulness, and a repertoire of cross-cultural skills.

In order to get a sense of your current level of cultural intelligence, go to the back of the book and complete the short form of the Cultural Intelligence Assessment in the appendix. The higher you score on this assessment, the higher your level of cultural intelligence is likely to be.

As shown in Chapter 8 (Figure 8.1), cultural intelligence is developed through repetitive experiences over time, in which each repetition of the cycle builds on the previous one. The feedback from each cycle of experience leads to an ever-higher cultural intelligence quotient, or CQ. In this way, specific knowledge gained in both formal and informal ways is transformed into an ability that can then be applied to new situations.

Culture has a profound influence on almost all aspects of human endeavor. The culturally intelligent person has special knowledge. He or she understands the possible effects of cultural variation (e.g., differences in values) on his or her own behavior and that of others. The culturally intelligent person also knows how and in what circumstances these cultural differences are likely to have an effect. Culture matters, but it doesn't matter to the same degree in all circumstances all the time.

Cultural intelligence also requires the practice of mindfulness. Mindfulness is

- being aware of our own assumptions, ideas, and emotions
- noticing what is apparent about the other person's assumptions, words, and behavior
- using all of the senses in perceiving situations
- viewing the situation from several perspectives
- attending to the context to help interpret what is happening
- creating new mental maps of others
- creating new and more sophisticated categories for others
- seeking out fresh information to confirm or disconfirm mental maps
- using empathy

Knowledge and mindfulness are key elements of cultural intelligence, but in themselves they are not enough. Becoming culturally intelligent means acquiring cross-cultural skills. It is not just about becoming more skilled but also about developing a repertoire of skilled behaviors and knowing when to use each one. While everyone can learn to be culturally intelligent, certain characteristics of individuals, such as openness, extraversion, and agreeableness, support the development of cultural intelligence.

- Culturally intelligent decision makers understand the different ways in which people with different cultural backgrounds mentally simplify the complex decision-making process. They know their own motivation and goals in making decisions, and they understand how the motivations, goals, and decision-making methods of people from other cultures might differ from their own. They also know that cultural factors may sometimes outweigh Western concepts of rationality. They are mindful of the ethical components of business decisions and the relationship of ethical behavior to their underlying cultural values. Finally, they are able to adapt decision-making behavior, such as the type and amount of information gathered, the weighting of decision criteria, and the degree of participation in decisions that is appropriate to the specific cultural context, while at the same time respecting the universal rights of all those involved.
- Culturally intelligent communicators and negotiators know that cultural differences have a huge influence on the communication and negotiation processes. In organizations we spend most of our time in communication with others, and in no other activity is people's cultural grounding more influential. Both language and nonverbal behavior make it tricky to communicate across cultures. Culturally intelligent negotiators know how to anticipate communication differences, practice mindfulness by paying attention to both the context and the conventions of communication as well as its content, and adapt their negotiation behavior to make concessions, persuade, exchange information, and/or build relationships as appropriate for the negotiation and the cultural context.
- Culturally intelligent leaders know that leadership exists largely in the minds of followers. While all followers expect leaders to have a vision, to be able to communicate that vision, and to have skill in organizing followers, the specific behaviors that they use to do these things vary dramatically across cultures. The culturally intelligent leader understands that his or her leadership style will be largely either task- or relationship-oriented but that some adaptation of this style may be required depending on the characteristics of followers (e.g., their degree of collectivism). Culturally intelligent leaders do not unthinkingly mimic the leadership behaviors of another culture. Rather, they pay close attention to leaders like themselves who are effective in the cross-cultural environment and model their behavior appropriately.
- Culturally intelligent team members and leaders know that culturally diverse work groups and teams have the potential for very high achievement but also characteristics that make them prone to failure. The key to managing culturally diverse work groups lies in maximizing the benefits of diversity while minimizing the costs. Culturally intelligent team management also requires fostering cultural intelligence among team members. In order to do this, team members and team leaders must understand the effects of group processes and the steps to cultural intelligence. Team managers must consider the effects of group type, the nature of the group task, the cultural diversity of the group, and the group's internal processes to resolve conflict.

The development of cultural intelligence is an iterative process. Each intercultural interaction in which we engage offers the opportunity to enhance our cultural intelligence. Cultural intelligence can be developed at home. However, for a person seeking cultural intelligence, a period of time living and working overseas, either self-initiated or as a company assignment or training program, can be extremely rewarding.

We wish that we could somehow endow you with high cultural intelligence or that you could download it from the Internet. But developing cultural intelligence will involve hard work on your part. It is essentially a process based in experience. As such, it is often both physically and emotionally taxing. However, we think the sense of confidence and control in cross-cultural interactions that you will feel will make it worth the effort. We hope this book has helped you to start on this journey.

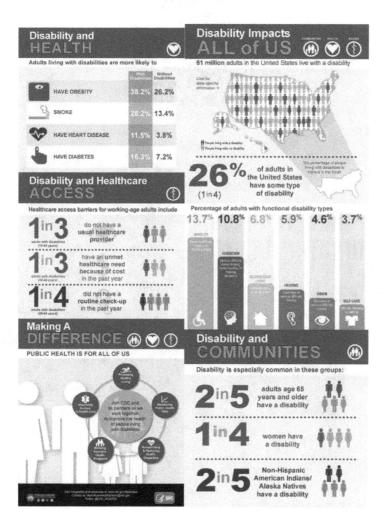

Figure 6.2 Disability Impacts All of Us

Nonverbal Communication

Sometimes we forget that over half of communication if nonverbal. In fact, studies suggest that the words we say are smallest portion of our communication. Therefore, an awareness of the nonverbal messages we are sending is important. Knowing how to stand or gesture with authority may help you project leadership and competence, while fidgeting and using many nonverbal fillers may make someone doubt your abilities.

Etiquette

Etiquette may seem like an old-fashioned concept, but it is essential for business success. Etiquette may involve niceties like saying please and thank you, opening doors, knowing how to dress and address other people, and more. Being polite and following commonly accepted business etiquette never goes out of style.

Take the online assessment: How smooth are you? Take the business etiquette quiz

Figure 6.3. **Business Etiquette Around the World**

Summing Up Unit I: Foundations

After completing the lessons in Unit I, you have a good foundation on which to build your skills throughout the course. After completing Unit I, you should be able to:

- Understand how to properly introduce yourself and someone else
- Identify and apply the 5Cs of communication
- Deliver constructive feedback
- Use the editing and revising process
- Demonstrate the ability to write concisely and clearly
- Apply a variety to stylistic writing elements effectively (e.g., vocabulary, pronouns, parallelism, etc.)

You may want to review the 5Cs of communication and various writing activities as the course progresses because they will continue to be the foundations for effective communication.

Unit II

Formats

Written Business Communication Formats

Business communications have very specific formats and types; it is important for you to know and use these formats effectively. Following formatting conventions indicates your knowledge of the standards, attention to detail, and desire to present you and your company in the best possible way. Some companies will have specific style guidelines to follow; when such guidance doesn't exist, you should follow the standard formats you learn here.

In Part II, you will learn about different written formats (e.g., letter, memo, email) and when to use them, business meetings, and writing for the internet and social media. The chart below briefly describes and compares the various types of business communication.

The most common types of business communication are:

- Letters
- Memos
- Emails
- Meetings
- Reports
- Internet and social media

Document Medium Comparison

Characteristic	Letter	Memo	Email	Online	Social Media
Audience	External	Internal	External or Internal	External or Internal	External or Internal
Use of visual enhancements (bold, italics, subheads, bullets etc.)	✓	✓	✓	✓	✓
Tone	Formal	Impersonal	Friendly Pro-fessional	Friendly Pro-fessional	Informal Pro-fessional
Single Spacing, with blank line between paragraphs	✓	✓	✓	✓	✓
Salutation & Closing	Yes, formal	No	Yes, less formal	Based on Situation	Based on Situation
Signature	✓				
Short paragraphs	✓	✓	✓	✓	✓
Sections with descriptive subheads	✓	✓	✓	✓	✓

Figure II.1 Infographic: Document Comparisons

7

Letters and Memos

Two common business communications are letters and memos. Letters are the most formal of business communications. Letters are typically meant for an external audience (i.e., someone outside of the company, such as clients, customers, or business partners). Memos are very different: they are internal documents, meant for employees and departments. The following readings will describe letters and memos in more detail. After completing this lesson, you will:

- Know when to use a business letter or business memo
- Know and demonstrate use of business letter format
- Know and demonstrate use of business memo format

Reading 7.1

Write Effective Letters and Memos

By Everett Chasen and Bob Putnam

> *"If I had more time, I would have written a shorter letter."*
>
> —T.S. Eliot

The Parts of a Letter

Many large organizations have correspondence guides that describe how people should write letters on -company stationery. Even if you work in one of those organizations, there are likely to be times when you can't consult the manual. And if you don't work for an organization that has a manual, you'll need some help. For your ready reference, here are pointers for how a letter should be organized.

At the very top of the letter is the *letterhead*, which identifies your company and provides the address where any return correspondence should be sent.

Right beneath the address at the left margin, put the *date* on which you've written the letter or the date you intend for it to be mailed—whichever is later. You'd be amazed at how important the date is—people file your letter using it; it's a great way to avoid confusion in responses ("In your April 23 letter, you said …"); and it's a reminder to your correspondent that her reply is timely or not—so please, do not omit the date.

Some people add a reference line below the date, which is useful when you're writing to a large company and don't know to whom to send your letter, or if you're answering a specific letter. This is also a good place for reference numbers, such as a case number or purchase order number.

Next comes the *name and address* of the person to whom you are writing. In many large offices, most mail is opened by someone other than the addressee, and sometimes the envelope gets lost in the transfer—which is why you have to put the name and address inside, too, to make sure the letter gets where it's supposed to go.

After that comes the *salutation*, or greeting, a traditional ritual followed by letter writers for hundreds of years. In business letters, the salutation almost -always begins with "Dear," and is followed by either "Ms. Smith," or "John" or "Sir or Madam" or some variation on one of those themes. Follow the salutation with a colon—not a comma.

Some people include a *subject line* to follow the salutation (don't bother if you've already inserted a reference line below the date.) Emails, which almost -always have subjects, have influenced letters because in the past letters did not have subject lines. Subject lines help your reader know, at a glance, what your letter's about. If you use one, keep it short. Finally, you get to the body of the letter. We'll discuss this in more detail below.

After the *body* of text, end your letter with a closing. This is a phrase like "Sincerely," or "Very truly yours," or "Best regards." If your organization doesn't specify the phrase to use in your closing, pick something that reflects the tone of your letter, as long as it's respectful.

Leave five blank lines after that and type in your name. As a manager, you should put your title and your company name on lines under your name. Of course, the blank space is for you to sign your name—so that whoever gets the letter knows you've at least seen it, even if you ascend far enough up the ranks that someone else writes your letters for you.

The Body of a Business Letter

Even if you skipped over the previous section because your current company has a style manual that determines what all letters will look like, here's the part you should not skip—unless you want to write lots more cover letters before your next promotion. What makes a good business letter? It's a letter that:

- **Is brief:** People don't have time to read long letters anymore. Ask yourself the question: "What do I want my audience to do or to know after reading this letter?" Then answer that question as close to the beginning of the letter as possible.
- **Is warm and friendly, not cold and impersonal:** Part of the goal of most business letters is not only to convey information, but also to build a business relationship. A letter filled with legalisms, fancy words, or Latin phrases will not be perceived as an example of your extraordinary intellect or vocabulary. It will only appear pretentious and wordy. The KISS acronym "keep it short and simple," originated in the design community, but it applies here.
- **Is written at an appropriate level of familiarity:** In making the letter friendly, you have to consider your audience. The person you write to also plays an important part in determining the tone of your letter. You can be more familiar, of course, with someone you know than with a

stranger, but you must also write differently to your boss than to your colleagues or to anyone who reports to you.

- **Is organized in a logical manner:** In every good letter—in fact every good written document—-sentence follows sentence in a logical way, just as B follows A. Don't jump around between topics. If you introduce more than one concept, make sure you've completed your discussion of the first topic before you move on to the second.
- **Is persuasive:** In most cases, you will ask your readers to take some action after they read what you have to say. You need to persuade or educate them to take the action you want. Provide them with the information they need to agree with you, presented in a logical and factual manner.
- **Emphasizes the positive:** Avoid using negative words such as can't, won't, and impossible. Instead, a good letter emphasizes what you can do. Instead of "We no longer make those widgets," try "Although our popular widget model A-123 is sold out, we have a new model A-124 that may fit your needs. I've enclosed a product brochure that describes its features."
- **Uses the writing skills described in chapter 3:** Always write using active voice, not passive; keep your words short; cut whatever you can; avoid jargon and foreign phrases; and above all, be courteous. Even if you're writing a complaint letter, or responding to an angry customer who, in your opinion, is way off base—keep your cool. You can, indeed, catch more flies with honey than with vinegar, and even if your objective in writing is something other than catching flies, being civil in your correspondence is the right thing to do for your company and your own reputation.

Before starting to write, think of a one-sentence description of what you hope to accomplish through your words. Use that description to create your first draft—and then pare down the draft to what is essential. Don't put that description in your letter. Review your logic, check vocabulary for readability and negativity, proofread carefully, confirm the gender of your recipient, and send it out. Of course, if others draft letters for your review or signature, it's doubly important you look for all these things before giving your approval, since your staff may not have the same point of view as yours. You may have to send many letters back for a while, marked up with your corrections, but eventually your staff will figure out what you're looking for.

Expert Tip

As the director of executive correspondence for a large government agency, **Katrice Pasteur** and her staff of 12 review between 5–10,000 letters, memos, and reports every year. "Letters are still extremely important in business," she says. According to Katrice, a good letter:

- **Addresses all of the correspondent's concerns, without dancing around the issues.** "Get to the bottom-line issues in the beginning—and make sure the writer doesn't have to write back again and tell you that you didn't answer his question."
- **Doesn't beat around the bush.** If the answer is no, it's no. "And don't try to overwhelm your correspondence with information they didn't ask for, either—that just invites them to write back again and ask more questions."
- **Is consistent with other correspondence you've written.** "It's OK to say the same thing to different people."

A Sample Business Letter

The Balmy Lip Balm Company
123 Sunny Day Lane
Key West, FL 33040

Ms. Angelina Jolie
The Mansion On The Hill
Beverly Hills, CA 90210

Subject: Our new lip balm product

Dear Ms. Jolie:

Thank you for your letter praising our company's former lip balm product. The reason you can no longer find the old version of Balmy's Lip Balm in Beverly Hills, California is because we are in the process of replacing it with a newer version we are confident you will appreciate and enjoy.

The rumor you have heard is true: We will be replacing the secret ingredient in our formula. This is because bats are becoming an endangered species, and it was increasingly difficult to obtain sufficient quantities of the bat waste by-product we were using. (Of course, we would never harm any actual bats!)

I hope you will agree that our new synthetic formula lip balm, which uses no human or animal product or waste material, will be as good as, if not better than, our previous product. I am enclosing a free sample of the new Balmy's Lip Balm, so you can see for yourself just how good it is. I am sure the career successes you attribute to our old lip balm will continue once you've tried our new one.

Thank you for being such a good customer in the past, and enjoy the sample!

Sincerely,

I.M. Balmy
President, Balmy Lip Balm

Figure 6.2

Writing Memos

Writing coaches and college business courses focus most on letter writing, but it is the humble memo, or memorandum, that still makes the business world go around. Memos can be addressed to a group of -people. Even when they are addressed to one person, there will be other readers. A well-written memo can make or break a career. It actually did for one of us. As a brand new government employee, Ev wrote a memo on the operating hours of a lock and dam in Troy, New York, and got noticed by senior leadership as someone who could make a coherent argument in writing.

Typically, memos are to the point. Most memos do one of four things: they provide information or directions to their readers; they record agreements between groups (these are often called "memorandums of agreement" or "memorandums of understanding"); they allow an action to take place; or they make an -argument in favor of, or opposed to, a course of action. To maintain clarity and directness, you should limit the number of points you make in a memo. If you have several points to make, you should separate them into more than one memo, or call for a meeting.

Because memos are usually internal documents, they are more informal than letters but are more formal than emails. Also, because they are internal, most organizations have templates for preparing them. If you're managing a small business, however, and develop your own forms and procedures, Microsoft Word has several memo templates you can use. They include a:

To: line, in which you enter the name of the memo's principal audience, or the group or organization it is being sent to.

From: line, in which you enter your name, your title, or both.

Date: line, in which you enter the date (but you knew that, didn't you)?

Subject: or **Re:** (for reference) line, in which you explain the subject of your memo. Take time to write a subject that will get the attention of your reader, while still being appropriate. With all the emails today's business executive receives, and all the letters and other -information they read, your memo needs to stand out. So make sure the subject line interests them.

The body of the memo follows the subject line. What you put in the body depends on your purpose for writing the memo.

- If you're *providing information* to your readers, it's usually to help them make a decision. Give them good, solid information, simply presented. As a manager, it's your job to present not only the good news, but also the bad. Don't bury the truth under an avalanche of words. Remember the letter will be a permanent record. Try to anticipate what your readers already know. It's no use to anyone to go into detail about general, easy issues. If you do, they won't read what's really important.
- If you're *recording an agreement*, be comprehensive. Make sure to include all the pertinent details. In the future, it will be an important record, and will be used when there are questions about what each party in the agreement actually meant.
- If you're *allowing something to take place*, be especially brief. "Effective June 1, Jane Jones will be acting director of our Marketing Division," tells readers all they need to know (unless, of course, you want to add a brief biography of Jane to introduce her).
- If you're *making an argument,* which is the most difficult form of memo writing, keep your writing simple, so your argument is understood. Summarize your argument in the first paragraph—not the last—so readers understand right away what you're thinking and can follow your thoughts clearly. Make transitions from one step of your argument to the next; order your thoughts in a logical manner (using topic headings can help you do that); and write a conclusion that sums up everything you said and what you want readers to do.

Many people use numbers or bulleted lists to make the information they present easily accessible. Whether you use these or not, you should write short, concise paragraphs. The usual writing rules apply for any memo, especially about using active voice, using easy-to-follow vocabulary, and being civil. In memos about assigning responsibility, make sure it's clear to whom those responsibilities have been assigned.

For many years, it was commonly accepted practice in memos to close without a signature or a closing other than "For additional information, please contact…" Nowadays, many people sign off on their memos, either with a signature above their typed name or with a close like "Sincerely." Remember that in a memo, your title is in the From: line, so it's different from letter writing, where your title is at the bottom with your typed name and signature. It is a good new trend to sign memos.

As a manager, you should read all the memos you receive carefully—not only for their content, but also to help you conform memos you write to the organization's accepted style. And keep this last rule in mind: If you're writing to an outside organization, use a letter; if it's within the organization, write a memo; and if your memo is more than two pages long, consider a report instead.

A Sample Memorandum

To: All Organization Members

From: Avon Barksdale, Chief Executive

Date: August 15, 2012

Subject: Appointment of Stringer Bell as Acting Chief Executive

As many of you know, I have recently been called out of town on a special assignment. While I am endeavoring to return to headquarters as quickly as possible, and will remain in touch with the organization via phone, email, and occasional face-to-face meetings, I believe it is necessary to appoint someone to manage the day-to-day aspects of our organization while I am away.

Accordingly, I have asked Russell 'Stringer' Bell to assume the role as Acting Chief Executive during the period of my absence. Stringer has been my right-hand man in the past, and is fully familiar with all aspects of our operation. In addition, he and I will consult on a regular basis, so you may assume that any direction he provides has my full approval.

I hope you will provide Stringer with the same level of cooperation and loyalty you have provided me in the past. As I have only a limited capability to receive phone calls and emails on my current assignment, please contact him directly if you have any questions regarding this memo, or any other subject.

Thank you for your continued support,

Avon Barksdale

Figure 6.3

Reading 7.2

Basics of Document Design

By Janet Mizrahi

One of the most important elements of workplace writing is a document's appearance. Writing in professional contexts requires as much attention to the way a document appears on the page or the screen as its content. The reason is that as writers, we must make the task of reading easy for our audience. If you have ever waded through dense pages of text with long paragraphs or tried to follow a single line of type that goes across an 18-inch computer screen, you know that reading can become tedious if good design is not factored into what your eyes must look at.

In this chapter, we'll cover the basics of document design for print and screen. We will discuss the conventions of document design as they pertain to specific genres in the remaining chapters.

Print Document Design

Writing for a printed page differs from writing for a screen not just in the words we write but in the way the words look on the page. This is called **page layout.** You are probably aware of certain elements of page layout without knowing it. For example, use of columns and choice of landscape or portrait view are part of page layout.

When composing a document that will be printed, first consider page size. Is your document for standard sized paper (8.5 × 11 in.) or smaller? If you are creating a trifold brochure, for example, you will be laying out the words very differently than if you are writing a report. In both cases, however, consider the z pattern. The z pattern (see Figure 7.2.1) is the way readers of English approach a page. Our eye begins at the top left of the page and scans to the right, going back and forth, left to right, until we reach the bottom. This pattern is significant because words or images that fall along the z hold the eye's attention more than the areas surrounding the z. Savvy writers will put words and images they want the reader to focus on along this path.

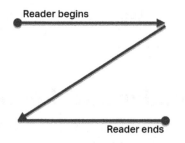

Figure 7.2.1 z pattern of reading.

Elements of Page Layout

Each page contains design elements you will want to consider as follows.

Color

Although black is always the preferred color for body type, some color can add visual interest to print pages. Color can be used for document headings, in charts and graphs, or as ways to highlight information. Avoid using bright colors for type and understand that the way a color appears on the screen will likely differ from its reproduction on the printed page. Also remember that you will need a color printer for your color scheme to show!

Graphical Elements

Adding graphical elements to your documents such as boldface, bullets, enumeration, italics, or underlining serve varied functions. **Boldface** calls attention to words and phrases. It is commonly used for headings and sparingly used to highlight words or phrases. **Bulleted points** are used to list items and to attract the reader's eye. Bulleted points break up text, too. **Enumeration** (listing items 1., 2., 3., etc.) is used to indicate a series in order. *Italics* are used for emphasis, to indicate a word in a different language, for proper names, and for titles. **Underlining** can indicate a title or emphasis.

A quick word on the use of CAPS. Beware that the reader will interpret type in all caps as a scream. The only time I use all caps is in a context in which I must conform to a text-only design. In that case, I use caps for headings. I never use all caps and boldface, however. It is not only redundant but also truly a signal for translating the words into a scream.

No graphical elements should be overused, and writers should avoid including too many on any one page. Doing so clutters the page and ends up having the opposite effect from what was intended.

Headings and Subheadings

Headings name categories of information. They summarize the content that follows and are organized by levels: first level heading, second level heading, and so forth. Headings can be viewed as the points of an outline, and their use is a primary way writers organize content. For the reader, headings serve as graphic markers that signal a new topic. They help the reader easily focus on specific areas of interest. Headings break up text, making material more visually attractive and easier on the eye.

Subheadings are mini-headings, or subsections of a heading. They, too, break up long text and enhance visual appeal.

In a print document, headings are indicated by use of a graphical device such as centering, boldface, or caps. Headings often use a contrasting type font. For example, if the body of a report were Times New Roman, you might want to use Arial for headings.

Header and Footer

Using a header and footer is a way to unify a document. Headers and footers also provide a location of page numbers or add graphic design features such as a company logo.

Margins

Most business documents have page margins all around of 1 to 1.5 in. Page margins are important because they create white space to make a page look uncluttered. Another aspect of margins is **justification**.

Word processing programs give you four-options for your margins: left justified with a ragged right edge, centered, right justified with ragged left, and fully-justified. Table 7.2.1 illustrates the types of margin-justification and when each should be used.

Table 7.2.1 **Type justification**

Type justification	Functionality
This margin is left justified, ragged right type. This margin is left justified, ragged right. This margin is left justified, ragged right.	Notice how the left margin forms a straight line, while the right edge is jagged. This is considered the easiest alignment to read and should be used in nearly every writing situation.
This is centered type. This is centered type. This is centered	Centered type is inappropriate for most reading tasks but is a good choice for headings, such as the headings in this table.
This is right justified type with a ragged left margin this is right justified type with a ragged left margin	Readers' eyes would quickly tire if having to readjust to locate the beginning of each line of type. Use right justified type to align short phrases only.
This line is considered fully justified. This line is considered fully justified. This line is considered fully justified. This line is considered fully justified.	Notice the awkward spaces between the words when using fully justified text. This occurs because the word processor does not hyphenate words so it has to create spaces to fit the type into a rectangle. Those spaces slow down reading. When full justification is needed for particular documents, you will need to use your own appropriate word hyphenations to reduce the space gaps that otherwise occur.

Paragraph Length

In college papers, it is not unusual for a paragraph to take up an entire typed page. However, that this is unacceptable in all business documents. To aid our readers, business writers limit paragraph length to no more than eight lines (not eight sentences.) This is a rule of thumb that should be taken very seriously. Long, dense paragraphs scare readers away.

Spacing

Again, in college, papers are usually double spaced and new paragraphs are indented. However, in business documents, single spacing is the norm; new paragraphs are signaled by adding an extra space. Because the extra space is clearly a marker of a new paragraph, it would be redundant and unnecessary to also use a tab.

Typeface

Type fonts are divided into two basic families: *serif* and *sans serif*. Serif fonts such as Times, Garamond, or Palatino have feet and tails under the letters that form a line to help the eye track the words and sentences, which is why graphic artists choose serif fonts for long documents such as books. Serif fonts have an old fashioned feel. For business documents that will be printed, using a serif font will help your reader move through the content faster.

Sans serif fonts like Helvetica, Arial, and Verdana have a cleaner, simple line that translates better to the pixel-based display on screens.

Look at the following example to examine the difference between font families:

This is 12-point Garamond, a serif font.

This is 12-point Arial, a sans serif font.

Notice the difference in the two 12-point fonts. Both are 12-point, but Arial appears much larger than Garamond. When you choose your font, you will want to take into consideration how large or small it appears on the page.

White Space

Space on a page without any visual or type is called white space. White space breaks up text and frames the words on the page. It also helps balance a page. It is helpful to view your page in the *preview* function of the word processing tool you use to see how the white space is arranged on the page. This is an excellent way to adjust pages that are off balance or too densely packed with words.

Notes

1 Nielsen (1996).
2 Nielsen, J. February 1, 1996. "In Defense of Print." Nielsonnormangroup.com. http://www.nngroup.com/articles/in-defense-of-print/ (accessed January 19, 2015).

Business Letter

Business letters are the most formal business communication. Your writing style and the formatting details (e.g., punctuation, salutation, and closing) contribute to the formality and demonstrate your understanding of business communication. A sample letter and checklist to use when editing your work appear below.

Assess Your Document Here:

Letter Sample and Checklist

☐→ Sender's Address Here
Street Address
City, State, Zip Code

☐→ Date Here

☐→ Addressee's Name Here
Street Address
City, State, Zip Code

☐→ Salutation Here:

☐→ Introduction Paragraph: Open with the main idea (deductive approach). Include your reason for writing and an outline of information to follow in the document (outline statement).

☐→Body Paragraph 1: Start with topic sentence. Include supporting information. Use specific details and in-text citations when appropriate.

☐→Body Paragraph 2: Use basic body paragraph organization. Use visual enhancements and design elements as needed, including bullets, bold, italics, and subheadings. Remember and apply the 5 Cs of communication.

☐→Body Paragraph (if needed):

☐→ Conclusion: Provide a sense of closure. Remind reader of main point; include action steps if needed. Include a forward-looking statement and include contact statement (who reader should contact for more information).

☐→Complementary Close,

☐→ Signature Here

☐→ Sender's Name

Sender's Title, if appropriate

☐→ Enclosure Notation, if needed

Applying This Skill: Identify Parts of a Business Letter

Form student groups of 3–4 people. Your instructor will distribute envelopes containing parts of the business letter. Work to arrange the puzzle pieces into formal business letter format.

Assignment: Introduction Letter

Please write a business letter introducing yourself. The letter must be kept to one page and must follow the business letter format. The font size should be no less than 11 pt. and should be Times New Roman.

This assignment is designed to help me know more about you, your writing skills, and your ability to create professional-looking and -sounding documents.

Please address the letter to me, your professor.

Your introductory paragraph (3–4 sentences) should tell me a little about yourself. You can tell me a little about your family, where you were born, your high school activities/graduation date, any other postsecondary education, and so on.

The body (2–4 short paragraphs) should address the following:

o **Education background.** Tell me about your major and how you chose that field (if you haven't selected a major, what direction do you think you might go?), how many credit/courses you are taking this quarter, university participation/involvement, any study-abroad experiences and/or travels in other countries, any internship experiences or plans to intern prior to graduation, and so on.
o **Work experiences/volunteer commitments.** Tell me about your current work situation: where, how many hours, major responsibilities, and so on. Also, what job title would you like to have when you graduate, long-range job goals (after you've worked ten years), and so forth? Where do you volunteer, and why?
o **Communication experience.** Tell me about your strengths and weaknesses in the area of communication (e.g., written, oral, technological usage, etc.), types of communication you do on your job, what you expect to get out of this course, and any other relevant information.

Your closing paragraph should provide a sense of closure. Mention any concerns, hopes, or expectations you have about the course. Please include the best way to contact you.

Memos

Memos are among the most common business documents, although they are frequently being replaced or sent via email. Memos are internal documents, generally sent from department to department or from a department to a group of people. They are often purpose-driven documents (e.g., when a company needs to update its human resources policies). Sometimes memos will be printed and posted on company bulletin boards; other times, memos will be emailed to employees. Memos are written in a particular format, which is shown below.

Memo Layout and Checklist

Assess Your Document Here:

☐→ To:
From:
Date:
Re: (subject line here, 3–5 words)

☐→ Opening Paragraph: State main purpose for writing/reason for writing. Outline topics and organization of body paragraphs.

☐→ Short, descriptive subhead (if needed)

☐→Body Paragraph 1: State main topic with supporting ideas and details.

☐→ Body Paragraph 2: State your second main topic (topic sentence) with supporting ideas and details. As needed, use subheadings, bullets, and in-text citations.

☐→ Body Paragraph 3: Start with topic sentence. Include supporting information. Use specific details and in-text citations when appropriate

☐→Short, descriptive subhead (if needed)

☐→Body paragraph (if needed):

☐→ Conclusion: Restate main point/reason for writing. Include forward-looking statement, reminder of action steps, and who to contact for further information/action (contact statement).

8

Email

Email is the most common form of business communication—so common, in fact, that email overload is a serious problem for most people. Studies show workers may spend an average of 28%—nearly thirteen hours—of their workweek on email. Checking email may reduce worker productivity by up to 40%.

For these reasons, writing effective emails is essential. In the deluge of email, you want to make sure your message is read and your information gets to the receiver. Your email reflects on you, your boss, and your company, so presenting a polished, professional image is essential to career success. The following article highlights some of the pet peeves people have about email, ways to write effective subject lines, and ways to manage your email effectively.

After completing this lesson, you will:

- Know and demonstrate use of business email
- Know how to write effective subject lines
- Understand ways to manage email

Create an email signature block

....

Reading 8.1

Master Emails and Electronic Communication

By Jack E. Appleman

Overview

- Enhance email efficiency.

- Craft explicit, action-generating subject lines.
- Follow email etiquette.
- Compose mobile-friendly emails and professional text messages.

How did we ever manage without email? Some of us remember the last century when we mailed letters, sent faxes, and left lots of voice-mails. Today, email rules as the number one business communication method, despite the explosion of social media (see Step 10) and other new channels that continue to emerge.

Email is an amazing tool. Well-constructed email messages can provide clear directions that promote efficiency, build morale, solidify key relationships, generate leads, and offer many other benefits. But emails can also cause problems that didn't exist in the pre-Internet era. It's the ultimate double-edged sword—and we all have our share of horror stories, including emails that were sent to the wrong person or shouldn't have been sent at all. And you've undoubtedly been on the receiving end of nasty or condescending emails that make you want to punch the screen or throw your mobile device against the wall!

Plus, email is an enormous time waster. A study by Inc. revealed that the average U.S. worker spent six hours a day checking emails (James 2015). Are you kidding me? How do organizations get anything done? And the number of emails continues to skyrocket, about 120 per day per person in the latest count— thanks in part to mobile devices that allow us to easily send emails 24/7, according to the Radicati Group (2015). The more emails we send, the more replies we receive—and the more precious time we spend processing them. Every five emails sent generate an average of three replies; eliminating one out of every five emails would cut the number of incoming emails by 12 percent and free up our time for other tasks (Song, Halsey, and Burress 2007).

This step will explain the most important practices for maximizing efficiency with emails and other electronic communication tools.

Reduce the Number of Emails

Given the startling amount of time spent on electronic communication in the workplace, everyone should strive to become more efficient with emails. Still, some of the strategies that follow may need to be adjusted based on the culture of your organization, as well as the preference of your supervisor, client, and other readers.

Don't Always Reply All

We all receive emails that we couldn't care less about. Let's say the purchasing administrator emails 15 team leaders asking what supplies they need. By force of habit, 12 of them hit reply all, filling everyone's inboxes with every detail. Does every other team leader need to know that Maria needs two boxes of copy paper, 75 three-ring binders, and a dozen staple removers?

While you can't control others' email habits, you can help unclog co-workers' inboxes by not hitting reply all unless necessary. And when requesting information from many colleagues, consider asking them to "reply to me only."

See what happens when everyone continues to cc everyone in the original email chain:

Email String

1. From Suman to Jennifer (cc Carlos)

Carlos and I are in the process of modifying ABC Industries' cybersecurity plan and we need the one-page technical guidelines you developed last year.

2. From Jennifer to Suman and Carlos

Please see the attached guidelines and keep me posted on how the project is going or if you have technical issues.

3. From Carlos to Jennifer (cc Suman)

Thanks very much, Jennifer.

4. From Carlos to Suman (cc Jennifer)

I'll revise the text and incorporate the technical specs from Jennifer's guidelines.

5. From Suman to Carlos (cc Jennifer)

Perfect, Carlos. I'll await your revisions. Meanwhile, I'll schedule a date when you and I can meet with Julie at ABC to show her the new plan.

6. From Carlos to Suman (cc Jennifer)

That sounds good, Suman. Please make it Wednesday or Thursday in one of the next two weeks.

7. From Suman to Carlos (cc Jennifer)

No problem, Carlos. Those days should work for me too.

After email 3 (Carlos thanks Jennifer for her assistance), Jennifer no longer needs to be copied. Emails 4 to 7, dealing with drafting the cybersecurity plan and arranging a meeting with Julie at ABC Industries, don't involve Jennifer. So by copying her on those four emails, Suman and Carlos are clogging up Jennifer's inbox and wasting her time.

A better approach: Suman and Carlos should wait until the new cybersecurity plan is approved by ABC Industries (assuming no technical problems requiring Jennifer's assistance) and then email Jennifer a brief update about the client's reaction, while thanking her for her support.

Don't Acknowledge Every Email

In your effort to be courteous, you may be wasting your time—and the reader's time. Check out this all-too-common exchange between two colleagues, even when they work on the same floor:

Andre: I misplaced your suggestions for the status update that you emailed last week. Please resend.

Mia: See the requested suggestions below.

Andre: Thanks, Mia.

Mia: No problem.

While few would disagree that Mia's "No problem" wasn't necessary, Andre's "Thanks, Mia" was also a waste of time. I'm not telling you to be rude; just differentiate between a useful reply and a needless "thank you." As long-time colleagues, Andre and Mia shouldn't waste their time on trivial acknowledgments. But if you're the devil's advocate, you may ask what the big deal is. It takes less than 30 seconds to read and delete the email, right? Yes, but those half-minutes can quickly turn into hours of unproductive time.

Use discretion before sending that acknowledgment. Consider the topic, time sensitivity, and the sender's expectations.

Avoid Instinctive "I'll Get Back to You" Replies

Many individuals are conditioned to respond immediately to nearly every email, to notify the sender that they received it and are working on getting the required information. That's another time-waster—which I'm guilty of frequently, including a few years ago, while replying to an affiliate with whom I had been working for three years:

Brian (September 20, 11 a.m.): I need your vehicle information for our October 10 presentation at YXZ Company. Please email it to me by September 25.

Jack (September 20, 12:30 p.m.): I'm tied up in a workshop all day so I'll email this to you as soon as I can.

Jack (September 21, 9:30 a.m.): Below is my vehicle information that you requested.

Soon after I sent my September 20 email, I realized how unnecessary it was. The next morning, I sent Brian the requested information, four days ahead of his deadline. In most cases, you don't need to update the person that you will take care of their request later; just wait until you're finished and send it.

Do some individuals want an immediate response for every email to make sure you've received it? Sure, so identify them and try not to send unnecessary replies to those who don't need them. Again, it goes back to your organization's culture and the sender's preferences.

Know When to—and When Not to—Email

An email (or text) is not always the most efficient way to communicate. Still, many of us get caught in a string of emails that ends up wasting everyone's time. See the following email conversation between two co-workers from different offices looking to set up a conference call:

May 5—Alison (Houston office): I suggest we set up a call with the Houston and Atlanta supervisors during the week of June 20 to discuss changes in the corporate advisory practice. What day and time would work on your end?

May 6—Ramón (Atlanta office): I don't know. Our managers have told me that they don't believe these calls are very productive.

May 7—Alison: I'm aware that they weren't happy with prior calls, so we've prepared a detailed agenda.

May 8—Ramón: The other issue with previous calls, according to our managers, was the lack of follow-up.

May 9—Alison: Are they talking about weekly or biweekly updates, follow-up phone calls, or other issues?

Five emails and several days later, Alison and Ramón still haven't scheduled the call. Both neglected a critical business tool—the telephone! Had one of them called the other, the meeting could've been scheduled in two minutes. Then, Alison or Ramón could've sent a brief email documenting the agreed-upon details.

If you find yourself in the middle of a useless email string, pick up the phone! You could save a lot of time on both ends. For those in organizations that use Outlook Invite or other calendar programs, follow the protocol for arranging meetings—but don't waste time on an email string to nowhere.

Write More Productive Emails

To further boost productivity, construct concise and explicit emails that make it easier for the other person to reply and help you work more efficiently.

Be Explicit About What You Want

Your emails should address the big picture to determine, for example, how to complete a project as efficiently as possible. Take this approach whether you're starting an email conversation or replying to one of the messages. See how efficiency improves with each version of an email dialogue between Susan and Omar:

Email Dialogue 1: Lots of Wasted Emails

Susan: Please prepare your Q1 expense summary. Let me know if you need expense reports for any prior months and if you can email it to me by April 20. (Sender clearly states action required)

Omar: OK, I'll see what I can do. (Worthless response)

Omar: I'm working on the summary now and will soon let you know which expense reports I need. (Another worthless response)

Omar: I need the January and February expense reports. (Finally, he explains what he needs.)

Susan: I'm tied up for the next week. By when do you need these expense reports?

Omar: I need them by April 10, so I can finish the summary by April 20.

Email Dialogue 2: A Bit Better

Susan: Please prepare your Q1 expense summary. Let me know if you need expense reports for any prior months and if you can email it to me by April 20.

Omar: I need the January and February expense reports.

Susan: I'm tied up for the next week. By when do you need these reports?

Omar: I need them by April 10, so I can finish the summary by April 20.

Email Dialogue 3: Efficient, With Explicit Emails From Both Parties

Susan: Omar, please prepare your Q1 expense summary. Let me know if you need expense reports for any prior months and if you can email it to me by April 20.

Omar: Please email me the expense reports for January and February by April 10, and I'll submit the expense summary by April 20. (He explains what he needs and by when.)

See this other example illustrating the importance of being explicit, where Larry is trying to schedule a training for his staff with Fang, the conference manager:

Larry: I need to arrange a leadership training course for midlevel managers in March. Are there any training rooms available?

Fang: Let me know how many managers need to be trained so I can provide a suitable room.

Larry: We're looking to put 15 to 20 people through the course.

Fang: I suggest the Royal Conference Room on the fourth floor, which will easily accommodate 20 people.

Larry: Sounds good. Will that room be available during the weeks of March 12 or 19?

Fang: I have Monday, March 12, and Friday, March 23.

Larry: I'd like to avoid Mondays or Fridays. Is there any availability on Tuesdays, Wednesdays, or Thursdays during those weeks?

Fang: The room will be free on Tuesday, March 13, but only until 2 p.m.

Larry: That'll work, because the course is four hours. We can run it from 9 to 1.

Fang: You're confirmed for the Royal Conference Room on March 13, 8 a.m. to 2 p.m. (You can use the extra time for setup and breakdown.)

It took 10 emails for Larry to arrange the training with Fang. Let's see what happens when Larry is explicit from the start:

Larry: I need to reserve a room for a leadership training course for midlevel managers in March. Please review the details below and let me know what's available.

- Leadership training:

  o 4 hours
  o 15 to 20 midlevel managers
  o Tuesday, Wednesday, or Thursday during the week of March 12 or 19.

Fang: I can give you the Royal Conference Room on the fourth floor, which can easily accommodate 20 people, on Tuesday, March 13, from 8 a.m. to 2 p.m.

Larry: That's perfect! We're confirmed for then.

Spur Action With Explicit Subject Lines

How do you decide which emails to open first—or at all? Naturally, it depends on the sender; you'll probably open emails from your boss, a client, or another important party as soon as possible. Otherwise, the subject line is the most critical factor. If a subject line is vague or confusing, you may disregard that email, at least for the time being. Plus, when reading emails on your mobile device, you're more likely to just scan subject lines without reading the body of the messages—which you may read later or not at all.

So as the sender, make your subject lines precise and engaging to increase the chances that the reader will open your email sooner and take the desired action, which will ultimately enhance your productivity.

Compare these three pairs of subject lines:

Vague: Reps' Latest Rating

Explicit: Reps' Rating Down 12% | Need Training

What receiver may think upon reading: "I better start planning a training program for the reps."

Vague: Upcoming Budget Meeting

Explicit: May 6 Budget Meeting | Agenda May 3

What receiver may think upon reading: "I need to begin working on the agenda."

Vague: Launch Date

Explicit: Please Approve June 8 Launch Date

What receiver may think upon reading: "I need to decide whether to approve June 8 as a launch date."

Not only is each of these emails with an explicit subject line more likely to be opened sooner than its more-nebulous version, it should prompt the reader to take action—before they read the text of the message.

Pointer

Write explicit subject lines so recipients open your emails quickly.

Don't Be a Lazy Subject Liner

When emailing someone with whom you haven't corresponded in a while (say several months), you may be tempted to search for the last time this person emailed you and simply reply. That's fine, but don't be too lazy to modify the original subject line, which may be unrelated to the topic of your new email. See what happened when Rich didn't bother to change the subject line:

From Christina to Rich (February 20)

- Subject line: Q2 Budget Forecasts
- Text of email: Please email me your Q2 budget worksheet by March 1.

Eight months later, Rich needs Christina's input on performance reviews. But he's too lazy to change the subject line.

From Rich to Christina (October 22)

- Subject line: Re: Q2 Budget Forecasts
- Text of email: I'm working on performance reviews. Please email me your scores for the three clerks on your team by October 29.

When Christina, inundated with emails, quickly scans her inbox and sees Rich's subject line, she thinks to herself, "Why is Rich contacting me about the budget worksheets from more than six months ago?" Then she might move onto other emails, leaving Rich without the information he needs before his deadline. Had Rich been more diligent and inserted a new subject line, such as Need Clerks' Reviews by Oct. 29, he probably would've received Christina's input in time.

To further improve email efficiency, sharpen your overall writing ability. The other skills addressed in this book—including brevity, organization, persuasion, tone, and grammar—can all be applied to emails.

Mind Your Etiquette

While many organizations have their own set of rules for sending and receiving emails—frequently related to compliance—follow these practices, universally accepted as proper etiquette:

Make Sure Each Email Would Meet Everyone's Approval

An email is a permanent and documented message, which can be retrieved at any time. Only send messages that comply with your organization's rules and that you would be comfortable showing to any individual at any level or an outside authority. For example, as a midlevel manager, you should never send this type of email criticizing direct reports and the organization's hiring practice: The new IT assistants don't know the first thing about technology. Where do they find these losers? If HR department employees or company leaders were to see this email, it would reflect poorly on you as a manager.

Pointer

When writing emails, don't cheat on grammar and don't use funky fonts or text-messaging abbreviations.

Don't Take Shortcuts With Grammar and Syntax

Working professionals used to print out letters, memos, reports, and other documents, sometimes on company letterhead, and mail them out (occasionally, this is still done). The act of producing a physical document compelled employees to carefully review their text and revise if necessary. But the ease of delivering a message with a few keystrokes has resulted in carelessness with spelling, punctuation, capitalization, and sentence structure, not to mention sheer laziness in not using actual words.

Some write emails like a text message (more on texting later). So instead of sending a polished request, See the operations report for January and email me your comments, they shoot off emails that read, c op rpt 4 jan coments bak 2 me. Once the reader deciphers what the text-speak means (a waste of time and drain on productivity), they will likely consider you less professional.

Avoid Blank Subject Lines

Give your readers a break and clue them in on what the message is about. With the hundreds of emails business workers receive every day, people tend to treat subject lines like headlines in a newspaper or online news outlet: They scan the subject lines and decide which email to open first (as discussed already). A blank subject line can give others the impression that you assume they will open their emails by default, despite not knowing what to expect.

Don't Put the Entire Message in the Subject Line

We've all worked with this co-worker before: You boot up your email in the morning and run into Can you please review the budget analysis and provide me feedback on the key sections by Feb. 10. Such a long subject line, while not as bad as no subject line, is difficult to read on mobile devices (see more on making emails mobile-friendly later in this step). A better way to convey this request would be to use a specific subject line, while including the details in the body of the email:

> Subject: Budget Analysis Feedback by Feb. 10

> Text of message: Please review the budget analysis and provide feedback on the key sections by February 10.

Avoid Putting "Urgent" in the Subject Line

If you want to be known as the panicked employee who needs an immediate response to every issue to avoid a nervous breakdown, then write urgent in the subject line. Otherwise, keep urgent out of your subject lines. While teaching an undergraduate course several years ago, I had one student who repeatedly wrote urgent when sending me emails. Then the message read something like this: "Professor, on the next assignment, should it be three paragraphs or four paragraphs?" In this case, urgent was in the eye of the beholder.

Instead, use explicit subject lines and then persuade your reader to action with concise, explicit, and well-organized text. Tool 8-2-1 offers additional advice to help you keep your email professional.

Tool 8-2-1: Email Etiquette Quick Tips

For Important Audiences, Use Salutations and Sign-Offs

When emailing senior executives, clients, and other important readers (use your judgment), don't simply begin your message, which can be perceived as too informal. Start with a salutation such as, "Dear Ms. Walker, "Hi Steve," or simply, "Emily." And sign off with something like, "Thanks," "Best regards," or "Best."

Close With a Friendly Outreach

Some argue that ending an email with, "Please contact me if you have any questions," is unnecessary, because the reader knows that they can reply with inquiries. Still, this type of closing sets a positive tone and conveys an important message to the reader—that their opinion matters.

Don't Use All Caps—AND I MEAN IT

An email written in all caps is the written equivalent of shouting. Avoid using email to express anger at someone (See Step 6 on tone).

Avoid Funky Fonts

Not only do artsy and cutesy fonts come across unprofessionally (in most organizations), they can become garbled and unreadable in other email systems.

Stay Away From Colored Backgrounds

Like funky fonts, colored backgrounds can be construed as unprofessional and can make text hard to read.

Save Religious and Spiritual Signatures for Personal Emails

Religious and spiritual messages don't belong on business emails (unless your organization is an institution of this type). Feel free to use an uplifting signature like, "Make it a fulfilling day," but nothing stronger than that.

Lose the Emojis and Emoticons

In many situations, emojis and emoticons can come across as unprofessional. Still, I must admit that some clients and respected colleagues have sent me emails with emojis. Stay away from them unless you're certain that your supervisor or other key people in the company would approve.

Make It Mobile Friendly

Today, more than 60 percent of emails are opened on mobile devices rather than on desktop or laptop computers (Lewkowicz 2016). And this percentage will continue to rise along with the use of mobile devices. Here are the most important tips for ensuring that mobile readers can easily process your emails:

Increase the Font Size

Use at least 12- or 14-point type so the reader doesn't need to squint to read your message. And consider making links even larger.

Limit Subject Lines to 40 to 45 Characters

If you've got too much information to fit within this limit, put the most important message first, as in this example:

Audit Report Revisions May 7 | Senior Partners Must Approve

Be Careful With Bullet Symbols

The different styles of bullet points that Word offers don't always display properly in an email (mobile or otherwise). So stick with simple hyphens or asterisks, as in these two examples:

Among the most profitable products:

- sports drinks
- energy bars
- flavored water.

The keys to marketing success:

- an engaging message
- integrated tactics
- timely follow-up.

Use Single Columns

Text in multiple columns sometimes appears condensed and can be difficult to navigate with certain mobile devices and email systems. Stick with single columns, which will also help you highlight key content.

Be Sure Your Call to Action Stands Out

Make your desired action clearly visible and clickable if you're directing readers to a link. In the following example, the hyperlink to the shipping protocol is bolded:

Please review and approve the shipping protocol.

Separate Links With White Space

Avoid closely stacked links, which may cause users to click the wrong one. Compare these two versions (hyperlinks are bolded):

Too Tight—Can Lead to Errors

Learn more about these options for configuring the training room:

- classroom
- u-shaped conference table
- clusters.

Breathing Space—Easier to Click the Right One

Learn more about these options for configuring the training room:

- classroom
- u-shaped conference table
- clusters.

Avoid Large Images

You don't want mobile-device readers frustrated by long delays before your image downloads. Consider shrinking images that may be too large—and then emailing them to yourself so you can test on your mobile device.

Text Like a Professional

Today, business texting (usually through SMS or IM) plays a critical role in helping working professionals communicate faster, internally and externally. About 80 percent of businesspeople text as part of their jobs, according to a 2015 survey conducted by Instantly and commissioned by RingCentral. And nearly 70 percent of employees think their organizations should use texting to communicate internally, according to a 2014 survey by the Vitiello Communications Group.

The first step for enhancing your workplace text messaging is to follow the same guidelines for emails: Keep them brief, get to the point quickly, give clear instructions, check your grammar, and use actual words. Still, texting presents other challenges and opportunities. Here are some tips to for efficient workplace texting:

Avoid Acronyms and Abbreviations

Don't use acronyms or abbreviations (a staple in personal texting) unless you're certain that the receiver knows what you mean. Overusing any type of shorthand could leave your recipient confused and force them to seek out a definition in another app, all to avoid appearing dumb or naive by not knowing it right away.

Divide Long Messages Into Multiple Texts

Instead of cramming too much information and overusing abbreviations to avoid exceeding the character limit, send two or three separate messages. Though that means the individual will receive multiple rings or vibrations, they'll appreciate the more readable messages.

Limit How Much Information You're Asking For

Unlike an email, which can accommodate extensive information (such as with bulleted lists), a text message should be limited to one or two requests. While some people have honed their typing dexterity on mobile devices, you still put a strain on them and less-dexterous users when asking them to type a long reply. Plus, if you ask the reader to research an issue and then report back through text, you're likely asking them to toggle between devices (a computer to research, and a mobile device to reply).

Enable the Reader to Reply Quickly

Structure your text message so the reader can reply immediately with a minimum number of words. An example:

We will ship your parts by May 8, 10 a.m. CT. Please provide reply with this information:

- Building number and floor:
- On-site contact and cell number:
- Preference—1 large or 3 small containers (indicate 1 or 3):

Know When to Text—and Not to Text

Based on the situation and your organizational culture, determine when text messaging would be the appropriate communication channel as opposed to email or phone. For example, if you need a response within 24 to 48 hours, an email may be the most appropriate medium. But if you're facing a tight deadline and need your supervisor's approval within the hour, a text would probably work best.

Respond to Texts as Soon as Possible

Text messages carry an inherent immediacy about them. Recognize that the sender probably needs your reply within 20 to 30 minutes, just as you do whenever shooting off a text message to a co-worker. You don't want to be known as the one in the office who demands an instant response but doesn't return the favor.

Your Turn

Enhancing the efficiency of your emails and texts requires a variety of strategies to help you save time and compose more effective messages. To hone your email and texting skills, try these exercises:

1. Review this string of messages between two colleagues who have worked together for several years, and determine which of these emails (one or more) aren't necessary:

> Rosa: Please complete the Q4 progress report for XB within two weeks (by January 21) so I can submit it to management for approval.
>
> Marc: I'll get it to you as soon as I can.
>
> Rosa: Thanks. I appreciate that.
>
> Marc: Should it include a summary of prior XB progress reports? And, if so, how far back should I go?
>
> Rosa: Can you access these prior reports?
>
> Marc: Yes, I can access XB progress reports from the past two years.
>
> Rosa: Email the past three XB progress reports covering the first three quarters of last year.

2. Write an explicit subject line for this email to your supervisor—designed to get them to open the email as soon as possible:

> Our team has developed a plan to significantly increase the number of inquiries while lowering online marketing expenses. By dividing these costs equally among all the divisions, we could send 12 more email blasts in a year and expand our reach with mobile advertising by 25 percent. According to our analysis, by next year, this plan could produce an average of 30 inquiries a month instead of our current average of 15 per month.

3. Reorganize this text message to make it easy for the reader to quickly submit the required information:

> I need to confirm details for the June 1 presentation skills training. I need to know how many of your direct reports will attend. Which location (River Road or Sax Plaza) is best for them? And what are their preferred starting times? The trainer can begin at 8, 8:30, or 9.

The Next Step

While the majority of working professionals worldwide regularly write and receive emails, considerably fewer compose social media messages as part of their jobs. But that's changing, as an increasing number of organizations are calling on their employees to generate text for social media channels. So you need to be ready. That's what we'll cover in step 10 (Apply Writing Skills to Social Media Copy).

References

James, G. 2015. "New Study: The Average Worker Spends 30 Hours a Week Checking Email." Inc., August 27. www.inc.com/geoffrey-james/new-study-the-average-worker-spends-30-hours-a-week-checking-email.html.

Lewkowicz, K. 2016. "April Email Market Share: Mobile Rises to 56%, Its Highest Point Yet." Litmus blog, May 10. https://litmus.com/blog/mobile-rises-to-56-market-share-longest-sustained-growth-in-2016.

Radicati Group. 2015. "Email Statistics Report, 2015-2019." Palo Alto, CA: Radicati Group. www.radicati.com/wp/wp-content/uploads/2015/02/Email-Statistics-Report-2015-2019-Executive-Summary.pdf.

Song, M., V. Halsey, and T. Burress. 2007. The Hamster Revolution: How to Manage Your Email Before It Manages You. San Francisco: Berret-Koehler.

Email Format & Checklist

Assess Your Document Here

☐ → Sender's email address
Receiver's email address
Date
   Autogenerated by email program

☐ → Subject line: 3-5 words

☐ → Salutation Here:

☐ → Opening Paragraph: State main purpose for writing/reason for writing. Outline topics and organization of body paragraphs.

☐ → **Short, descriptive subhead (if needed)**
Body paragraph 1: State main topic with supporting ideas and details.

☐ → **Short, descriptive subhead (if needed)**
Body paragraph 2: State main topic #2 (topic sentence) with supporting ideas and details. As needed, use sub-headings, bullets, in-text citations.

☐ → Body paragraph (if needed):

☐ → Conclusion: Restate main point/reason for writing. Include forward looking statement, reminder of action steps, who to contact for further information/action.

☐ → Complementary Close,

☐ → Sender's Name
Email signature block
Position/title
Contact information

Figure 8.1 Email Format and Checklist

Applying This Skill: Write Email Subject Lines

Write email subject lines for the following emails. There are many possible solutions.

1. A question about what time the test is on Friday, explaining that you lost your printed schedule.

2. A question about whether or not children are allowed to play ball games in the communal play area. You have seen children playing near the building and fear that they might break the windows.

3. An email to a book supplier. Your company has run out of stock of a popular book, *Fun Language Exercises*, and you need to order more copies urgently to fulfill increasing orders from customers.

4. An email delivering a final report that you have completed, requested by the chief of operations two days ago. You have studied the results of a recent product trial and have presented your findings with tables, graphs, and detailed conclusions.

5. An email answering a colleague's request that you swap shifts next Tuesday. You wish to suggest switching for your Wednesday shift so that you can visit your parents, who live on a boat that is in town from Wednesday to Friday.

6. An old friend from university is in town and you want to arrange a meeting in the coming week. You are free on Thursday and Friday, and if possible would like to meet near where you work. There is a good cafe nearby called Lou's Diner, where you think it would be best to meet.

7. A letter of complaint to the manager of a shop where you tried to return some trousers that were too small for you. The staff were rude and did not allow you to return the trousers, blaming you for picking the wrong size. You know the store has a policy that allows you to return any item within twenty-four days, so you wish to both arrange a refund and address the staff's impoliteness.

8. Someone has written to complain to you about a communal drinking area in the office. It has been left in a mess, and the water jug is not being regularly replaced. You have contacted the office manager and decided to put up a sign instructing office members on good drinking-area conduct. Your sign is ready to be put up, and you are writing to both announce these new rules and explain why they are necessary.

9. The mayor is visiting your office, and you are responsible for arranging his transport. There have been complications with the car hire company, however, and you need to suggest to your boss that he use alternative transport options instead. You have compiled a list of chauffeur services, taxis, and public transport choices and are prepared to discuss different options.

Exercise adapted from Phil Williams via English Lessons Brighton at: http://www.englishlessonsbrighton.co.uk/

Email Signatures

In addition to writing effective emails, knowing how to format and manage email contributes to your professional presence.

Email signature blocks are expected by most companies and most employers because they create or reinforce an image of the company and increase brand awareness. The email signature also provides essential information about you and the company, such as your contact information, the business's logo and website link, and more. Many people consider the email signature block a digital business card, so the presentation of the signature is important to how you are perceived.

The signature block can be created in your email program and then either automatically or manually added to each email you send. The following elements should be included in your email signature block:

- Your name
- Your position and department
- Your phone number
- Your email address
- Company name
- Company logo
- Link to the company's or your personal website
- Color, text, and formatting that is consistent with your company's image

In addition, other elements may be added to your signature block. However, you don't want to create a signature with too much text or too many links. Optional elements in an email signature block include:

- A picture of yourself
- Your preferred pronouns

- Links to social media platforms
- Any legal disclaimer, if needed
- A banner that advertises information about your company, products, announcements, and so on
- A call to action that encourages the reader to take action (e.g., follow a social media platform or view a new product)

Creating and using multiple email signature blocks can be helpful. One block may be used on emails sent to prospective clients while another is used on internal company emails. This helps reduce people's annoyance with large email signature blocks in short back-and-forth emails.

Email Signature Block Examples:

To an External Client:

 Beatriz Garcia (she/her/hers)
Accountant
ABC Company, *Create the Future*
555 4th Ave S, Madison, WI 53558
bgarcia@ABCcompany.com (o) 555-555-2222 (c) 555-555-2223
ABCCompany.com

View my profile on **Linked in**

To an External Client:

Eric Miller

 Associate Sales Representative
emilller@ABCcompany.com
ABC Company, *Create the Future*
555 4th Ave S, Madison, WI 53558
Like us on Facebook | Follow us on Instagram

For a Return Email:

Eric Miller
Associate Sales Representative
(555) 555-2223
emilller@ABCcompany.com

For a Return Email:

Beatriz Garcia
My work day may look different than your work day. Please do not feel obligated to respond out of your normal working hours.
She/hers
Accountant
bgarcia@ABCcompany.com (o) 555-555-2222 (c) 555-555-2223

For a Student:

Best Regards,

Gabriel Johnson

Information Systems Undergraduate

Information Systems Club | IT Chair

St. Cloud State University

9

Bad-News Messages

Delivering or receiving negative news is never pleasant, but it's unavoidable. Negative news may be as simple as the inability to attend a meeting or as complex as laying off employees. In most business communications, you put the main point first to save your receiver time and money. But when delivering bad news, you will follow a different organizational format, which is explained below. After completing this lesson, you will:

- Learn and demonstrate the ability to write a bad-news message
- Demonstrate your ability to follow proper message format

Reading 9.1

Persuasive and Bad News Messages

By Janet Mizrahi

Writing Negative or Bad News

Delivering unwanted news is a fact of life in the world of work, and when an organization must inform its stakeholders of negative news, there are basic goals that a message must attain:

- Confirm that the bad news will be understood and accepted
- Deliver the message in a way that the reader will continue to look at the writer or organization in a positive light
- Minimize future contact with the writer or organization about the negative situation

In some cases, delivering bad news uses the direct strategy. For example, anyone who has ever received a rejection letter from a college (certainly bad news!) knows that the bad news comes in the first line. This is done so that the anxious student does not overlook the information. If you think your reader would prefer to read the bad news first or if the situation demands firmness, use the direct approach for bad news. Begin with the bad news itself, explain the reasons for the bad news in the body, and close politely but firmly.

However, bad news is frequently delivered using the indirect strategy. This structure has four main elements, as Table 9.1.1 illustrates.

Table 9.1.1 Bad news message: indirect strategy elements

Indirect strategy elements	Writing strategy
Neutral or buffer statement	Describe a point on which both parties can agree Express appreciation Begin with good news Offer praise
Reasons leading to message	Include details supporting the denial Omit apologizing Use positive language wherever possible
The negative or undesired news	Clearly state the bad news to eliminate any misunderstanding Deemphasize the bad news by placing it in a subordinate clause
Polite close	Aim to build goodwill by offering an alternative, if possible, or a simple forward-looking statement

Begin your negative news correspondence with a **buffer or neutral statement** about which both the writer and reader can agree: *The recent renovation of the University Club has made it a much sought-after venue.*

Alternately, you may wish to start with a statement of **appreciation**: *Thank you for your well researched proposal to include Mayweather House in this year's Giving Back® volunteer day.*

You can offer any **good news** that is part of the message (as long as it doesn't mislead the reader into thinking the message contains all good news) or offer praise to open your bad news message: *All departments have done a great job decreasing their operating budgets.*

Start the second paragraph of the bad news message by providing logical **reasons** leading to the bad news itself. Slip in the **bad news** in a subordinate clause, and never repeat it. Make sure the negative message is clearly stated so you don't create misunderstanding or encourage further communication. For example, following the previous buffer statement, our next sentence might read:

Since we have expanded our facility to accommodate parties of over 100 and added a gourmet chef, the number of organizations and individuals requesting to use the University Club for events has tripled. Our bylaws require that we give priority to members of the club before opening up our schedule to nonmembers, so we are unable to accommodate your request to use the Dean's Room on the date you have requested.

The **closing** of the bad news message must be polite and promote goodwill to the reader, who has just heard unwelcome news. Avoid being too conciliatory by offering to provide "additional assistance" or to "call us if you have further questions." If you are able to offer an alternative, do so. For example, if you know that another facility is available to accommodate the faculty retreat mentioned earlier or you can hold it on a different day, say so. If not, simply end on a positive note: *Thank you for considering the University Club for your event, and we look forward to helping you in the future.*

References

Guffey, M., and D. Loewy. 2015. *Business Communication: Process and Product.* 8th ed. Stamford, CT: Cengage Learning.

Marsh, C., D. Guth, and B. Short. 2012. *Strategic Writing: Multimedia Writing for Public Relations, Advertising and More.* 3rd ed. Upper Saddle River, NJ: Pearson Education.

Janet Mizrahi, "Persuasive and Bad News Messages," *Writing for the Workplace: Business Communication for Professionals*, pp. 52-54. Copyright © 2015 by Business Expert Press. Reprinted with permission.

Applying This Skill: Write a Bad-News Message

As a group, consider the scenario below and the indirect strategy elements discussed in the article above. Plan and draft your message below.

Scenario: At Walding Company, a financial services group, you've been helping consumers save for retirement for over 25 years. Recently, however, you learned your company computer system had been hacked, and the personal records of nearly all of your customers have been compromised. Write an email telling your customers about the breach and that they may be affected. Develop your message by answering the questions below. Be prepared to share your message with another group.

- How will your audience react to this news?

- What is your neutral opening statement? How can you open with a statement that identifies the topic without sounding negative or too positive?

- What are the issues that led to the bad news? What facts or reasons are relevant to the bad news? How can you give the facts/reasons without sounding negative or too positive?

- What is your bad-news statement? Can you write about the bad news without explicitly stating it?

- What alternative counterproposal or "silver lining" could you offer your audience? How might you use "you phrases" to soften the bad news?

- What is your forward-looking statement? What might you say to maintain a positive relationship between you and your audience?

- *Draft your bad-news message here:*

Assignment: Write a Bad—News Message

As assigned, select one of the scenarios below and write a bad-news message for the situation. You may add details as needed.

Scenario 1: Shipping Surcharge

Assume you work at a shipping company that has seen a large rise in orders since the beginning of the COVID-19 pandemic in 2020. While the increase in business has been welcome, the increase in fuel costs, coupled with the need to increase wages, has done nothing to increase revenue. In fact, your profit margin has narrowed.

After some consideration, you have decided to implement a new shipping surcharge and minimum order payment. The changes will take effect on the first of the month.

Write an email message to your customers notifying them of the changes.

Scenario 2: SnowDog Sleds

Assume you work at a snowmobile company called SnowDog. Since the beginning of the COVID-19 pandemic in 2020, SnowDog has faced increasing expenses, from parts to shipping to wages. After some consideration, you have decided to make changes to your policies about dealership minimum purchases.

Starting next season, dealerships will be required to purchase a minimum of ten sleds in order remain a SnowDog dealer. The purchases are also subject to a new shipping surcharge and minimum order payment.

Write an email message to your customers notifying them of the changes and encouraging them to place orders for next season.

Scenario 3: Membership Changes

Assume you are the newest sales representative for Weight Loss Clubs, a gym and weight-management company. While the company is about five years old and growing steadily, the president is eager to increase membership and revenues. Because of high real estate rental prices in your city, your club must raise membership rates effective next month. Clubs in nearby suburbs are not subject to the membership rates, but your facility is the flagship club for the company.

Write an email to club members telling them of the membership price increase. Consider the following:

- You do not want to lose members to other clubs.
- Your job depends on your ability to attract and retain memberships.
- You may be noticed for a promotion if you increase memberships.

10

Business Meetings

Some companies hold many meetings—sometimes up to 70 a week! Other companies are doing away with meetings or implementing alternative meeting formats via electronic means, walking, standing, and others. But statistics show there are about three billion meetings held each year. To prepare you for business meetings, we will conduct several business meetings over the course of the semester.

The articles and information below will help prepare you for the business meetings held in class and business meetings you'll attend in the workplace. After completing this lesson, you will be able to:

- Demonstrate the ability to present yourself professionally
- Develop the ability to adapt to changing directions/assignments
- Demonstrate the ability to conduct an interview
- Demonstrate the ability to effectively present information in a group setting

....

Reading 10.1

Productive Virtual Team Meetings

By Debbie DuFrene and Carol Lehman

While those who lead virtual meetings must perform all the same tasks required for effective face-to-face meetings, the technological component heightens the importance of preparation, leadership, and follow-up. Meeting participants might live in different time zones, speak different languages, and be uncomfortable with virtual interactions. Alternately, meeting participants might be in the same region or city but find virtual communication to be more efficient in terms of time and money.

In your virtual meetings, avoid trying to reproduce what happens in a face-to-face meeting. While the virtual meeting experience will differ from organization to organization, depending on the needs, resources, and intended meeting results, it will most certainly differ from face-to-face meetings that take place in the same organization.

Appropriate Technology Choices

Many different types of virtual meeting technology and software products are available, depending on the needs of your organization. Technology can provide a high-end telepresence experience at significant cost or more economical basic web conferencing. Choosing the most effective technology is not a simple process and is influenced by the organization's budget, the nature of the team task, and members' access to various technologies. Each organization must explore options and select the technology most suitable to its needs. We will not explore all available options nor make recommendations; rather, our primary purpose is to discuss a number of technology choices you might consider for your virtual meetings.

Telepresence Virtual Meetings

Some large organizations want a telepresence experience for participants; this technology creates the impression that people in different locations are actually in the same room. For example, Cisco's TelePresence is a system that uses ultra-high-definition life-size screens and lag-free voice over Internet protocol. Advanced features enhance the "high-intensity collaboration" capability needed for sophisticated planning sessions and problem resolution.[6] In this virtual boardroom, participants feel as if they are sitting across the table from someone a thousand miles away. As an alternative to purchasing such systems, however, many organizations desiring the telepresence experience are turning to their own in-house IT experts to find cost-effective alternatives that can deliver high-quality video and audio, natural eye contact and motion, life-size images, and intuitive operation. Such inside solutions allow companies to avoid major capital expenditures.

Web-Conferencing Options

Many organizations use web-conferencing software to set up virtual meetings. Such products are less expensive than the technology that provides a telepresence experience and are affordable for even small entities. Available products include the following:

- Cisco's WebEx is one of the oldest and most commonly used online meeting services and works well with Windows, Mac, smartphones, and tablets. Users receive high quality video and phone conferencing, screen sharing, and online collaboration tools, such as whiteboarding, note-taking, and annotations. Integration with other desktop applications such as Outlook makes it easy to schedule an appointment and add a meeting to it, e-mail the attendees quickly, and join a meeting on a mobile device.[7] The product starts at $49 per month for unlimited meetings and allows up to 25 participants per meeting.[8]
- Citrix's GoToMeeting integrates software such as Microsoft Office with features including videoconferencing, screen sharing, chats, invitation options, meeting info, recording capability, drawing tools, and the ability to annotate shared content in real time.[9] The product is available for about $50 a month for up to 25 attendees and can be accessed from a Mac, PC, smartphone, or tablet.[10]
- MeetingBurner is a free online meeting service for up to 10 attendees. It has an easy-to-use interface, has fast load times, and includes Skype integration and screen sharing. Facilitators receive analytics that show how participants interact with the content.[11]

---

[6] Perez (2012, March 27).
[7] Henry (2012, January 22).
[8] WebEx (2015).
[9] Online meetings get better: GoToMeeting 3.0 (2007).
[10] GoToMeeting (2015).
[11] Fance (2012).

- Google+ Hangouts is another free service that has gained in popularity with the addition of screen sharing and document collaboration via Google Docs.[12]

Adobe Connect and iMeet are other examples of available conferencing services. New products are introduced each year, and the number likely will increase significantly as more businesses turn to virtual meetings as a means to save time and money.

Other Examples of Virtual Meeting Technology

Here are two additional options that may appeal to some organizations as they select virtual meeting solutions:

- IBM/Lotus offers virtual world meeting features through its product Sametime. These features include a virtual-reality meeting (similar to Second Life) with 3-D avatar attendees and presentation graphics displayed on a large movie-like screen. The virtual room is equipped with softphone voice communications and a whiteboard.[13]
- While not designed specifically for meetings, Skype is a free application that enables video and audio transmission and can compensate in part for a lack of face-to-face communication. The popular application bundles the capabilities of phone, traditional chat, and videoconferencing and works with Windows, Mac, and Linux operating systems.

Regardless of the collaboration tools used, the work of virtual teams can be enhanced by use of a dedicated website or intranet where information, data files, graphic materials, schedules, and reference collections can be stored and shared.

Meeting Preparation

An important question to ask before scheduling a virtual meeting is, "Should we meet?" You must determine if the purpose of the meeting is worth the time and cost of everyone's time. Answering the questions in Table 10.2.1 will help you answer the main one: Should we hold a virtual meeting?

Table 10.2.1 **Should we hold a virtual meeting?**

	Yes	No
Would e-mails or phone calls be as effective as a meeting?		
Is the input of participants needed, and will it be acted on?		
Does everyone have time to prepare for the meeting?		
Is enough information available to make the meeting productive?		
Can the desired end result be best achieved with a meeting?		

If the meeting's purpose is to share information, then e-mails, file postings, and informal conversations might be just as effective as a meeting. However, if participants need to share opinions and knowledge and develop common thoughts, a meeting may be needed. In some cases, simply sharing information might be a legitimate reason to meet if spontaneous exchange is needed while everyone is together in real time. Knowing the desired end result defines the purpose of the meeting.

---

[12] Henry (2012, January 22).
[13] Fontana (2008, January 23).

Additionally, the leader must decide the best time for the meeting, which may involve different time zones. For this reason, most virtual teams select a standing meeting time and stay with it for the duration of the project. Once the decision to meet has been made, preparation for the meeting can begin, following these steps.

Identify the Meeting Objective

The meeting objective should be determined and communicated to those who will be in attendance. A productive meeting depends on clearly defined objectives that participants can work toward and against which progress can be measured. Rather than simply "discuss," the objective should be to "discuss and decide," or "discuss and plan," or "discuss and identify key barriers to success."[14] Following the meeting, participants need action steps and a plan, not simply a list of what happened in the last meeting.

Become Familiar with Meeting Elements

Conducting a virtual meeting takes preparation and special skills to ensure that everyone is engaged. An effective leader must demonstrate the skills discussed earlier, as well as comfort in leading a virtual meeting. If the leader or facilitator in charge of the meeting is not comfortable with the technology, a practice session may be necessary to ensure success. For example, in one business, a senior-level executive tried using a headset during a practice session and found that it was much easier to use his own speakerphone. If a practice walk-through is needed, use this time to test and make needed adjustments to the technology as well. The technology should facilitate, not overpower, the meeting's agenda.

Send an Advance Agenda

As with face-to-face meetings, virtual meeting agendas and supporting materials should be sent to participants 24 to 48 hours in advance. The more preparation work is done, the more likely the virtual meeting will be efficient. A sample agenda format is shown in Table 10.2.2.

Table 10.2.2 **Sample meeting agenda**

Meeting title:	Project update	
Date/Time:	Thursday, June 9, 10 a.m. (EDT)	
Meeting objective:	Assess progress on project and assign remaining tasks	
	Topic	**Speaker**
8:30–8:45	Progress since last meeting	Team leader and members
8:45–9:00	Update on manufacturing issues	Production manager; member discussion
9:00–9:15	Discussion of adjusted delivery timeline	Team leader and members
9:15–9:30	Recap and wrap up; individual member assignments	Facilitator; member input

If new members or guests will be participating in the meeting, they will benefit in particular from receiving in advance an overview of meeting attendance such as the one in Table 10.2.3.

---

[14] Krattenmaker (2008, February 27).

Table 10.2.3 **Meeting attendance overview**

Table 10.2.3 **Meeting attendance overview**

Invited participants	Attending	Not attending
Name—Represented area		
Name—Represented area		
Name—Represented area		
Name—Represented area		
Name—Represented area		

The meeting should be planned to last for a reasonable length of time. If it must exceed 90 minutes or so, include short stretch breaks in the agenda.

Facilitation of Effective Online Meetings

Virtual meetings have unique challenges that must be anticipated and addressed by the leader. The following actions increase the likelihood of a smooth, productive meeting.

Assure a Smooth Start

The meeting should start at the time announced in advance, so participants should assemble themselves slightly ahead of the announced starting time to gather materials and check connections. Starting late costs the organization money and wastes the time of participants. At the start of the meeting, all participants should introduce themselves by name so everyone knows who is in attendance and has a sense of the group composition and locations. Following introductions, the leader or meeting facilitator should review where the group is with their progress and refer to the meeting agenda.

Appoint a Facilitator

In addition to the team leader, a moderator or facilitator may be appointed to help the meeting move along. This person can keep track of the participants who are waiting to speak and assist with technical aspects of the meeting if needed. The leader can then focus on the meeting purpose and objectives. For some organizations, a designated support person may be assigned to monitor all aspects of the technology. Other roles may be assigned as needed, including a recordkeeper to prepare official meeting minutes and provide follow-up communication to all participants. For meetings where most of the participants are in one room, the facilitator might tie a balloon on the phone or webcam to remind team members of the remote participants.[15]

Control Speaking

Spoken words should be carefully chosen. If participants are connected only by audio, they will not understand if the leader points to a line item and says, "Let's talk about this." Questions and comments should be repeated if there is a chance that some cannot hear all speakers. Sometimes a problem occurs when participants try to talk over one another. However, software products typically include a feature allowing participants to click a particular key on their keyboards to signal that they want to talk. The leader or facilitator can then recognize participants in turn.

---

[15] White (2014).

Seek Consensus Frequently

Frequent summaries of what has been discussed and decided help ensure that everyone is on board with the meeting's progress. Roll-call voting should be conducted for important decisions. Polling is a typical technological feature the leader can use to have participants respond to questions presented in true or false, yes or no, or multiple-choice formats. Results can be instantly displayed for all participants.

Keep Everyone on Task

As with all meetings, virtual meeting participants must not be allowed to get sidetracked. Keeping participants engaged in a virtual meeting is particularly challenging, as people can easily "multitask" by reading something else, checking e-mail, or moving about for food or drink. If some participants are obviously not participating or responding, the leader or facilitator may need to single them out for response to encourage them to rejoin the meeting. However, the more engaging and focused the meeting, the less likely participants will lose interest.

Evaluate Meeting Effectiveness

A meeting evaluation should be completed at the end of each meeting. Items to evaluate should include the overall focus on the issues, efficiency regarding time and discussion of issues, participation, and results. The leader may schedule a few minutes at the end of the meeting to ask for feedback from participants on the meeting effectiveness. This activity provides useful input for planning future meetings and also encourages involvement and collaboration from meeting participants.

Meeting Follow-Up

Meeting follow-up actually is more easily achieved in virtual settings than face-to-face because of the permanent archive of communication exchanges afforded by electronic environments. Notes and recordings from the meeting should be converted to meeting minutes and made available to all participants within two days of the meeting. Minutes from all meetings should follow a consistent format and include a "Decisions Made" section to highlight actions. A sample template for meeting minutes is shown in Table 10.2.4. Other templates are available at the Microsoft Office Online website: http://office.microsoft.com/en-us/templates/ct101172601033.aspx.

Table 10.2.4 **Meeting minutes template**

Subject:	
Leader:	
Facilitator:	
Location:	
Date/Time:	
Attendees:	
Key points discussed		
No.	Topic	Highlights
1		
2		
3		
Decisions made		
1		

2		
3		
Agreed upon actions		
No.	**Action item**	**Person responsible**
1		
2		
3		

Minutes and related documents can be e-mailed or posted to a common space where they can be reviewed and referred to later as needed by the various team members.

Case 10.2.1: Lullabot Employees Share Insights for Virtual Workers

Lullabot, formed in 2006, is a 100 percent distributed company with no central office. According to Jeff Robbins, the company's cofounder and CEO, while all of Lullabot's employees work virtually from home or a distant location, they are not remote workers because they stay well connected.[16] In a distributed organization, both communication and culture must adapt to accommodate for the lack of a centralized workplace. Lullabot's intercontinental work team offers the following list of highly effective habits for virtual workers:[17]

- Get dressed as if you are going to work. Productivity is boosted when you shower, dress, and report for your workday. While dress may be a bit more casual, readying yourself for a purpose helps you get in focused work mode.
- Have a schedule. A distinct advantage of virtual work is being able to find your own ideal schedule and pattern for productivity. No matter how off-beat your schedule may be, sticking to the pattern helps you use time effectively and avoid working all the time with reduced productivity.
- Have a dedicated workspace. Keep organized, and do what you can to differentiate work and leisure.
- Get out. Just as leaving a physically located job for lunch can help you rejuvenate, the same is true for leaving your home workspace. Run an errand, exercise, or at least retreat for a while from the computer.
- Connect. Create situations for face-to-face time with clients or colleagues using videochat via Skype, Google Hangouts, or GoToMeeting rather than sending an e-mail. Take part in meetings and gatherings of a professional organization or group in your area.

Lullabot personnel remind other virtual workers that there is no single right or wrong way to work from home. They encourage virtual workers to try various strategies to find their own best practices.

Reflect

What other highly effective habits of distributed workers would you add to the list developed by Lullabot personnel?

Apply

Interview one or more virtual workers to learn more about the advantages and challenges of their work arrangement. Prepare an oral presentation with appropriate visuals to share your findings.

---

[16] Robbins (2014, May 22).
[17] Lee (2013, March).

Case 10.2.2: Accenture Keeps Its Virtual Workforce Connected

Accenture, a multinational and widely distributed consulting firm, has offices located around the globe. With thousands of global employees working mostly at client sites in more than 100 companies, Accenture must focus continually on keeping its virtual workforce connected with one another and with the company.[18]

Accenture has made 13 consecutive appearances on Fortune's "World's Most Admired Companies" list and has been recognized with various awards that recognize its strides in diversity and employee development. Completing an extensive "new joiner" orientation program is a requirement of every new consultant hired at Accenture. Following orientation, each new hire is assigned a career counselor to help identify career paths and navigate various work-related obstacles. Each time an employee is promoted, more training is provided, with the average Accenture employee spending about 75 hours in training each year. Managers receive specific training in leading virtual teams, including topics such as how to be sensitive to time zone issues and how to encourage initial chitchat in online exchanges.

A variety of technology tools assists Accenture in keeping its employees connected. Cisco's TelePresence web-conferencing platform facilitates communication, and the company also has a People Pages site (the company's version of Facebook), which allows employees to read personal profiles and send messages to each other. The Careers Marketplace website provides employees with information about careers with Accenture and links them to open positions. Keeping more than 300,000 worldwide employees connected is no small task, but Accenture's management works concertedly to make sure it happens.[19]

Reflect

What additional technical and nontechnical strategies could be employed to promote connectedness among virtual team members?

Apply

Develop a handbook for "new joiner" orientation to help people assimilate effectively into virtual teams. Your handbook, suitable for posting electronically, should include guidelines, tips, resources, and other useful information.

References

Accenture. (2015). Accenture website. Retrieved from https://www.accenture.com/us-en/company#

Fance, C. (2012). Online meeting and web conferencing tools—best of. Hongkiat. Retrieved from http://www.hongkiat.com/blog/online-meeting-tools/

Fontana, J. (2008, January 23). Lotus toying with Sametime features including virtual world meetings. Network World. Retrieved from http://www.networkworld.com/article/2282565/software/lotus-toying-with-sametime-features-including-virtual-world-meetings.html

---

[18] Accenture (2015).
[19] Marquez (2008, September 22).

GoToMeeting. (2015). Plans and pricing. Retrieved from
https://www.gotomeeting.com/meeting/pricing?c_name=becauselpvar2

Henry, A. (2012, January 22). Five best online meeting services. Lifehacker. Retrieved from
http://lifehacker.com/5878067/five-best-online-meeting-services

Krattenmaker, T. (2008, February 27). Make every meeting matter. Harvard Management Update. Harvard Business Review. Retrieved from https://hbr.org/2008/02/make-every-meeting-matter/

Lee, E. (2013, March). How working at home works (for us). Retrieved from
https://www.lullabot.com/blog/article/how-working-home-works-us

Marquez, J. (2008, September 22). Connecting a virtual workforce. Workforce Management, 1–25.

Online meetings get better: GoToMeeting 3.0. (2007, August 21). PC Magazine, 43.

Perez, J. C. (2012, March 27). Cisco boosts telepresence system with new collaboration features. PCWorld. Retrieved from
http://www.pcworld.com/article/252642/cisco_boosts_telepresence_system_with_new_collaboration_features.html

Robbins, J. (2014, May 22). What is a distributed company? Business. Retrieved from
https://www.lullabot.com/articles/what-is-a-distributed-company

WebEx. (2015). WebEx meetings pricing. Retrieved from http://www.webex.com/pricing/

White, M. (2014). The management of virtual teams and virtual meetings. Business Information Review, 31(2), 111–117. doi:10.1177/0266382114540979

Assignment: Business Meetings

Over the course of the semester, the class will conduct business meetings. Topics for the business meetings will be distributed during class about a week prior to the scheduled meeting.

For business meetings, you will be evaluated on your content, quality of source (research), and professionalism. Professionalism includes body language (e.g., sitting up straight, not fidgeting, etc.), composure, and presentation of information (e.g., vocabulary, filler words, etc.).

Each person should be prepared to speak for 2–4 minutes during the meeting. The professor (or TA) will not call on people; it is your responsibility to contribute to the meeting and make your points. You are not required to dress up for the meetings, nor are you required to have visual aids (unless otherwise instructed in class).

An agenda similar to the one below will be distributed about a week before the meeting. It will include details about the topics of the business meetings.

Business Meeting 1 Agenda

Location: Classroom

Date: As assigned

Time: Regular Class Time

Preparation details:

For the business meeting, you will be asked to:

Here is what you need to do:

Presentation details:

Remember, this is a department meeting, not a formal presentation. So, you do not need any visuals, and you do not need to dress up.

We will sit in a circle, as a department would in a conference room. Participants must voluntarily add their information; I will not call on people. In addition to presenting your information, you should ask questions or make comments on other people's topics.

Professionalism is a portion of your score for this assignment. Professionalism includes posture (sit up straight, feet on floor), attention to others (not on phone or computer, paying attention to speaker), tone and clarity of voice (minimal "ums" and "ahs," volume etc.), minimal nervous gestures/repetitive motions (tapping, knee bouncing).

You will be evaluated on the information you present and your professionalism.

11

Writing for the Internet and Social Media

With the prevalence of the internet and the increasing use of social media, writing for those mediums is becoming more and more important. Often, companies will assume new graduates are experienced in writing for the internet and social media and expect them to have and use those skills. Many of the conventions of business writing that you've learned so far apply to writing for the web and social media. However, these electronic mediums have some particular conventions about which you should be aware. After completing this lesson, you will:

- Understand how social media has changed the communication model
- Understand how people access content on the internet and via social media
- Know and demonstrate the ability to write for the internet and social media

Reading 11.1

Apply Writing Skills to Social Media Copy

By Jack Appleman

Overview

- Prepare for the surge in on-the-job social media writing.
- Speak one-on-one to readers.
- Craft compelling headlines and chunk your content.
- Extend conversations with your replies.
- Write engaging LinkedIn and Twitter posts.

If you're a small business owner, independent contractor, freelancer, or public relations and marketing professional, you recognize the power of social media to achieve business goals. The rest of you have probably gotten fairly adept at using platforms such as Facebook, Instagram, Pinterest, and Yelp. And you may have posted your profile on LinkedIn, where you interact with workplace peers, friends, and acquaintances.

Over the next several years, get ready for more frequent and intensive workplace "socializing." Many companies have already expanded their use of social media platforms to connect with their staff, customers, potential hires, consultants, and others. That means you'll need to build and continually fine-tune your professional presence on LinkedIn and become more adept at using other social media tools.

Those of you who work for a major corporation may soon participate in (or are already participating in) "employee advocacy," where organizations call upon workers at all levels to help build their brands and deliver key messages to target audiences on Facebook, LinkedIn, Twitter, and other platforms. These initiatives are apparently paying off. A study by Bambu (2017) revealed that companies with employee advocacy programs increased revenues by an average of 26 percent in the first year of implementation.

On top of this trend, an increasing number of organizations are creating their own social enterprise networks to enhance internal communication—beyond the scope of its corporate communication specialists. According to a study by Deloitte, business leaders use social enterprise networks to create a "highly engaged workforce to support them in achieving business goals faster." These networks can enhance a company's capability to share best practices, crowdsource for quicker answers, discover new technology solutions, recognize high-performing employees, and drive cross-functional collaboration.

Whatever the reason, you'll likely be writing more social media copy related to your job or business. And all your Facebook experience crowing about your daughter's gymnastics award or describing the bliss of your tropical vacation may not help you write the results-driven social media text required in the workplace.

To be an effective social media writer, hone the skills addressed in earlier steps, such as simplicity, brevity, flow, organization, persuasion, and tone. Then learn some of the techniques and nuances for writing in various platforms.

Maximizing the impact of social media often requires strategies such as integrating images and videos, timing posts, linking to websites, inserting keywords for search engine optimization, creating hashtags, and more. For our discussion, we'll stick with crafting copy that helps you achieve the desired results. Following are the most important social media writing skills to master, especially for LinkedIn and Facebook. (Plus, the final tips two address specific tips for LinkedIn profiles and Twitter posts).

Stop Readers With Compelling Headlines

If you don't entice readers with an engaging headline, bid them farewell because they won't stick around for the rest. Advertising legend David Ogilvy explains, "On the average, five times as many people read the headline as read the body copy" (Dahl 2007). As with email subject lines (see Step 9), a compelling social media headline (such as for LinkedIn, Facebook, or a blog post) can dramatically increase readership.

Two of the best approaches for headline writing are to be explicit (highlighting the message to follow), or to be intriguing (offering a short tease and compelling readers to stay with it and discover something valuable or fascinating). Here are examples of each type of headline:

Explicit

- To Write Persuasively, Address Readers' Hot Buttons
- Reduce Taxes: Fund an IRA

Intriguing

- Drop Your Cable Plan?
- 5 Tips for Breakthrough Interviews

Speak One-on-One to Readers

Take the conversational style preferred in business writing (see Step 1) to a more personal level. For example, if you're talking with a friend about your frustration contacting a software provider for assistance with your new mobile platform, your dialogue—and social media post—could start like this:

Do you ever feel like software companies hate talking to real customers?

To embrace this style, imagine yourself in a one-on-one conversation about the topic you're writing about. Don't be afraid to be a bit edgy, as in the previous example. Just keep it civil and professional.

Chunk It

The more we get overloaded with information from traditional and social media channels, the more our attention span shrinks. Most people prefer to process messages in brief sound bites. So keep paragraphs super short and, where appropriate, break up text with subheads (see more in Step 4).

In her blog post offering advice on addressing workplace bullying, Catherine Mattice Zundel (2017), president of Civility Partners, uses a colloquial and captivating lead-in followed by three simple subheads to explain why employees fail to act:

I've been thinking lately about WHY people don't take action against workplace bullying, and I've come up with three reasons:

1. Fear. In the case of workplace bullying, taking action means standing up to the bully. It possibly means standing up to managers who aren't willing to acknowledge it's a problem. What happens if people don't listen? Will the bully retaliate? What problems will taking action create? These questions are answered in the context of fear, so the answers lead people to avoid taking action.

2. Spotlight. Many people don't want to be in the spotlight. Why would someone volunteer to be in the spotlight if it meant they will be punished by the bully? Or worse, by the organization?

3. Apathy. Some people just don't care enough to take action. Maybe the bullying doesn't bother them personally. Or maybe they think it's normal to be treated that way, so they don't feel compelled to take action against normalcy.

Ask Questions That Prompt Actual Responses

When writing website copy, a newsletter article, or an email blast, you might ask a rhetorical question like, "Are you ready to enjoy higher returns on your IRA?" But on social media sites like LinkedIn, Facebook, and Twitter, you can engage your audiences by asking questions that seek out responses.

For example, as a realtor looking to build relationships with prospective sellers, you might pose this question: "How satisfied are you with the choice of urgent care centers in your community?" Many readers, especially those who believe these choices are limited, may take advantage of the voice you've given them to air their concerns and opinions. Getting readers to engage is more than half the battle with social media. Once you have their attention, try to convince them to take the desired action, such as signing up for a webcast, attending a conference, or purchasing a product.

Extend the Conversation

Typically, when replying to messages on social media, you want your comment to be meaningful, bettering the chances that the other party will engage with you. Say you're a leadership development consultant and see a tweet from a prominent management consulting firm about a recent trend on managing Millennials. If you respond with a request to set up a meeting to discuss your expertise with Millennial workers, you may be perceived as too aggressive—and there go your chances of starting a relationship. Instead, embellish what was said, perhaps offering a different perspective. Let's play out this scenario on Twitter:

ZY Management Consultants tweet

Over 50% of Millennials disappointed with communication from supervisors.

Your response as leadership consultant

@ZYMgmtConsult Millennial workers want more face-to-face communication from bosses, says study.

Through this thoughtful post, you've extended the conversation with the individual at ZY, who will likely view you as a valued source on this topic—and may reply or continue the online dialogue, which could help develop a meaningful relationship.

With LinkedIn Profiles, Immediately Convey Your Value

Anyone who wants to know more about you—recruiters, new business prospects, potential partners, and others—goes to your LinkedIn profile, probably your most important personal branding tool. Even as a small business owner with a dynamic website, you may find that those deciding whether to contact you go first to the LinkedIn profile.

Grab attention with a compelling headline followed by an engaging summary of what you can deliver and your approach—speaking directly to your targeted readers. Use a conventional or off-beat style, depending on factors such as your industry, role, and target audience. For more on writing LinkedIn profiles, see Appendix B.

Write Short, Captivating Tweets

Twitter, the ultimate "sound-bite" channel, permits 140 characters to get your message across, but as with all business communication, if possible, strive to go shorter. With so few words to convey your idea, make each one count with simple, direct messages that spur responses.

Among the strategies for composing effective tweets—depending on the subject—are conveying a clear call to action, creating urgency, evoking an emotional response, and piggybacking on breaking news or trends. Let's look at some examples of engaging tweets:

HubSpot (@HubSpot)

72.6% of salespeople using social media outperformed their colleagues who were not on social media.

Maria Shriver (@mariashriver)

What do you do if you're told you're too aggressive?

YearUp (@YearUp)

Hiring a cookie-cutter team can stifle innovation. Why employers need to look outside the box.

Deloitte (@Deloitte)

Thirsty for a change: The untapped potential of women in urban water management.

Your Turn

To get others to read your social media copy, you need to captivate them instantly with as few words as possible. Try this exercise to hone your skills in grabbing attention:

Imagine that you're either applying for a new job or trying to land a new client. The decision maker has asked all candidates to tweet something compelling about yourself or your company. Compose a tweet that summarizes your most important value-added quality (perhaps from information on your LinkedIn profile) to convince the individual to select you.

References

Bambu. 2017. Q1 2017: Essential Data to Launch Your Employee Engagement & Advocacy Strategy. Chicago: Bambu. https://getbambu.com/data-reports/engagement-to-advocacy.

Dahl, G. 2007. Advertising for Dummies, 2nd Edition. Hoboken, NJ: Wiley Publishing.

Mattice Zundel, C. 2017. "Increase employee professionalism in 30 mins." LinkedIn Pulse, March 20. www.linkedin.com/pulse/increase-employee-professionalism-30-mins-catherine.

Reading and Activity: Jigsaw Activity—Web Writing

This activity combines the Reading and Applying This Skill activities. Each group will be assigned one piece of the puzzle detailed below. Your group will read the included information, discuss it, and answer the questions assigned. You will be the "experts" for the assigned piece. Groups will then be rearranged so there is one expert on each puzzle piece in each group. In the new groups, each person will "teach" the other group members the information they learned for their puzzle piece. In the end, each student should have a complete picture of the web-writing puzzle.

Piece #1

1. What is electronic communication? What are its advantages and disadvantages?

2. How has social media changed the communication model?

Electronic communication is anything created and transmitted electronically. It includes documents, texts, files, social media, songs, and videos. While electronic communication is more and more prevalent—93% of documents are created digitally, and only 70% ever migrate to paper—there are still times when you want to use printed documents. You'll use printed messages to:

- Make a formal impression
- Provide legal information, like original or notarized signatures
- Protect sensitive information, like emailing tax documents or financial information that requires extra levels of security
- Stand out from the flood of electronic messages. It's increasingly difficult to get people to read your messages in a world full of information overload.
- Provide a permanent record. It's easier to store electronic documents, but they:

    o need to be updated frequently to maintain accessible file format; and
    o are sometimes lost due to computer crashes, file corruption, or file deletion.

- Read. Sometimes it's easier to read complicated documents on paper and share documents with others.

    Any communication done electronically is electronic communication. This includes:

- Adobe pdf
- Word document
- PowerPoint
- Rss feed

    Social media is a form of electronic communication, but not all electronic communication is social media.

    Social media has caused a fundamental shift in the way we communicate. It has:

- Transformed passive audiences into active ones
- Caused a shift from old "monologue" model (we talk, you listen) to a "dialogue" model (transparent, authentic, vibrant, consumer driven)

    o Companies are no longer broadcasting a tightly controlled message.

- Become about initiating and participating in conversations where people

    o Share content
    o Revise content
    o Respond to content
    o Contribute new content

Users are contributing to conversations and listening to them. This has changed:

- Relationships between companies and stakeholders so they are more dynamic and interactive
- Ways companies are managed, such as marketing strategies
- Behaviors and expectations of consumers and employees

People rely on social media and content sharing to get information that's both personal and professional.

Monologue

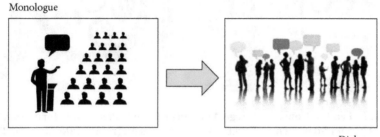

Dialogue

Figure 11.1 Single presenter to audience vs group discussion.

Piece #2

1. How do readers consume content on the web and mobile devices?

2. What is the F pattern, and why is it important?

People read web pages the way they do books in several ways. They read from top to bottom and left to right. Images receive the most attention, and readers use headings to locate information.

But web users don't read large chunks of text. In fact, only 16% of users read online content word by word. They skim and scan. They pick out key words, phrases, and fragments and look for headlines, subheads, and bold text. They pay attention to only some parts of page and are guided by headings, links, and bullet points.

This type of reading is often called "content snacking." This means consumers and readers consume large numbers of small pieces of information. They taste headlines and the first paragraphs of pages.

In one study, researchers tracked the way 232 people looked at thousands of web pages. This study revealed people consistently read web pages in an F pattern.

First, people read horizontally across the upper part of the page. This is typical of the Western style of reading: left to right, top to bottom. This line formed the top part of the F.

Figure 11.2   People Tend to Consume Large Amounts of Small Pieces of Information from Different Sources—Often Social Media Sites such as Facebook, Twitter, Instagram, LinkedIn, YouTube, and Pinterest.

Next, people tended to move down the page and read in a second horizontal movement. Reading of this second line was typically shorter; this is the second horizontal line in the F.

Third, people vertically scanned the left side of the page. Sometimes this was a slow and systematic movement, which is shown in a solid strip of red on the images. Sometimes, people read faster, which is indicated by the spottier red dots on the vertical axis.

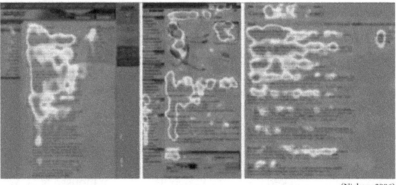

(Nielsen, 2006)

Figure 11.3 F-shaped Reading Pattern

On these images, the red indicates where people's eyes spent the most time. Yellow is second, followed by blue. This tells us people are skimming and looking for information. They are not reading the text thoroughly.

- Fun fact: people read 25% more slowly on screen than on paper.

Piece #3

Because people read content on the web differently, pages must be written differently.

1.   What are some factors to consider when writing for the web?

2. What is the inverted pyramid?

People read 25% more slowly on screens than on paper, and people don't read word for word on screens. They skip around and "snack" on content. Readers approach the web in a nonlinear fashion. It's been described as the difference between a novel and a department store. In a novel, the reader starts on page 1 and reads straight through to the end. The web or mobile readers enter a department store and go directly to the department where they expect to find the content they want.

Because people read differently online, you must write differently for web pages. It means the way you design your page and the way you write has a great effect on whether or not people read and spend time on your page:

- Fun fact: you have about 3–4 seconds to get your readers' attention.

One way to think about delivering content is the inverted pyramid model:

The inverted pyramid is how journalists tend to write; it differs from academic and research writing, which typically has writers lay a foundation with lots of supporting research (base of pyramid) and build to a logical conclusion.

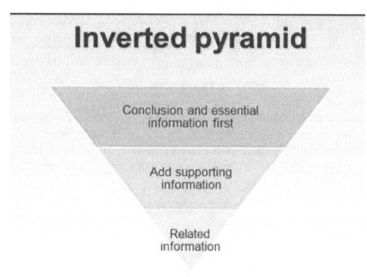

Figure 11.4 Inverted Pyramid

The journalist's inverted pyramid style starts with the conclusion and follows with details. The writer needs to catch readers' attention in the first few words. You start with the conclusion, maybe a summary or 1–2 sentences that give the reader an idea of what the longer piece is about. Then you fill in with supporting information, background, and, finally, details. Basically, your most important information must be first.

You should also limit yourself to one idea per paragraph. You want to use about half the word count of traditional writing. A typical Microsoft Word document is about 500 words per page. Google recommends a web page have between 250 and 300 words per page. Clearly, conciseness and brevity are even more important than in standard business writing.

Use half the words online

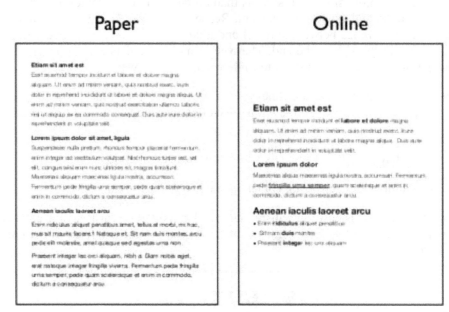

Figure 11.5 Half Words

Finally, in journalism (in newspapers in particular), the old idea was that readers don't look at what's "below the fold," so the most important information was always printed "above the fold." Now, that idea translates to screens. Generally, you can't count on people scrolling beyond the first screen. So in the first few words and lines, you must focus on key facts and make your main points.

Piece #4

1. How do you plan to write for the web and social media (audience)?

2. How do you think about content for web pages?

Throughout this class, we've talked about "you attitude" and reader focus. We've talked about being concise and clear. Now, we need to apply these concepts to writing for the internet and social media.

Before you write, you have to think about your audience. Who are your visitors? Are they frequent visitors, young or old, casual versus engaged, technical versus nontechnical? How would you describe them? Are they busy, curious, and worried? Do they know the subject/company/product? What's their computer/web experience? What's their reading ability?

Knowing your audience will help you tailor your message to different segments. For example, the audience you write for on LinkedIn will likely be different from your Instagram audience, which may be different from your Facebook or blog audience. Consider all of these differences as you are planning what to write.

Next, think about your purpose for writing. Do you want to sell products? Inform people? Tell them how to do something?

Your purpose should align with your business's strategy and goals. The best purposes are specific and measurable. When you write a proposal, what do you want to happen? When you write an email, are you asking for funding or asking people to attend a meeting? If you're writing instructions, what do you want to happen?

After you define your purpose, rethink of it in terms of "you attitude" and your audience. Your purpose should be audience focused and talk directly to reader. You want the audience to:

- Feel involved and identify with your content
- Be part of the conversation

Make sure you're talking to the audience; make them feel engaged, as if they're talking *with* you. This is a conversation or a dialogue, not a monologue.

As with all business documents, readers want to know "What's in it for me?" and "Why should I care?" To make sure your pages and content are reader focused, you should use "you" four times more than you use "I" or "we." So, your goal is to:

Not this	This
Sell products	Have people buy products
Inform people	Answer people's questions about X
Tell customers how to do something	Have people learn to do a task correctly

Lastly, as a web writer, you think about content. Most users get to web pages from search engines, links on other websites, or links within a website. This means pages should be written as if the user hasn't seen the rest of the site. Make sure all relevant information is present (What's relevant? Consider your audience) and make sure your page links easily to other places.

To attract the internet-savvy audience, your content must be:

- Useful: This requires you to know something about your audience. What do they want? What do they know? How can you best give them information?
- Current: Provide the most recent, up-to-date information available, which means constant updating.

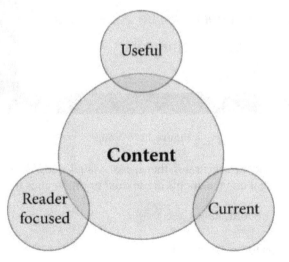

Figure 11.6 Intersection of Factors for Creating Content

Piece #5

1. Explain voice in relation to web writing and social media.

2. How are visual enhancements used in web writing and social media?

When you write, "voice" describes the personality of writing. Voice is determined by the words you choose, the tone you use, the point of view, and personality. Web and social media are fairly informal types of writing, but informal and casual doesn't mean being sloppy and careless with spelling, grammar, and the like.

In general, you want the voice you use to be personal, friendly, and, ideally, unique. Consider the different voices in the following sentences:

- Web users may subscribe to the free email newsletter below.
- Sign up for your free email newsletter!

Depending on the type of electronic communication, you'll use different voices. If writing for a corporate website, you'll likely use an efficient and informative but approachable voice. An internet piece would use a less formal voice that is community focused ("us," "we") and inclusive. Blogs tend to be informal conversations that invite feedback. Before writing or posting, reading previous company posts or competitors' posts will help you identify the appropriate tone to use in each medium.

How would you describe the voices in the examples below?

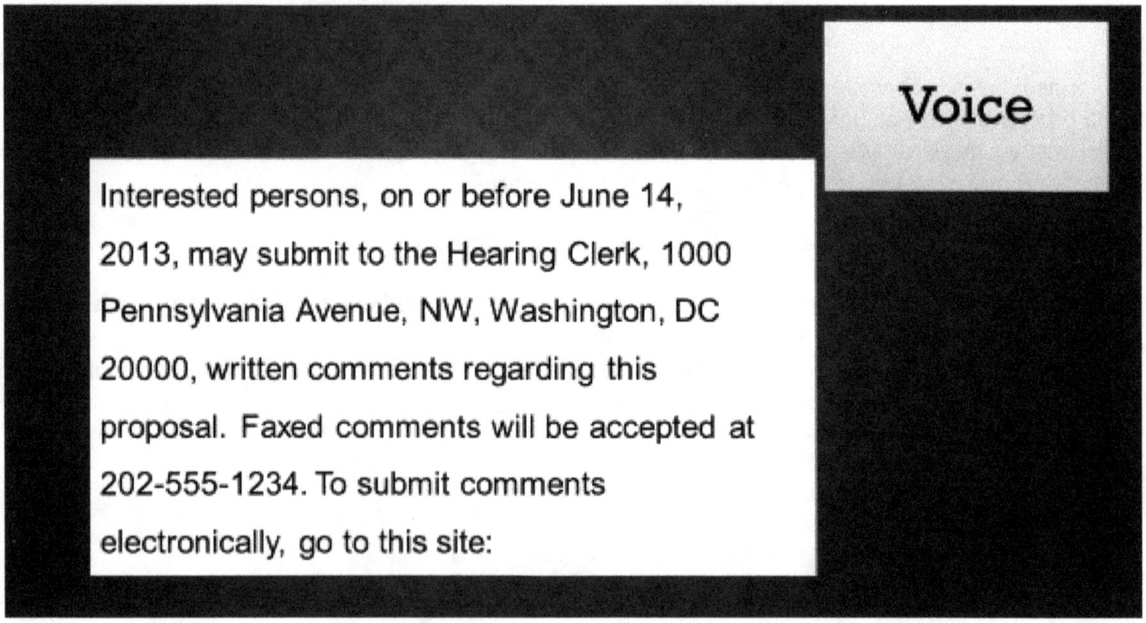

Voice

Interested persons, on or before June 14, 2013, may submit to the Hearing Clerk, 1000 Pennsylvania Avenue, NW, Washington, DC 20000, written comments regarding this proposal. Faxed comments will be accepted at 202-555-1234. To submit comments electronically, go to this site:

Figure 11.7 Voice

The example above also demonstrates the use of visual cues. We've been talking about visual enhancements all semester. Visual enhancements are textual or photo cues to help the reader. They include:

- Highlighted words (e.g., bold, italics, etc.)
- Bulleted lists
- Headings and subheads to break up text
- Chunking and white space to break up long blocks of text

Figure 11.8 Voice (2)

These typographical cues help make written text manageable. They create visual separation on the page and draw eyes to specific sections.

Consider the following examples:

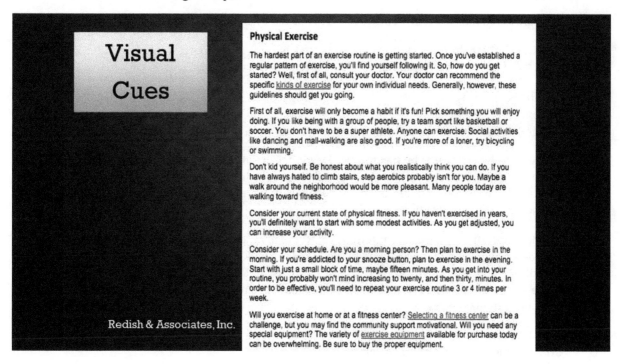

Figure 11.9 Visual Cues

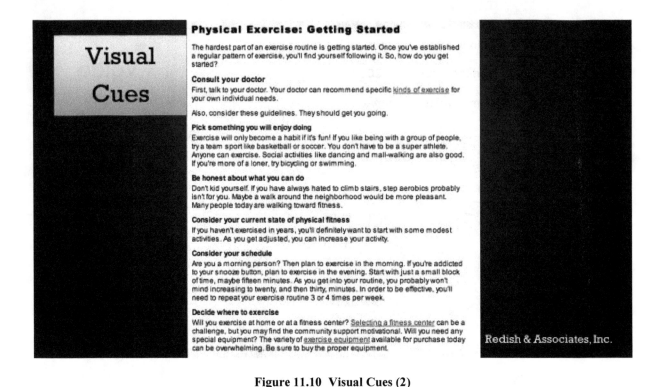

Figure 11.10 Visual Cues (2)

Piece #6

1. Why is writing concisely important in web writing and social media?

2. Why are verbs important in web writing? How are they used?

In all business communications, concision and brevity are important. Web writing should have about half the word count of conventional writing. As a general guideline:

- Headlines: eight words or less
- Sentences: 12–20 words
- Paragraphs: 40–60 words; 2–3 lines

One way to be concise is by headlining. Headlines are short, specific, concise statements that get the main point across in just a few words. People tend to read the headlines, so this is your chance to capture your readers' attention. As information overload becomes more and more problematic, effective headlines become more essential. Your headlines need to:

- Be short, specific, concise, and informative: Remember, people are "snacking" on information.
- Include keywords that will be found by search engines: Keywords are terms or phrases (usually 2–3 words) your customers would likely use to describe your products or services.
- Make sense on their own: They may be all the audience reads, so make them clear and memorable without being too cutesy.

Consider the headline examples below:

Figure 11.11 Consider the headline and image

Figure 11.12 How does this headline draw you in?

Some of the most effective headlines include verbs. In audience-focused content, talking directly to the reader makes them feel involved and part of the conversation. The verbs tell the audience what you want them to do. The web audience often wants direction: What should they do next? Do you want your audience to take a quiz, set up an appointment, or download a free worksheet? Do you want them to take action on the site? After they leave the site?

Consider the two examples above. How do they use verbs and calls to action? How does that work with the headlines?

Applying This Skill: Jigsaw Activity for Writing for the Internet and Social Media

Piece #1

- What is electronic communication? What are its advantages and disadvantages? When should you use paper communications?

- How has social media changed the communication model? Explain the monologue versus dialogue models of communication.

Piece #2

- How do readers consume content on the web and mobile devices?

- What is the F pattern, and why is it important?

Piece #3

- What are some factors to consider when writing for the web?

- What is the inverted pyramid?

Piece #4

- How do you plan to write for the web and social media (audience)?

- How do you think about content for web pages?

Piece #5

- Explain voice in relation to web writing and social media. Give an example of different voices.

- How are visual enhancements used in web writing and social media?

Piece #6

- Why is conciseness important in web writing and social media?

- Why are verbs important in web writing? How are they used?

Assignment: Social Media Audit

Assume your team has been asked by a small or midsized company to evaluate its social media presence and make suggestions for improvement. You will assess several of the company's social media platforms and provide recommendations for ways the company may advance its goals.

Social Media Audit Overview

For this project, you will complete several different assignments. The Social Media Audit is the entire project—an umbrella term. The specific assignments under the umbrella may include some or all of the following:

- Progress (status) report
- Pitch Day presentation (with visuals)
- Letter to client (2–3 pages)
- Sample social media posts (two per platform)

Below is a step-by-step outline for completing the project. In addition, review the Applying this Skill: Planning the Social Media Audit worksheet on the following page.

Step 1. Select a company

As a team, select a small or midsized company that interests you. Small, local companies work well for this assignment. The company should have some social media presence but should not have a social media manager. Large or chain companies (e.g., Starbucks or Target) will have social media managers and are not appropriate choices for this assignment. Look at a variety of company websites and social media before determining the company with which you would like to work. The company you select should have at least one social media platform but does not need to have a presence on all social media platforms. You may suggest the company begin to use a certain platform.

List your team's company here:

Step 2. Select social media platforms

Each person in your team will research one social media platform. You may select from the following list of social media platforms or suggest your own:

- Facebook
- Twitter
- LinkedIn
- Instagram
- YouTube
- Snapchat
- TikTok
- Reddit
- Website
- Blog

Each team member will focus on *one* type of social media.

List your social media platform here:

Step 3: Competitors

As a team, select 2–3 competitors for your company. Competitors may be large companies, franchises, chains, or small local companies. Selecting a variety of competitors will help you provide a comprehensive overview of the market. Everyone in your team should compare the same companies.

List your company's competitors here:

Step 4: Campaign

Create a campaign for your project. The team will eventually create sample social media posts to share with the client. All posts should relate to the same topic or event. Successful campaign ideas include holidays (e.g., 4th of July, winter, etc.), attracting certain demographic (e.g., college students, mothers), increasing business at a specific time (e.g., during sporting events, lunch hour), and more. When you create your social media sample posts, they will be related to your campaign theme.

List your ideas for a campaign here:

Step 5: Research

Each team member will conduct research about their social media platform. The research will include:

- Your company's presence on the social media platform: Do they use it? How often do they post? What types of posts do they make? How much engagement do they have with each post?
- Competitors' presence on the social media platform: Do they use it? How often do they post? What types of posts do they make? How much engagement do they have with each post?
- Best practices for the social media platform: How should the company use the platform to reach its goals? For best practices, look at the platform's FAQs or guides for small businesses, Social Media Examiner, Hootsuite, and the like.

Step 6: Write and Create

Following the best practices for your social media platform (e.g., length, use of images and hashtags, etc.), create two sample posts. These are posts that the company could use if it wanted to. You are giving the company examples of posts that would be effective. The posts should be related to your campaign.

The sample posts may be created on the platform, in a Word or Google document, using Canva, and so on. You may use Creative Commons free-use images.

You will not post these sample posts.

Step 7: Present

Assume the company has asked you to present your findings to them. You may be asked to do an oral pitch presentation with slides and/or a written report. Often, firms will do both. Check with your instructor about the requirements for presenting your information and findings.

As a team, work together to compile your information into one cohesive report that you would submit to the company in a real-world situation.

12

Reports and Pitches

Two additional forms of business communication you will encounter in the working world are reports and pitches. In many companies, reports are extremely common; reports may be written in a variety of formats and styles. Occasionally, depending upon your position and company, you may be asked to pitch a product, proposal, or idea. The content in this chapter will help prepare you to write reports and prepare and deliver pitches. After completing this lesson, you will be able to:

- Identify formal and informal analytic and informative reports
- Compose reports
- Define a business pitch
- Create and deliver a business pitch

An Introduction to Reports

Business reports are a way to share information within a company. Most often, reports will be written documents, but occasionally you may be asked to orally deliver information, such as during a business meeting. Sometimes, people will orally report on a project (e.g., during a meeting or to their boss).

Reports are, at the most basic, a way to describe and deliver information. In a business setting, they are used to clearly and concisely provide information about events, issues or problems, projects, or occurrences in a company. They may be formal or informal and are informative or analytic. Common report types include:

- Progress
- Feasibility
- Personnel
- Expense
- Annual
- Meeting minutes

An informal progress report may be simply telling your boss about the events of the day or sending an email with those updates. A more formal report may detail the possibility of purchasing new office furniture or making a proposal to a new client. Because of the variety of report types, they may also be written in a variety of styles, including memo, email, and letter reports. Formal reports, such as a company's annual report, use a very stylized type of reporting that typically includes an abstract, table of contents, multiple parts, charts, graphs, tables, and more. Should you need to write a formal report, your company may have specific guidelines for you to follow or you can research the part of a formal report.

The progress report is one of the most common report types. A progress report updates a supervisor, manager, client, or other team members on the status of a project. The report may be formal or informal, depending upon the situation. Progress reports within a company allow managers to track projects, determine success and struggles so far, and step in to make adjustments and changes as needed. Internal progress reports keep teams connected and in alignment with project goals and increase the likelihood of successful project completion. External progress reports are reports sent to clients. They will provide updates on large projects, including timelines and cost projections. Such reports build and maintain trust between the company and client, which is essential to keeping customers.

The Progress Report

Preparation

This is the first phase when the team reviews the project. What were you asked to do? What have you done so far? What steps will you take next to complete the project on time? Consider any problems/successes you've had so far, how you've overcome them or how you plan to handle them.

Writing

Each team member should write several paragraphs about his/her tasks assigned, steps completed, and next steps. The team lead will compile and proof-read the progress report and review it with the team members. The report should include and introduction and conclusion reminding the reader of the project tasks and deadlines.

Editing

The progress report should have one voice (not sound like several people wrote different paragraphs). All team members should contribute to editing and proofreading the report before submission.

Figure 12.1 The Progress Report includes Preparation, Writing and Editing

Progress reports should do the following:

- Summarize the project/expectations
- Update the status of the project
- List steps completed

- Identify any problems or issues encountered
- List costs so far and cost projections, if relevant
- Estimate a completion date

Progress reports help teams and companies successfully complete projects.

Another common type of report is the personnel report. Often, the personnel report is a human resources document; it may be about assignments, benefits, or performance. Outside of human resources, many employees will be asked to provide feedback or evaluate coworkers at some point. In this case, a personnel report may be compared to a peer review; it is an assessment of another person's work and performance. Personnel reports may be useful to managers and supervisors when evaluating the success of projects and employees' work, including promotions.

Online resource: Please visit "Report purposes and types" by Susan Oaks

Assignment: Progress Report Email

For this assignment, you will write an email reporting on your team's progress regarding the a team project. You will use the email formatting discussed in class. The progress report team member is responsible for coordinating this portion of the project, editing and submitting the progress report.

Progress reports, also called activity or status reports, are common in the business world. They inform a supervisor, coworker, or client about the status of a project. The report may cover a variety of topics, including project design, steps taken, problems faced, monies spent so far, and the like. The report also indicates the next steps of the process, including any changes, predictions on timelines for completion, and projected budget going forward.

The progress report for this assignment will identify:

- The project you are working and why
- Who is assigned to which tasks
- Work each team member has completed
- Work each team member has yet to complete and next steps

The progress report should discuss any challenges or problems your team has faced so far and clearly identify steps you plan to take to complete the project by the assigned date. Each team member will contribute a section on their progress so far.

The report must include the following:

Introduction

State the purpose of the email and indicate what information will follow in the email.

Body

The following details must be included:

- Requirements of the project (cite/summarize from materials or class discussions)
- Work accomplished and problems encountered (including individual steps and specific detailsregarding how/when; discussion of problems and how they were overcome)
- Work remaining (including individual steps and specific plans regarding how/when)

Conclusion

Provide an honest overall assessment of your team's progress, including timelines, quality of work, and so on. Remember to close by stating whom readers should contact if they have follow-up questions.

Assignment: Write a Personnel Report Email

After you complete your team projects, you will submit a personnel report email to your professor. In this case, the personnel report is a reporting and evaluation of each team member's work and participation in the team projects over the course of the semester.

At various times in your career, you will have to provide feedback to peers or subordinates, such as in an annual performance review. Writing honestly, tactfully, and positively is essential to preparing personnel reviews and reports. In this case, the personnel report is a private document between you and your professor (your team members will not read it), but at other times, reports may be shared with other people, and tact is essential.

In this report, you will include the information detailed below. Use standard business email format, including a brief, detailed subject line. Do *not* include the information as an attachment; the email text will be the information.

Send Email

To:

Subject:

Message:

Greeting,

The introduction paragraph will state the purpose of your email. You will mention the assignment you completed, your leadership role, and provide an outline of information to follow in the body of the email.

The body paragraphs will include details about the following:

- Communication: How does your team communicate (e.g., group text, in class, email, etc.)? How is the group communicating? Are there any issues? If so, explain.
- Working in the team: How is the process so far? Is everyone participating as expected? Are deadlines being met? Explain.
- Meetings: List the date, time, place, duration of, and members present at meetings. Discuss the meeting process; has it been effective?
- Evaluate each team member: Provide a percentage score for each team member's contribution to the project.
- Contribution must be indicated by a percentage and must average out to 100% for the team.
- Contributions must be in 5% or 10% increments (85% or 90%, not 92.5%).
- A percentage of 0 must be given to a team member who did not participate

See the examples below:

Example 1:

Team member	Contribution
John	90%
Ali	110%
Shun	100%
Emmy	100%
	400/4

Example 2:

Individual	Contribution
Nischal	110%
Colin	90%
Karlee	110%
Yanran	90%
Chris	100% 500/5

Write at least 2–3 sentences about each person (including yourself) explaining the rating you assigned each team member. Provide specific, verifiable evidence for each person. For example:

- Ally was present for all of our team meetings and participated actively in our group text. She asked questions when she had them and responded to other team members' questions as well. Ally sent me the required information before the due date and made changes when I asked her to. For these reasons, I assigned Ally a 100% score.
- Sven attended two of our four team meetings; she texted us once to say she wouldn't be there, but the other time, she just didn't show up. Sometimes Sven responded to group texts. She sent me the required information a day after the due date, so I had to spend extra time incorporating her piece into the group project. Overall, I thought Sven could have been more involved, so I gave her an 80% score.

Provide a sense of closure; comment on your team overall and your feelings about working with this team so far, for example. Include a contact statement (whom to contact if the reader has any questions) and close with any goodwill statements as appropriate.

Type your name at the end

Include an email signature block

An Introduction to Pitches

In some positions and companies, you will be expected to sell products or ideas. Often, these presentations are called pitches. A pitch is basically a short presentation convincing others to accept your idea. The pitch may be to sell a product, garner funding for a new company, or convince a company to hire you. A pitch might be an advertising pitch to promote a new brand or product, or it might be pitching an idea to investors or trying to find funding. Pitches are common in sales, advertising, entrepreneurship, and writing. The pitch typically includes two parts: the oral pitch and the slide deck.

The oral portion of the pitch is when you present the product or idea. This is similar to an oral presentation (see chapter 18 for details about oral presentations). During the oral pitch, you clearly and concisely deliver persuasive information about your idea. The oral pitch is like an elevator speech for your business or idea (see chapter 16 for details about elevator speeches); it is short, anywhere from 3–10 minutes.

The basic structure of a pitch presentation is as follows:

1. Identify the problem and position your idea/suggestion/company as the solution.

2. Propose a solution; describe your solution as unique, and detail its features and benefits.

3. Identify the target/goal; show that you understand the audience's needs by addressing their needs with you as the solution.

4. Provide a timeline/schedule.

5. End with a call to action; ask the audience to act (e.g., provide funding, hire you, etc.).

The slide deck portion of your pitch follows these steps in visual format. See the infographic below for details about creating a slide deck for the Social Media project in this course.

Figure 12.2 A social media pitch presentation includes many elements.

Summing Up Unit II: Formats

After completing Unit II: Formats, you have an understanding of the standard business communication formats. Using these formats appropriately will ensure you present your best self in the workforce. After completing Unit II, you should be able to:

- Format and write effective business letters, memos, and emails
- Write bad-news messages
- Present yourself and information at a business meeting
- Understand reports and pitches
- Understand the characteristics of writing for the internet and social media

You may want to review the formats as the course progresses. For example, when completing team projects or job application documents, you may want to review the guidelines and suggestions discussed in the chapters in this unit. The formats and stylistic elements learned in this unit should be used throughout the course and in the business world.

Unit III

Preparing to Apply for a Job

As you near the end of your college career, you will be looking for a job. Finding a job can be a huge undertaking, requiring a lot of time, effort, and attention to detail. In Unit III, we will focus on a variety of skills that will help you stand out when applying for a job. You will learn about LinkedIn; writing a reference page, resume, and cover letter; and interviewing skills. Competition in the job market is fierce, but after completing this section, you will be prepared to find your ideal job.

13

LinkedIn

LinkedIn has become the largest professional networking site, with about 467 million total users and 106 million active users every month communicating in 24 different languages. LinkedIn has over three million active job listings, and hiring managers and recruiters are constantly looking for desirable candidates (Chaudhary, 2017).

Creating an effective profile on LinkedIn has been written about extensively and is reviewed in the article below. Here, the goal is to encourage you to use LinkedIn. Recruiters and hiring managers are more likely to see your profile and be interested in the skills and talents you have to offer if you are actively using LinkedIn.

Once you have an excellent profile, you need to actively use LinkedIn. Recruiters are most likely to spot people who are engaged and active on LinkedIn. The following activities will help you become active on LinkedIn. After completing this lesson, you will:

- Know how to share articles, photos, or videos on LinkedIn
- Connect with an alumnus to increase your network
- Understand how to request a recommendation
- Demonstrate your ability to recommend someone
- Network with other professionals

....

Reading 13.1

Write a LinkedIn Profile That Draws in Recruiters

By Samantha White

LinkedIn serves as a window into your professional capacity. The platform is used by employers to post vacancies and by recruiters to identify and approach suitable candidates. So it's worth investing time in your profile to create the right impression.

Duncan Brodie, FCMA, CGMA, a coach, trainer, and speaker at U.K.-based training provider Goals and Achievements, explains how to present your skills and experience to attract opportunities.

Use the Headline Section to Promote Skills

Many LinkedIn users dedicate valuable space in the headline area of their profile to describing their employer. Instead, they should focus on promoting their professional skills.

Brodie often coaches people for whom English is a second language. "I encourage them to mention that they are a multilingual accountant," he said. "Those language skills grab the attention of a recruiter and could potentially open up opportunities."

Another aspect to highlight in the headline area is the sectors in which you have experience. "Your headline might read 'Senior management accountant with 20 years' experience in FMCG/telecoms/public sector,'" Brodie said. "If you've worked internationally, include that, too.

"For members in practice, it's a good idea to mention how you benefit clients. For example, 'supporting SMEs to improve bottom-line profits', or to 'minimize tax liabilities.' Or, if you specialize in cost reduction or finance team transformation, talk about that."

Offer Clarity in the Summary

In the summary area, give a clear picture of your experience, skills, and management and leadership qualities.

"If you are not in a formal leadership position in your day-to-day work, mention something you do outside work which demonstrates these skills," Brodie said. "This could be something you're involved in a voluntary capacity."

The summary section is also the place to talk about your areas of expertise—are you good with budgeting and forecasting? Do you have expertise in foreign currency?

Information technology skills are increasingly important for accountants, so make sure you highlight these. Involvement in major business projects or accounting system implementations can help demonstrate your breadth of experience and perhaps differentiate you from everyone else, Brodie said.

"Recruiters will also be looking for the core management accounting skills," he said. Most management accounting jobs require experience with month-end reporting, budgeting, forecasting, balance sheet management, cash management, and working capital management. "You want to make sure that those terms are listed amongst your technical skills," Brodie said.

Nontechnical skills sought in management accounting job descriptions typically include good communication and presentation skills, the ability to build relationships with different parts of the business, negotiation, influencing, problem-solving, sound decision-making, and managing multiple deadlines.

"If you can get some of those terms into your summary, the chances of you being found by a recruiter will greatly increase," Brodie said.

The headline and summary sections of your LinkedIn profile are optimized for search engines, so using the right keywords in those areas will help recruiters and hiring managers with relevant vacancies find you. However, it's important not to overload your profile with keywords, as there's a danger it won't read naturally. Brodie encourages job seekers to adopt a conversational style.

"You might say something like: Qualified management accountant with 10 years' experience of monthly management accounts, budgets, and forecasts in X, Y, and Z sectors. Team player with proven track record of working successfully with nonfinance managers to improve financial control and risk management."

In the experience section, professionals should include every relevant role they have had. "Describe the role in one or two lines and then focus attention on your main achievements in the role," Brodie advised.

A high-quality photograph that shows you as a warm, friendly individual is essential to making the right impression, he said.

Line Up Strong Recommendations

Another part of your profile recruiters will focus on is the recommendations others have written about you. A handful of strong recommendations from a line manager and peers who have worked with you is better than a long list of them from acquaintances.

The quality-over-quantity approach also goes for your number of connections. If you receive a connection request from someone you don't know, look at the person's profile.

You may share an interest or a contact, or he or she may be a member of a group you're in. "If it's not clear why they want to connect, you can send a message that says, 'Thanks for reaching out…. What motivated you to make the connection request?'" Brodie said. "If they are genuine, they'll get back to you."

Maintain Your Profile

Brodie suggests users update their profile three or four times per year.

"If you have made a significant achievement in the past few months and had really positive feedback on it, you might add that to your key achievements in your summary. If you've recently switched sectors, you might add that sector to your headline after three months or so in the new role," he said.

Once your profile is polished, you can start to explore other aspects of the platform. "There are a lot of people sharing ideas and good content on there that you can actually learn from, for your personal development," Brodie said.

Join groups that are relevant to your profession, sector, or location. These are good ways to make new connections and raise your profile, particularly if you contribute to the discussion or respond to requests for advice.

And although posts help to keep your profile fresh, you don't necessarily have to create your own. Sharing other people's posts or endorsing them for a particular skill is another way to contribute to the network.

The original version of this article, "4 Ways to Write a LinkedIn Profile That Attracts Recruiters' Attention," by Senior Editor Samantha White, is available at tinyurl.com/jszzsxc.

Figure 13.1 LinkedIn Profile tips

Applying this Skill: LinkedIn Profile Self Review

Complete the rubric below to evaluate your LinkedIn profile. Complete each section.

Aspect of Profile	Developing	Advanced	Comments (What is good about your profile? What needs improvement?)
Required Sections			
Photo (a clear headshot with plain background)	Picture is missing or casual. Clothing is not industry appropriate. Quality of photo is poor. Background is distracting.	Business professional headshot. Photo is clear and shows face. Plain background is used.	
Headline (a memorable blurb about you in a professional context)	Missing or default headline.	Brief, informative, uses keywords, skills and interests that relate to career goals. Connects current position to future goals.	
Summary (concise, confident description of qualifications, goals and background)	Missing or minimal information.	Describes current status, relevant skills, interests, coursework or experiences. Connects background to position, goals or industry. Uses action, key or industry specific words.	
Education (schools, dates attended, degree, field of study, activities and memberships, GPA (opt))	Missing or minimal information.	All information included with relevant details and experiences.	

Experience (work and/or activities with bullet points to describe tasks and accomplishments)	Missing or minimal information. Statements do not describe tasks or duties of position. No action statements used; accomplishments /results were not quantified.	All company information included. Statements clearly describe tasks, duties, transferrable skills. Accomplishments/results quantified.	
Spelling/Grammar	Many and noticeable errors in spelling, grammar, verb tense, pronouns, punctuation etc.	No errors in spelling, grammar, verb tense, pronouns, punctuation etc.	
Recommended Sections			
Organizations (clubs or organizations in or outside of school)	Missing or minimal information.	Complete listing of clubs or organizations with descriptions of activities within each organization.	
Volunteer Experience	Missing or minimal information.	Information is given to validate skills, interests and abilities.	
Skills & Expertise	Missing or minimal information.	At least 5 skills listed.	
Honors & Awards	Missing or minimal information.	Complete listing of honors and awards.	
Courses	Missing or minimal information.	Complete listing of relevant courses that highlight skills and interests.	
Projects	Missing or minimal information.	Complete listing of relevant projects that highlight skills and interests.	

Recommendatio ns	Missing or minimal information.	Several recommendations from a variety of people (managers, professors, classmates, co-workers)	
Connections (connect with members of your MKTG 333 group)	Few or no connections.	Over 250 connections.	
Groups (join at least 2 groups, including SCSU Current students & alumni Group)	No group memberships.	Many group memberships.	
Companies (follow 3 companies that could be potential employers)	Not following any companies.	Following companies relevant to industry and interests.	
Overall assessment of Profile			

Assignment 1: Sharing Ideas, Questions, Articles, and Links

For Assignment 1, you will post and comment on an article, link, video, or idea. In this assignment, you are not writing an article. You will post content, summarize it, and comment on it.

From your homepage:

1. Sign in to your LinkedIn account.

2. At the top of your homepage, click the "Share an article, photo, video, or idea" field.

3. Type your summary and comment into the text box. Attach the URL link for the article on which you are commenting.

4. Click "Post."

From a partner page:

1. Sign in to your LinkedIn account.

2. On the article page, click the "LinkedIn" icon and complete the following options.

3. Click "share."

Remember to include your own summary and comment.

Assignment 2: Requesting Advice from an Alumnus

For Assignment 2, connect with an alumnus from you school using the LinkedIn search or groups features. Ask that person for some advice about your career search/field of study or the person's career path. Alumni are usually happy to help students from their alma mater.

1. Sign in to your LinkedIn account.

2. Locate an alumnus working in the field or at a company where you would like to work when you graduate.

3. Send a message to the alum to introduce yourself and ask a question.

4. Make a screen capture of the sent message (and responses, if you receive any before the assignment is due).

5. Submit the screen capture electronically.

Assignment 3: Asking for a Recommendation

For Assignment 3, you will ask someone to recommend you on your LinkedIn page. Recommendations are important to help recruiters see and value your skills.

1. Sign in to your LinkedIn account.

2. Identify a coworker, mentor, friend, and so on who may write a good recommendation for you. On your connection's profile page, click the "More" icon in the top section of the profile.

3. Select "Request a Recommendation."

4. Fill out the "Relationship" and "Position at the time" fields.

5. Add a short comment (2–4 sentences) that personalizes your message. Explain your situation, and remind the person of where you worked together. Be gracious, and say thank you.

6. Make a screen capture of the request.

7. Submit the screen capture electronically.

NOTE: This recommendation activity is not the same as endorsing someone's skills on LinkedIn.

Assignment 4: Writing a Recommendation

For Assignment 4, you will write a recommendation for someone you know. Consider recommending a coworker, classmate, or committee or organization member. Write a brief paragraph or two explaining the person's skills and talents.

1. Sign in to your LinkedIn account.

2. Identify a coworker, mentor, friend, and so on who you want to write a recommendation for. On your connection's profile page, click the "More" icon in the top section of the profile.

3. Select "Recommend."

4. Fill out the following prompts.

5. Personalize the message by entering text in the message field.

6. Make a screen capture of the recommendation.

7. Submit the screen capture electronically.

Assignment 5: Connect with a Classmate

For Assignment 5, you will send a connection request to a classmate. The people you are in school with are also the business people you may work with in the future. Developing relationships now will improve your future career.

1. Sign in to your LinkedIn account.

2. Identify someone in one of your classes.

3. Select the "Connect" icon.

4. Customize your connection request.

5. Make a screen capture of the connection request.

6. Submit the screen capture electronically.

Assignment 6: Join a Group

For Assignment 6, you will ask to join one of the many groups on LinkedIn. Being a member of a group allows you to connect with other members of the group and demonstrates your interest in the area.

1. Sign into your LinkedIn account.

2. Type keywords (major, areas of interest, schools) into the search bar.

3. Filter results by clicking "Groups."

4. Click the group you're interested in.

5. Click "Request to join."

6. Make a screen capture of the connection request.

7. Submit the screen capture electronically.

14

Job Application Documents

References and Resumes

When applying for a job, two of the essential documents are a reference sheet and a resume. A reference sheet lists the names of people a company may call to ask about you: your performance, personality, traits, and habits. You will want to carefully select the people you list as references and carefully format your reference sheet. A resume is a brief summary of your education, experience, skills/accomplishments, and activities. A perfect resume is essential to getting an interview with a company. Many recruiters will eliminate your resume based on a single spelling or grammar mistake. It is important that these documents be perfect so you shine as the great candidate you are. After completing this lesson, you will:

- Identify people to act as references
- Have created a professional reference sheet
- Identify elements of a professional resume
- Have created a professional resume

Assignment: Job Application Packet

One goal of this course is to help you have a completed job application packet ready to use for internship or job searches. By the end of the course, you will have a professional:

- Resume
- Reference sheet
- Cover/job application letter

The activities in Chapters 14 and 15 will help you prepare your job application documents. As assigned by your professor, submit the documents listed above and your internship or job posting to complete the Job Application Packet assignment. (Save the job posting; you will need it several times during the course.)

The Job Application Packet assignment will collect all of your job application documents into one portfolio. After receiving feedback on your reference sheet, resume, and cover letter, you should make changes and edits before submitting the final documents in the Job Application Packet. The final Job Application Packet will include:

- Reference sheet
- Resume
- Job Application/cover letter
- Copy of the job advertisement/posting to which all documents are targeted

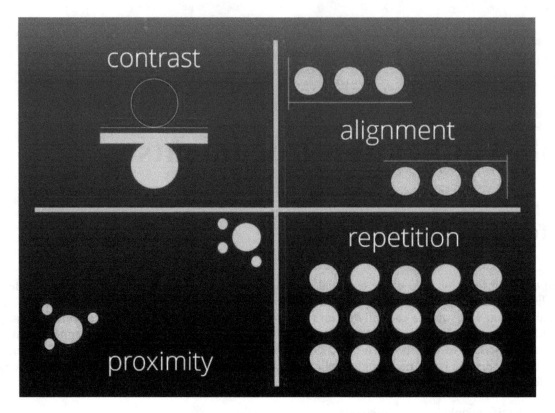

Figure 14.1 CRAP Elements

Enhance Your Writing with Graphic Elements

By Paul R. Timm and Sherron Bienvenu

Four Basic Design Principles

As we develop graphic elements in our documents, we need to be aware of four key principles:

- Contrast.
- Repetition.
- Alignment.

- Proximity.

Contrast

Contrast has to do with the variances in such things as typefaces (fonts) and other graphic elements. The simple rule for effective contrast is that it must be significantly distinctive. If, for example, you wear a navy blue blazer with dark grey slacks, you are not showing much contrast. In fact, people may have to look closely to see if they are really different colors. The same navy blazer with khaki slacks exhibits dramatic contrast. In other words, contrast needs to be significant. Little contrast provides no advantages. Look, for example at the two business cards below. Which grabs your attention better?

| **Influential Consulting**
Adam W. Young

916 Old River Road
Buffalo, NY 14602
(801) 422-1212 | **Influential Consulting**
Adam W. Young

916 Old River Road
Buffalo, NY 14602
(716) 555-1212 |

Figure 14.1.1 **Examples of Contrast in Design.**

Contrast needs to be significant, not subtle.

On a simple list, contrast in fonts can help categorize ideas for better reader comprehension. The list below illustrates this.

List without contrast:

CD ROMs

—Children's CDs

—Educational CDs

—Entertainment CDs

Educational

—Early learning

—Language arts

—Science

—Math

Teacher Tools

—Books

—Teacher guides

—Videos

Same list using simple contrast to categorize:

- CD ROMs

    o Children's CDs
    o Educational CDs
    o Entertainment CDs

- Educational

    o Early learning
    o Language arts
    o Science
    o Math

- Teacher Tools

    o Books
    o Teacher guides
    o Videos

Although this principle is simple, it can be a powerful way to enhance reader comprehension. To recap, apply these principles to create graphic contrast:

- Avoid elements on the page that are merely *similar*.
- If the elements (type, color, size, line thickness, shape, space, etc.) are not the *same*, make them *very* different.
- Contrast is often the most important visual attraction on a page.

Repetition

The second basic design principle is repetition. This element involves consistency of design. Check documents to be sure they:

- Repeat the same *visual elements* of the design throughout the piece.
- Repeat color, shape, texture, spatial relationships, line thicknesses, sizes, etc.
- Use repetition to develop the *organization*, strengthen the *unity*, and add *visual interest*.

Inconsistent design and layout distracts readers and damages your professionalism. Always re-check visual elements and ask for feedback from others. Specifically, ask a trusted associate (preferably one with an eye for detail) to review your document checking for consistency.

Alignment

Be conscious of where you place elements on the printed page. Find something to align with. If you have a graphic or illustration, consider how text should be associated with it. You may choose to "wrap" around an illustration or use a standard point of "justification" (the margin line your text follows). Word-processing software provides four choices in justification: left, center, right, or "full" (which aligns both left and right by adding spaces as needed to fill out the line).

Avoid using more than one text alignment on the page (don't center some text and right-align other text). Also, use center justification sparingly. It can be effective but often comes across as unimaginative, harder to read. The ad for construction workers shown below uses center justification (among other design flaws) and appears busy and confusing.

Figure 14.1.2 **An Example of Bad Alignment.**

See how this same ad could be cleaned up using better justification and eliminating unnecessary graphic elements:

Figure 14.1.3 **An Example of Good Alignment.**

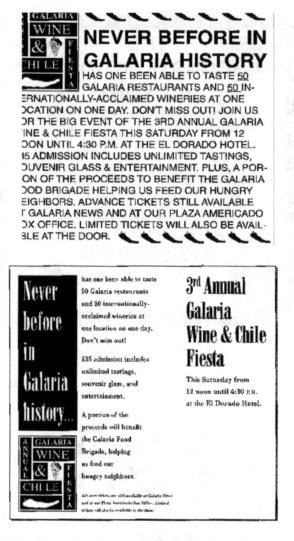

Figure 14.1.4 **Examples of Good (bottom) and Bad (top) Proximity.**

The other rules for alignment can be summarized as follows:

- Nothing should be placed on the page arbitrarily. Think about ease of reading, consistency, and appropriate contrast.
- Alignment creates a clean, sophisticated, fresh look.
- Every element should have some visual connection with another element on the page.

    This last point leads to the final basic design element, proximity.

Proximity

Readers often need to be shown how points in your document relate to each other. Proximity involves grouping related items close together. These grouped items then become one visual unit rather than several separate units. This helps organize information and reduces clutter.

    To illustrate the principle of proximity, look at the two advertisements below. The first does little to group elements, making it difficult for the reader to dig out the meat of the message. The second uses the principle of proximity to associate related information.

The design ideas we have shared in this section are, of course, very basic. If you produce documents requiring more sophisticated design, we encourage you to involve professional artists. That said, these ideas can improve even your routine documents. Keep in mind the four principles of contrast, repetition, alignment, and proximity (you can make that into an acronym if you like!), and you will enhance the impact and professionalism of your written documents.

Notes

1 Chip Heath and Dan Heath, *Made To Stick: Why Some Ideas Survive and Others Die*, New York: Random House, 2007.
2 Heath and Heath, p. 209.
3 Neither author is an attorney and this information does not purport to be legal advice. It is based on wide experience, however, and is intended to provide some commonsense guidelines.
4 See, for example, Scott Tambert, *How To Use Images Legally* (available online at www.pdimages.com/law/). Tambert is a specialist in public domain images research. He is not a lawyer, and you should always seek competent, professional counsel on legal matters. www.pdimages.com/web9.htm.

Reading 14.2

Line Up Your Personal and Professional References

By Diane Huth

Every employer is going to ask for references, so be prepared with a list of both personal and professional references before an employer asks for them. They will include your mentors, plus current and former employers, colleagues, vendors, customers, professors, colleagues from organizations you volunteer with. Select people who will write and say glowing things about you. Before you actively start your job search, call or talk with each of your mentors and ask if they will be willing to serve as a reference for you.

Once your mentors say yes to serving as a reference, make sure you have their contact information, which includes name, title, phone number, email and physical address. Create a nicely-formatted Word document with your contact information in the header or footer, and title it "References for <your name>." List each reference with contact information, and a brief one-sentence description of how you know or have worked with each person. Examples of suitable descriptions include:

- Served on the Board of the AMA chapter together from 2014–2016
- Direct supervisor at XYZ Corporation; can attest to my team work skills and attention to detail
- Ad agency account executive; worked together on the XYZ account

- Youth Ministry Pastor of XYZ church; worked together to host the summer Vacation Bible Camp in 2015
- Professor of Marketing for 3 courses from 2015–2016; can speak to my work ethic and dedication to my passion for marketing
- Customer from 2010–2013; provided accounting services to his family-run landscaping business Business executive, longtime family friend; familiar with personal background and values

Take several copies of this list of references to your job interview. If the company seems interested, leave one copy with the HR director. Keep one handy to use in filling out the Job Application, which they will probably ask you to complete, even though they have your detailed resume.

Save the file in both Word and PDF format, so you can forward it to your HR contact with a follow-up email to thank them for your interview.

TIP—Shortcut to Filling Out the Job Application Form

Even through you may have already filled out an online application, HR will undoubtedly ask you to fill out a long and tedious hard copy application form during an in-person interview. What they really need is your signature giving them the legal right to contact former employers for references and to perform credit and criminal background searches. So shortcut the application by filling out just the contact information, Social Security number (make sure you have it memorized), anything that's NOT on your resume or list of references, and signing and dating the application. Write in pen *"See attached résumé"* on all sections covered by your résumé. Then attach your resume and list of references to the application with a paperclip (which you will bring in your briefcase) and hand it in to HR. It will look much better than trying to hand-write lots of information into too-tiny spaces, and your application will be clean and neat. Five minutes and you're done!

Let Each Reference Know to Expect a Call—And Coach Them On a Suggested Response

After sharing the list of references with a prospective employer, call each listed reference and let them know that they may receive a call asking for a reference. Tell them something like, *"I just applied for a job at XYZ corporation working in social media marketing for their automobile insurance division, and I listed you as a reference. Hopefully, you will get a phone call. If you do hear from them, I'd really appreciate it if you mentioned what a good job we did together on the Jones account last year and how we grew sales by 27%."*

You don't want them to just say, *"Yeah, she worked for me—I don't remember when."* You can benefit from reminding them of dates, stats accomplishments, and specifics that they can mention so their talking points will be fresh on their mind.

Lastly, ask them to give you a quick call if they DO get contacted by HR to let you know specific questions they asked, if they appeared to have any concerns or interest, and what your reference said about you. It will help you gauge how likely you are to get an offer.

TIP—Understand What Former Employers May and May Not Say About You

In today's litigious society, employers are hesitant to say too much or too little about you for fear of being sued. Each state has a different law about what can and cannot be disclosed in response to a request for employment verification, from almost nothing to a great deal of information—some of which you may not want revealed. If a prospective employer calls an HR department, the information they will receive is limited. The most they might receive is confirmation of:

- Whether or not you were ever employed by the company
- Your title or position
- Your dates of employment
- Your compensation level—confirmation of what you stated you earned
- Whether or not you are eligible to be rehired—it's the legal way to find out if you were fired or left in bad standing

TAKEAWAY—Your list of references is very important because it gets beyond the barrier of the HR department to put a prospective employer in touch with someone who will give you a rave review.

TO DO LIST:

- Make a list of professional and personal references and have on hand at or after an interview.
- Include name, current contact information, and info on how you worked together in the past.
- Call or email to get permission to use each as a reference before finalizing the list.
- Call each reference when you expect a company to check your references to coach them on dates and key projects and achievements.

Assignment: Develop a Reference Sheet

An effective reference sheet includes 3–5 people who will speak well about you and your performance. Identify 3–5 people who would act as references for you. Create a reference sheet. Use appropriate header formatting, including your name and contact information. Your contact information should include your name, city and state, phone number, email address, and LinkedIn url. Companies today do not expect to see your street address, due to privacy concerns, but they do expect to see your LinkedIn url. Use the CRAP design elements discussed earlier in the chapter in reading 14.1 to effectively format your reference page.

Pre-Job Search Social Media Review

According to the Society for Human Resource Management, a majority of employers review candidates' social media content during the hiring process and, for many, the content they find affects whether or not they hire a specific candidate.

Your social media presence can help or hurt you in your job search. Since social media tends to be personal, it gives a company a good sense of who you are and whether or not you will be a good fit for the company. Having an attractive social media presence is important to getting the job you want.

Companies most often check LinkedIn, Facebook, and Twitter. LinkedIn, as a career networking site, is the most commonly viewed; on this site, you must create a professional image that highlights your accomplishments. Facebook, Twitter, and Instagram are more personal cites that companies use to get a sense of your personality.

Help companies see you as an excellent candidate by doing the following:

- Display a professional image with your photo and posts

- Post about your professional qualifications

- Demonstrate your accomplishments and creativity.

Recruiters admit to looking for reasons to support a candidate, so be sure to give them those reasons.

Some aspects of social media are warning signs to recruiters, however, and certain postings may disqualify you from employment consideration. Some of the warning signs to recruiters include:

- No presence or all accounts are private

- Posting negative info or controversial topics

If you have no social media presence, it may look like you have something to hide or nothing to show off and be proud of. About half of employers won't call a candidate if they can't find that person online. Companies do understand personal and professional social media accounts and are not concerned if some of your accounts are private. However, companies are interested in how you interact on social media. Using social media to build relationships and show your professional contributions shows engagement and professionalism. If you follow industry leaders or relevant groups, you demonstrate interest in the field. Creating and sharing content also allows you to share knowledge.

Avoid posting negative information or about controversial topics. Employers view the following types of content negatively:

- photos or videos that are provocative or inappropriate

- negative comments about people or companies you worked for or with

- discriminatory comments

sharing of confidential information

drinking and drug use

- criminal behavior

- poor communication skills

- an unprofessional screen name or other social media image

To improve your social media presence, review your current social media use. Then, improve your profiles by:

- Use keywords on LinkedIn and in posts to increase your searchability

- Make connections

- Edit your posts and profiles to eliminate spelling and grammar errors, controversial topics and profanity

- Participate in online conversations

- Post about your field of study or area of interest

Applying this Skill: Pre-Job Search Self Social Media Review

Most companies will look at candidates social media accounts during the job search, so having an attractive social media presence is important to getting the job you want. Follow the steps below to review your social media presence. Discuss your findings with your group.

General

- Google yourself.

  o Who can find you online and where can they find you?

- Which social media platforms do you use?

  o Are they professional or personal?
  o Are they public or private?
  o Are you active online?
  o Is your content professional?

- What first impression do you create online?

Facebook

A personal account may be used to promote your job search. Consider the following:

- Use professional profile photo
- Post about professional accomplishments
- "Like" companies you want to work for

Twitter

Twitter is often used professionally to broadcast content about your job search and field of study. Consider the following:

- Your bio

    - Be brief (166 characters max)
    - Use real name
    - Use keywords
    - Include college name, graduation, awards/activities

- As a job search tool

    - Follow people in your field
    - Re-tweet industry posts/articles

EXAMPLE

Kendrick Mossl

555 Birch Avenue South
Maple Lake, MN 55555
555-555-5555-|email@gmail.com| www.linkedin.com/in/url

References

Christian Crawford, CFO
Company Motors Inc.
555 555 Street NW
Clearwater, WI 55555
(555) 555-5555
Email@company.com

Relationship: Christian Crawford is currently the CFO that I assist with the day-to-day accounting within the company. Please speak to Christian regarding my experience and skills in the accounting department.

Annika Sheldon, Accounting Instructor
Unviersity of Minnesota- Duluth
555 Northway Drive
Duluth, MN 55555
(555) 555-5555
Email@company.com

Relationship: Annika Sheldon was my one of my accounting instructors. Please speak to her regarding my content knowledge, work ethic, and performance in the classroom.

Reis Cochran, Owner/President
Company Inc.
555 5th Avenue South
Buffalo, MN 55555
(555) 555-5555
Email@company.com

Relationship: Reis Cochran was my boss when I worked at Company Inc. for two years. Please ask Reis about my communication and problem-solving skills.

Table 14.1 Reference Page Example

Reading 14.3

Resumes and Portfolios for New Graduates

How to Showcase Potential

By Michelle A. Riklan

Today's Traditional Resume

Resume writers and career coaches can apply a variety of techniques and strategies to create relevant and effective resumes for fresh graduates.

Tie action verbs with numbers and statistics of the applicant's work performance. Many fresh graduates have worked in a retail or food business during at least one point in their college lives. It may be the only job experience that some graduates have. Unfortunately, job descriptions for retail and service jobs don't always translate well into the applicant's target industry.

What resume writers can do is translate unrelated job experience into relatable tasks and quantified information. Figures and specifics are more impressive than standard job descriptions for roles such as retail clerk or fast-food counter person. And even when specific performance results are not available, the numbers speak for themselves to verify the candidate's experiences and abilities.

Example for a store clerk: Part of five-person team that generated more than $30,000 in average daily sales.

Example for a fast-food associate: Worked in a fast-paced customer-service role assisting more than 1,000 customers each day.

Focus on the skills employers want. According to the previously referenced CareerBuilder survey, employers hire candidates who have the ability to communicate clearly, solve difficult problems, and think well under pressure. As career professionals, we need to find a way to translate our clients' skills and college education into those sought-after attributes.

According to Jaime S. Fall, Vice President of HR Policy Association, *"[fresh graduates]are very good at finding information, but not as good at putting that information into context."* He agrees that this generation is very good with technology, but adds that they're not that good in applying those skills in the real world of business.

We can help fresh graduates disprove this common belief by adding to their resumes a variety of accomplishments from undergraduate work experience, volunteer work, and extra-curricular activities. Try to emphasize situations where research skills and technological savvy were used to solve conflicts and demonstrate the ability to make logical decisions based on presented facts.

Example: Created an online check-out system for the Architecture Library, allowing users to process their own returns and saving more than four hours of staff time each week.

Example: Identified five potential new product lines to help local retailer attract more business from college students. Performed detailed marketing, sales, and profit analysis of each product and assisted owner in introducing two promising lines. Both products outperformed projections by at least 10 per cent in first six months.

Check to be sure the resume is well-written and easy to understand. Employers want candidates who can communicate well. The resume is where the employer will first check the candidate's communication skills, so it should be flawless.

The resume should also be written in the language and technical jargon of the job applicant's target industry, but it shouldn't read like a science or technology journal. Relevant certifications, memberships, and technical skills should be included to demonstrate the applicant's familiarity with the job and industry, but the resume should be easily understand by the average (non-technical) reader.

Highlight extra-curricular, volunteer, and other activities relevant to the position. If the applicant hasn't held a single internship or job before graduating from college, including the "extras" is one of the best ways to showcase his experience to potential employers.

Participation in clubs, volunteer efforts, and professional organizations shows dedication, responsibility, and willingness to learn. An affiliation with professional organizations related to the target job also counts as a plus to the job applicant's credentials and work experience, especially if he's done anything to improve the organization.

This is certainly an area where a professional resume writer or career coach can assist the graduate. Often, fresh graduates do not realize that their contributions had value. But experiences such as managing events, helping with fund-raisers, performing marketing activities, leading teams, engaging volunteers, communicating with school administrators, representing the organization to the press, and other activities can demonstrate a wide range of valuable
skills.

These activities, when well positioned, will elevate the resume of a fresh graduate from *total newbie* to *valuable intern* or *potential asset* in the eyes of recruiters. Take a look:

Example of fund-raising leadership: Chaired annual fund-raising event that generated more than $10K in support of arts enrichment program in local schools. Led a team of seven volunteers and managed all marketing, publicity, social media, and media relations.

Example of extra-curricular activity: Helped start the school's first table tennis club. Built awareness through public speaking and social media outreach. Negotiated with school administrators for use of facility and purchase of equipment. Published monthly newsletter. Set up tournaments and secured prize donations from local merchants. Attracted 30 players weekly and 80+ for year-end tournament.

The Rise of Unconventional Resumes

The traditional resume is still an effective and expected part of the application process. But in a competitive employment market, all job applicants—and especially fresh graduates—need to consider unconventional and creative approaches to capture attention. By extension, career professionals need to get creative, too. We need to stay on top of changing trends and be prepared to create additional documents to help graduates make a stronger case for their credentials.

Portfolios—The 21st Century Resume

Four out of five employers agree that electronic portfolios can increase the chances for an applicant's resume to get noticed. Why do fresh graduates need a portfolio when they haven't had actual professional work? Portfolios are a big deal, especially for creative and design work, because they are the physical manifestation of the applicant's creativity, technical knowledge, and professional skills. A portfolio provides supporting evidence of a candidate's skills, knowledge, GPA, coursework, and all the claims in her resume.

Writers and media practitioners can assemble a portfolio in the form of websites, clips, and press releases submitted to other publications. Published work is proof that the applicant does have the communication skills, research abilities, and technical know-how to work in the media and communications business.

For graduates of computer sciences and programming, their portfolio may come in the form of written programs, codes, and apps. Their digital portfolio could be their website or their app store.

For some industries, the portfolio might not be a literal portfolio or collection of completed works. Instead, it could be a collection of achievements, awards, journals published, studies, and distinctions.

The portfolio can be included in the traditional resume in a number of ways: URLs (live links) or scannable QR codes can be embedded in the resume, allowing an instantaneous link to the candidate's digital portfolio. In addition, details of the portfolio can be mentioned in the resume through listings of projects, programs, publications, and other distinctions.

Video Resumes—An Enhancement to the Traditional Resume

Please note, video resumes can't and shouldn't replace formal resumes and should not be used to tell the applicant's entire story. That would make the video resume too long and probably not very interesting! But a video resume can be a good supplement to a traditional resume and a way for the applicant to reveal personality as well as talents and skills.

A video resume should be short, ideally no longer than five minutes. Its purpose is to showcase the applicant's communication skills in a way that's not possible with a text-only resume. Aside from that, it could also be used to share creative materials, pitch a quick idea, and showcase the applicant's research skills by demonstrating knowledge of the company.

Career professionals can help their clients create compelling video resumes by evaluating what to present in the video, writing or editing the script, and coaching on presentation.

Each Resume Gets Only 5–7 Seconds

A recent survey from The Ladders (2012) reveals that recruiters spend an average of six seconds reviewing a resume, while another study from BeHiring (as quoted by Dr. John Sullivan on ere.net, 2013) says the time is five to seven seconds.

Considering this, the challenge faced by fresh graduates who don't have much experience rises. Of course, career professionals face the same pressure—How can we give fresh graduates a fighting chance when we have only six seconds to make an impression on their behalf? The answer lies in the numbers. According to TheLadders survey, about four seconds of the six-second interval is focused on four key areas of the resume:

Job titles

Previous companies

Start and end dates of employment

Education

The best approach, then, is to use Parts 1–3 of the resume (as listed above) to highlight internships, volunteer activities, related projects, and portfolio—all of the things that fresh graduates have to offer, written in language the potential employer can relate to.

References

Chronicle of Higher Education and American Public Media's Marketplace. *The Role of Higher Education in Career Development: Employer Perceptions* (2012). http://chronicle.com/items/biz/pdf/Employers %20 Survey.pdf

More Employers Finding Reasons Not to Hire Candidates on Social Media, Finds CareerBuilder Survey (2013). CareerBuilder.com. http:// cb.com/18kvlj1 http://www.hrpolicy.org/

Sullivan, John. *Why You Can't Get a Job ... Recruiting Explained by the Numbers* (2013). Ere.net. http://www.ere.net/2013/05/20/why-you-can'tget-a-job-recruiting-explained-by-the-numbers/

TheLadders.com. *You have Six Seconds to Make an Impression: How Recruiters See Your Resume* (2012). http://info.theladders.com/our-team/ you-only-get-6-seconds-of-fame-make-it-count

Assignment: Write a Resume

Write a resume.. Bring the rough resume to class for peer review and activities. Then, following feedback, edit your resume, incorporating changes you think are most effective for your situation.

Transferrable Skills

Job hunting often means you are looking for a different field in which to work. Maybe you are a college student looking for their first professional job, or maybe you are making a mid-career shift. Whatever the situation, identifying your transferrable skills is essential to your job search success.

Transferrable skills are skills you develop in one position that can be used and applied in other positions. Sometimes these skills are called "soft" skills. Some common transferrable skills include:

- Communication
- Active listening
- Computer skills
- Customer service
- Interpersonal skills
- Leadership
- Management skills
- Problem-solving
- Time management

These skills are transferrable because they are valuable in many positions. In contrast, a task is a job or duty specific to one job or field. For example, loading boxes at a shipping company is a task; you're not likely to need that in a task in a human resources position. Working in a fast-paced environment, or working with a team of co-workers, however, are skills you might use in human resources, so they are transferrable skills. Examples of tasks include:

- Delivered meals
- Sprayed weeds
- Fixed cars

Often, the tasks done in one position will help you develop transferrable skills that you will apply in your next job. By delivering meals you might develop oral communication skills by talking to people; or you might have worked independently while spraying weeds. To create the most effective resume you can, highlighting the transferrable skills you developed is important.

Applying this Skill: Resumes: Tasks vs Skills

Determine if the following phrases are task related or skill related. If they are task related, rewrite them to highlight transferrable skills.

1. Customer Interaction

2. Display strong motivation and initiative by completing tasks by specific deadlines

3. Patrolling around campus and providing safety to campus

4. Promote Husky baseball through merchandise sales

5. Finish products in a timely manner

6. Use exceptional attention to detail to create extremely clean cars

7. Serve food to customers while delivering my warmest hospitality

8. Developed strong interpersonal communication skills by providing quality service to customers

Applying This Skill: Student Resume Analysis: Find the Error

In your small group, review the resumes on the following pages. Order the resumes from best to worst and create a list of reasons for your decision. Indicate any changes you would make on the best resume(s). Bonus: Several semesters ago, students turned in these resumes. I was disappointed with all the students' work. On the best resume, I found an error that made me return all the resumes without grading them. Can you find the error that made me return all the resumes?

ERIC DONNAL

500 first Ave. S, Lawrence Hall #333
Saint Cloud , MN, 56301
edxxxl @stcloudstate.ed u
651-555-5555

EDUCATION:

Saint Cloud State University, St Cloud, M N   Expected May 2018
- Third year student
- International Business
- GPA 3.69

EXPERIENCE:

St. Cloud State University, St. Cloud, M N
- Community Advisor, residential life   August 2015- May 2016
                                               August 2016 -May 2017
- Conference Crew Manager   May 2016 -August 2016

Volunteer-
- Volunteered to cook in Anna Maries   Feb 9, 2015
- Volunteered to teach Basic English Language in Jalim Bihani Primary School
  and Arunodaya Academy for the primary level students, in Nepal.
                                               June 2013- Aug 2013

AFFILIATIONS AND ACTIVITIES
- College Senator position for Student Government   Aug 2016 – May 2017
- Public relation officer for the club Student Organized for Change (SOC Club).
                                                      October 2015
- Member of Nepalese Student Association (NSA).   August 2014 - present

ADDITIONAL SKILLS
- Communication, Counseling/ Advising, Customer Service, Dependable,
  Teaching/Training, Working in Teams
- **Computer Skills:** Software packages- MS PowerPoi nt, MS Word, MS Excel.
- **Language Skills:** Fluent in English, Nepali and Hindi.

ACTIVITIES AND ACHIEVEMENTS
- Got into **Dean's list** du ring the first semester and forth semester of college
                                               December 2014, May 2016
- Got acknowledged by Residential Life for **Academic Achievement** during my
  first semester.   December 2014

RESUME ANALYIS EXAMPLE 2
Rate 1 2 3 4 5

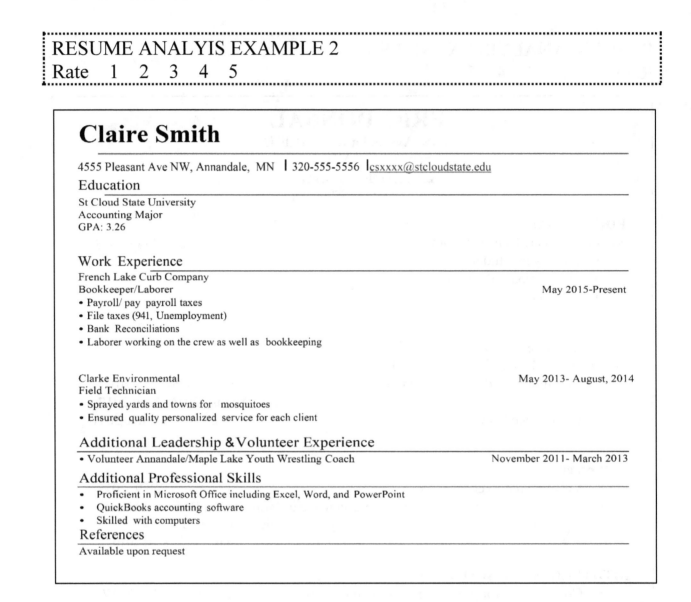

Claire Smith

4555 Pleasant Ave NW, Annandale, MN | 320-555-5556 | csxxxx@stcloudstate.edu

Education

St Cloud State University
Accounting Major
GPA: 3.26

Work Experience

French Lake Curb Company
Bookkeeper/Laborer   May 2015-Present
- Payroll/ pay payroll taxes
- File taxes (941, Unemployment)
- Bank Reconciliations
- Laborer working on the crew as well as bookkeeping

Clarke Environmental   May 2013- August, 2014
Field Technician
- Sprayed yards and towns for mosquitoes
- Ensured quality personalized service for each client

Additional Leadership & Volunteer Experience

- Volunteer Annandale/Maple Lake Youth Wrestling Coach   November 2011- March 2013

Additional Professional Skills

- Proficient in Microsoft Office including Excel, Word, and PowerPoint
- QuickBooks accounting software
- Skilled with computers

References

Available upon request

RESUME ANALYIS EXAMPLE 3
Rate   1   2   3   4   5

MARIE R. ANDERSON
5555 5 Ave • International Falls, MN 56649 • (555) 455-555 • maXXXX@STCLOUDSTATE.EDU

EDUCATION

BACHELOR'S OF SCIENCE, FINANCE   **Anticipated Graduation May 2017**
St. Cloud State University (SCSU), St. Cloud, MM
- Program nationally accredited by the Association to Advance Collegiate Schools of Business (AACSB)
- Recipient of Presidential Academic Scholarship
- Working over 24 hours bi-weekly while attending college full-time.
- 3.57 Cumulative GPA

STUDY ABROAD EXPERIENCE

PROPERTY SALES & COMMUNITY RELATIONS INTERN   **January 2016- May 2016**
First National Real Estate, Mosman, NSW Australia

- Compared a property with similar properties that were recently sold to determine a competitive market place
- Promoted sales of properties through advertisements, open houses, and participation in multiple listing services
- Developed and maintained a database of stored procedures, views and functions for hosted web applications

EMPLOYMENT

BUSINESS ADVISING DESK RECEPTIONIST   March 2015-
St. Cloud State University, St. Cloud, MN   Present

- Provide assistance to students to meet with an advisor
- Arrange records to increase functionality of the working environment and confidentiality of student files
- Manage office operations, including mail and a staff of five with a result to increase productivity

SERVER/BARTENDER   May 2016-
Cha Cha Resort, International Falls, MN   Present

- Identify customers' needs and problem-solve accordingly, using quick-thinking and strong judgment
- Display excellent work ethic and customer-focus during high-traffic shifts
- Demonstrate a positive attitude is high pressure situations to increase colleague morale and improve teamwork, resulting in stronger customer service overall

SERVER   May 2014-July 2015
Bond's Resort, Baudette, MN

- Developed strong interpersonal communication skills by providing quality service to thousands of restaurant customers
- Accepted credit card payments and worked with P.O.S registers to accurately secure payment and funds
- Learned how to multi-task and handle pressure of a fast-paced work environment in a professional manner

EXTRACURRICULAR EXPERIENCE

ADMINISTRATIVE OFFICER / SOCIAL COORDINATOR   **August 2016-Present**
Herberger Business School Investment Club
- Plan social gatherings for group members to get to know one and other better
- Send emails regarding what our meetings concluded to keep members updated

ADDITIONAL SKILLS

- Experience with Microsoft Office - Word, PowerPoint & Excel
- Excellent communication skills with an emphasis on customer service
- Proficient in organizing and planning

RESUME ANALYIS EXAMPLE 4
Rate 1 2 3 4 5

JOHN JOHNSON

1900 Maple Road, Saint Cloud, MN 56303 • (320)555-5555 • jjXXXXX@stcloudstate.edu

PROFESSIONAL OBJECTIVE
Seeking a Tax Accountant Internship for spring 2018

EDUCATION
Saint Cloud State University - Saint Cloud, MN
Accredited by Association to Advance Collegiate Schools of Business
Bachelor of Arts in Accounting
Expected Graduation: Summer 2018 with 150 credit hours
GPA: 3.92
Worked 25 hours per week while attending college full-time

EXPERIENCE
Accounting Clerk/Receptionist/Cashier
Eich Motor Company - Saint Cloud, MN   June 2014 - Current
- Journalizing, posting, and creating adjusting entries in ADP
- Met deadlines preparing and organizing monthly parts statements and audit trails for accounting purposes
- Manage opening and closing duties as assigned and provide quality service to hundreds of customers
- Display strong attention to detail, managing money transactions and daily receipts
- Work well as a member of a team, helping to maintain a positive attitude among team members
- Learn and use skills in efficiently executing cash transactions by operating own cash register
- Demonstrate ability to effectively multi-task in a fast-paced work environment

Independent Contractor
Saint Cloud Times - Saint Cloud, MN   October 2010 - January 2015
- Successfully controlled two Shopping News routes in a dependable and dedicated manner

VOLUNTEERING & SERVICE
Saint Michael's Church - Saint Cloud, MN   December 2008 - Current
- Leader of Vacation Bible School from 2010-2013
- Bring the Church Community together by providing refreshments after Mass

Saint Cloud State University - Saint Cloud, MN   September 2015 - May 2016
- Note taker for Student Disability Services
- Tutor for Accounting

AFFILIATIONS & ACTIVITIES
Beta Gamma Sigma - International Business Honor Society   April 2016 - Current
- Membership based on high scholastic achievement

Saint Cloud State Accounting Club - Saint Cloud, MN   August 2015 - Current
- Social Coordinator and set up annual Golf Outing

SKILLS
- Client-focused
- Detail oriented
- Microsoft Office, Excel, PowerPoint proficiency

- Quick learner
- Cooperative team member
- Specialized automotive accounting knowledge

AWARDS & HONORS
James W. Miller Family Scholarship   **Presidential Academic Scholarship**
Saint Cloud State University - August 2014   Saint Cloud State University - August 2014

- Rewarded for academic achievement & service   - Received based on ACT score of 28

RESUME ANALYIS EXAMPLE 5
Rate   1   2   3   4   5

Kris Manson

• Permanent Address: 7555 County Road 15, Bird Island, MN   55310
• Cell Number : 320-555-555
• E-mail: kxxxxxxx@gmail.com

OBJECTIVE

I am a full time student interested in gaining "hands-on" experience though an internship position. Graduating spring 2017.

EDUCATION

St. Cloud State University,   2014 - Present
St. Cloud, MN

- Major in Communication Studies with an emphasis in Organizational Leadership.
- Minor in Business Marketing.
- British Studies - Education Abroad Program Spring 2016.

WORK EXPERIENCE

St. Cloud State Athletics Department September 2016- Present
St. Cloud, MN

> Position: Marketing Specialist

Minnesota Viking's LLC June 2016 - Present
Eden Prairie, MN

> Position: Public Relations part time intern:
> - Training Camp summer 2016
> - Game Day 2016-2017 Season.

Bernick's Pepsi June 2016 - Present
St. Cloud, MN

> Position: Brand Ambassador

Harvest land Cooperative   May -August 2015
Morgan, MN

> Position: Marketing and Communications Intern

REFERENCES

Available upon request

Applying This Skill: Student Resume Analysis: Peer Review Best Resume Exercise

In your small group, gather all rough draft resumes into a pile. When instructed, pass the pile to another group. When you receive a new group of resumes, determine which one you like the most. List the specific design features and content elements that make this resume effective but not any suggestions for further improvement. Be prepared to share your document and findings with the class.

Applying This Skill: Peer Review Resume

Swap resumes with a classmate. Using the checklist below, review your partner's resume. Discuss areas of success and areas that need improvement.

Assess Your Document Here:

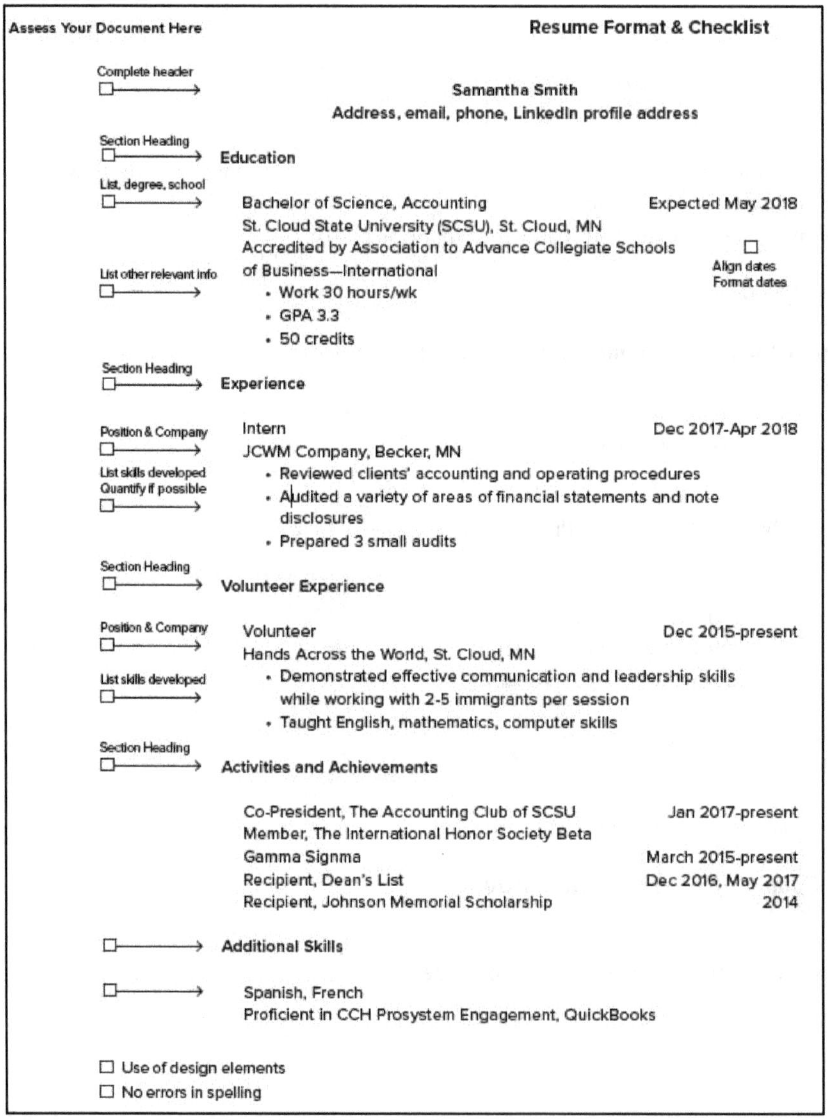
Assess Your Document Here

Resume Format & Checklist

☐ Complete header → **Samantha Smith**
Address, email, phone, LinkedIn profile address

☐ Section Heading → **Education**

☐ List, degree, school → Bachelor of Science, Accounting — Expected May 2018
St. Cloud State University (SCSU), St. Cloud, MN
Accredited by Association to Advance Collegiate Schools of Business—International

☐ Align dates / Format dates

☐ List other relevant info →
- Work 30 hours/wk
- GPA 3.3
- 50 credits

☐ Section Heading → **Experience**

☐ Position & Company → Intern — Dec 2017-Apr 2018
JCWM Company, Becker, MN

☐ List skills developed / Quantify if possible →
- Reviewed clients' accounting and operating procedures
- Audited a variety of areas of financial statements and note disclosures
- Prepared 3 small audits

☐ Section Heading → **Volunteer Experience**

☐ Position & Company → Volunteer — Dec 2015-present
Hands Across the World, St. Cloud, MN

☐ List skills developed →
- Demonstrated effective communication and leadership skills while working with 2-5 immigrants per session
- Taught English, mathematics, computer skills

☐ Section Heading → **Activities and Achievements**

Co-President, The Accounting Club of SCSU — Jan 2017-present
Member, The International Honor Society Beta Gamma Signma — March 2015-present
Recipient, Dean's List — Dec 2016, May 2017
Recipient, Johnson Memorial Scholarship — 2014

☐ → **Additional Skills**

☐ → Spanish, French
Proficient in CCH Prosystem Engagement, QuickBooks

☐ Use of design elements
☐ No errors in spelling

Figure 14.2 Resume Format Checklist

Applying This Skill: Partner Bullet Point Development

Partner with a classmate. Look at your partner's resume and select 2–3 bullet points to ask about. Say something like: "Tell me more about what you did here" or "Tell me more about this." As your partner talks, take notes about what they are saying. This will help identify words, skills, accomplishments, and so on that your partner may use to strengthen the bullet points.

Bullet Point:

Notes:

Bullet Point:

Notes:

Bullet Point:

Notes:

Top 12 Resume Mistakes

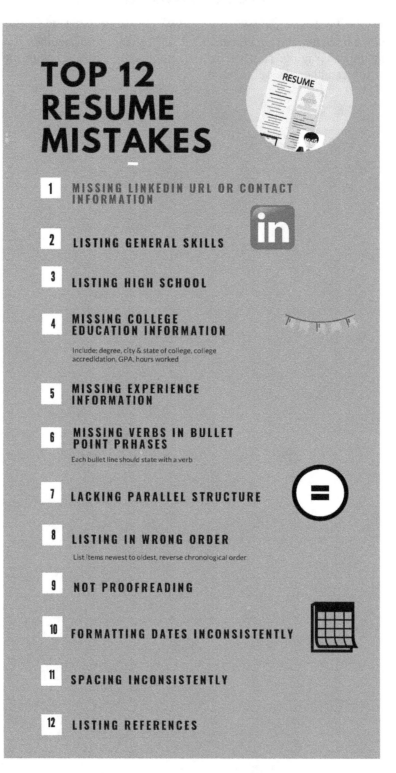

Figure 14.3 12 Top Resume Mistakes

Top Twelve Resume Mistakes Explained

1. Missing LinkedIn url or Header information

2. General Skills

3. Education: High School

4. Education Information

5. Experience: Missing Information

6. Experience: Bullet Point Phrases

7. Experience: Parallelism

8. Experience: Order

9. Proofreading

10. Date Formatting

11. Formatting/Spacing

12. References

SHELBY LAHJA

555 5ᵗʰ Ave S Apt 55   Cell Phone Number: 955-555-5555

St. Cloud, MN 56301   Email: studentemail@gmail.com

SKILLS

- Self-Motivated
- Hard Worker
- Organized
- Responsible
- Leader
- Good communication skills

EDUCATION

Farmington High School   September 2015 - June 2019

- AP Biology in 10th grade
- AP Statistics in 11th grade
- Full Time PSEO at Inver Hills Community College 12th Grade

St Cloud State University   August 2019 – Expected Graduation May 2023

- Double major in Finance and Management

EXPERIENCE

Capital One – Full Time - St. Cloud, MN   **November 2019 – current**

Job Title: Customer Protection Resolution Senior Coordinator

- Critical Thinking
- Communication Skills
- Fraud Detection
- Deescalating Skills
- Phone Experience
- Active Listening
- Customer Service

YMCA Kid Zone – Part Time - St. Cloud, MN   **September 2019 – November 2019**

Job Title: Childcare Provider

- Responsibility
- Organization
- Patience
- Problem Solving

Lahja Designs   **May 2020 – Current**

Business I started making customized signs, tumblers, coasters, and totes so I can start attending Craft Shows with hopes of having a store front someday.

- Responsibility
- Finance
- Determination
- Customer Service
- Time management
- Self-Motivated
- Money Management
- Marketing/Advertising

I

ACTIVATIES

Delta Sigma Phi -   September 2019 – November 2019

- Social Media Chair

References Available Upon Request

2

1. Missing LinkedIn URL or Header Information

Explanation	Recruiters expect your contact information to be complete, including your LinkedIn profile URL
Sample	missing information
Revision	in header, under email: linkedin.com/studentprofile.url
Reason	Most recruiters will look at your LinkedIn profile if they are interested in you.

2. Listing General Skills

Explanation	Skills have more validity and credibility if you list them where you developed them (job, experience). Skills sections are best for computer skills, language skills and other skills that don't fit elsewhere.
Sample	Skills: self-motivated, hard worker, organized, leader….
Revision	Skills: Oracle, Java, Fluent in English and Spanish" Used excellent organization skills to schedule appointments
Reason	Most recruiters will look at your LinkedIn profile if they are interested in you.

3. Listing High School

Explanation	Delete high school graduation information
Sample	Lists high school and graduation date
Revision	No high school information listed
Reason	If you are in college, recruiters assume you graduated from high school. In rare cases, like if you were valedictorian, it may be acceptable to list high school, but as a rule, leave it off.

4. Missing College Education Information

Explanation	The following information needs to be included in the Education section:
	
	a. List degree earning
	    i. **Sample:** "Going for Finance"
	    ii. **Revision:** "Bachelor of Science, Marketing" or "BS, Accounting"
	b. List city/state (St. Cloud, MN)
	    i. **Sample**: St. Cloud State
	    ii. **Revision**: St. Cloud State University, St. Cloud, MN
	c. List college accreditation
	    i. **Sample:** missing
	    ii. **Revision:** Accredited by Association to Advance Collegiate Schools of Business International (AACSB-I)
	d. GPA if 3.0 or above, or if in accounting
	    i. **Sample:** missing
	    ii. **Revision 1**: 3.2/4
	    iii. **Revision 2:** Major GPA 3.5/4, Cumulative GPA 2.9/4
	e. List hours working per week, if relevant
	    i. **Sample:** missing
	    ii. **Revision:** Working 30 hours per week

Reason	Providing the most accurate and relevant information possible will improve your chances of getting an interview

5. Missing Experience Information

Explanation	Job title or company location is missing
Sample	Target
Revision 1:	Target, St. Cloud, MN (dates of employment on right)
Revision 2:	Sales Team Member, Target, St. Cloud, MN (dates of employment on right)
Reason	Complete information provides the recruiter with accurate information; missing information makes you look sloppy or as if you're trying to hide something

6. Missing Verbs in Bullet Point Phrases

Explanation	Bullet point phrases listed under Experience sections should start with *verbs* and provide details about your skills
Sample 1	Critical thinking
Revision 1	Applied critical thinking skills to help team solve problems
Sample 2	Answered phone calls
Revision 2	Developed communication and problem solving skills while answering 50+ customer phone calls per shift
Reason	Skills are transferrable; you take them from one job to another. Recruiters want to know what skills you have and how you developed them. Focus on the skill, then how you developed it. Adding numbers quantifies your contributions.

7. Lacking Parallel Structure

Explanation	Bullet points need to be parallel in terms of all points start with verbs, all verbs are in the correct tense
Sample	• Customers called me • Helps supervisor • Detected fraud
Revision	• Answered customer calls (starts with verb) • Helped supervisor (all verbs in past tense) • Detected fraud
Reason	Using parallel structure helps the reader quickly scan a document. Start with verbs emphasizes your transferrable skills. Many recruiters say they immediately eliminate resumes with past/present tense errors in bullet point.

8. Listing in Wrong Order

Explanation	Experience (jobs or activities) need to be listed in reverse chronological order (most recent first) (usually)
Sample	
Revision	
Reason	Recruiters want to know what you're doing now, then work back to older jobs. List your most recent or current position first. If you have experience to highlight, like an internship, that is older, consider a "Relevant Experience" section to highlight that experience.

9. Proofreading

Explanation	A single spelling error will remove you from the job applicant pool.
Sample	Activities
Revision	Activities
Reason	Spelling, alignment and punctuation errors make you look sloppy and careless. Ask many people to proofread your resume; different people will see different errors.

10.   Date Formatting

Explanation	Dates should be aligned on the right margin and listed in the same format (Jan vs January; 1-2020, vs Jan 2020). Use "present" instead of "current."
Sample	Sept. – January 2019-2020)
Revision	Sept.- Jan. 2019-2020
Reason	Consistency shows good attention to detail and makes your resume look good.

11.   Formatting/Spacing

Explanation	All dates should be aligned, all bullet lists should be aligned, all formatting should be consistent (job title, place, dates). Text proximity indicates the content is related; white space separates information and makes documents easier to read.
Sample Spacing	See sample below.
Revision	Format jobs/experiences in single line spacing. Note: May need to adjust paragraph spacing; look for "Don't add space between paragraphs of same style" to reduce extra line spacing
Reason	An attractive resume is well-formatted and easy to read. Use "chunking" (related information is close together) to make your resume easy to read.

12.   References

Explanation	Remove "References are available"
Sample	References are available upon request.
Revision	Deleted
Reason	Recruiters assume you will provide references if asked. Resume space is at a premium. Use the space referring to references for something more important.

15

Cover/Job Application Letters

Whenever you submit a resume, you should include a cover letter. Sometimes they will be printed, like a resume, but most online application sites have a place for you to insert or upload your cover letter with your resume. If there is an option to include a cover letter, you need to do so. If you are emailing a resume, you may attach a cover letter to the email. If your resume makes it through the first round of review, a recruiter or hiring manager will read your cover letter. The cover letter is how you introduce yourself; it presents your personality, your uniqueness, and your interest in or passion for the position. An effective cover letter will help you make the best impression you can. After completing this lesson, you will:

- Understand how to and demonstrate your ability to create an effective cover letter
- Understand the importance of and how to target your job application documents

....

Reading 15.1

Techniques and Tools for Effective Cover Letters and E-Notes

by Kristin Johnson

For many job seekers, cover letters are either a mystery or a nuisance—generally not something positive. What if we, as career professionals, could empower them to view writing these documents in a more positive light? By providing some straightforward techniques and tools, we can make this task much easier and more effective for them.

Most of my clients tell me they don't hate writing cover letters; they just don't know what to say in them. They also have many questions about things they've read not to do anymore, how long their letters should be, or whether they need them at all. Sound familiar?

The purpose of this article is to provide support to you, the career professional, in encouraging job seekers to write these very necessary documents better and more quickly. But, before I launch into techniques and tips, a definition of the modern cover letter is in order.

According to a virtual seminar given by The Resume Writing Academy (2013), a cover letter "is a communication sent with a resume to convey a job seeker's qualifications." It is first-person correspondence that accompanies a resume to explain why the person is sending it, and to make the case for being the best candidate. Traditionally sent in the postal mail, cover letters are now primarily sent electronically. Either in the body of an email, as an attachment, or uploaded into an Applicant Tracking System (ATS) for an employer or job board, these electronic cover letters are called "E-Notes."

Now that we're clear on what a cover letter is, I'll clarify how you can answer the most common questions job seekers might approach you with. Also, you'll get some practical tips to writing these letters more effectively, as well as some helpful resources for future reference.

Question #1: Do I really need a cover letter?

The biggest question job seekers have is whether cover letters are even needed at all. They've heard that no one reads them anymore. Well, as was true with Mark Twain, rumors of the demise of the cover letter have been greatly exaggerated. It's true that many employers discard the cover letter and go straight to the resume, but it's also true that many don't.

In fact, according to Career Directors International's Global Hiring Trends Survey (2012), 26 per cent of hiring authorities state that they continue to read cover letters. That's more than one reader out of every four! So, yes, a cover letter is still something job seekers will want to use to gain the best odds of getting an interview. And while the cover letter doesn't need to be long—in fact, it should be short—job seekers should put all the effort into it that they would if they were 100 percent sure it was going to be read. Because they just don't know which hiring managers will read it.

Question #2: What is the point of the cover letter anyway?

The cover letter offers the candidate a chance to connect the dots between his resume, where he presents a more formal, professional skill set, to the enthusiastic, productive, engaged worker who perfectly matches the company's corporate culture. It's the chance to use the words, "I," "me," and "my," transforming the job seeker from a number in the ATS into a real, hirable person.

According to the RWA seminar, cover letters serve as a/an:

- Introduction of the candidate to the company.
- Marketing document to sell the candidate's skills and talents.
- Priority list of the job seeker's best qualifications, accomplishments, and other items that cause her to rise above all other applicants.
- Persuasive call-to-action, priming the employer to reach out to the candidate for an interview.

If job seekers don't make the most of this opportunity, they're going to be at a disadvantage. A cover letter provides them with:

- More keywords in their submitted documents, allowing for a higher ATS score.
- Additional accomplishments to strengthen the case for hiring.
- Personal stories or connections, explaining an interest in the company.
- Another avenue to demonstrate written communication skills and attention to detail.
- Persuasive language to inspire quick action.
- A tangible way for job seekers to show their reliability (if they follow up when they said they would).

The above points should convince any job seeker to take the time to write a cover letter or e-note. One of the CDI survey respondent's comment perfectly sums the value of cover letters: "They often provide insights two-dimensional resumes fail to provide."

Many people think that to accomplish all of those things, the cover letter would need to be several pages of densely packed, long paragraphs. This couldn't be farther from the truth, which brings us to the next question job seekers have.

Question #3: How long does it need to be? Can I just send it in an email?

In the current era of texts and tweets, with readers' attention spans quickly shrinking, brevity is crucial. And, yes, since so many cover letters are now emailed in the e-note format, an effective length could be as short as a couple of paragraphs with several bullets between. When recommending cover letter length to job seekers, keep in mind these statistics:

More than 8 out of 10 HR professionals spend less than one minute reading a cover letter, according to a SHRM survey (2005). Note that this survey was conducted in 2005—before the recession. Since then, the market has been flooded with applicants, putting even more demands on hiring managers.

According to a survey conducted in 2011 by Saddleback College in Orange County, California, of 87 respondents:

12.6 per cent preferred a full-page cover letter

43.7 per cent preferred a half-page

19.5 per cent had no preference

24.1 per cent stated "the shorter the better"

Whether writing an e-note or cover letter to mail with a resume, less is decidedly more. Condensing these career communications can be much harder than writing a longer letter, it's true. So, how do career professionals instruct job seekers to accomplish this seemingly impossible task of writing "tight"?

The book *Write Tight: Say Exactly What You Mean With Precision and Power by William Brohaugh* is a great resource for learning more concise communication. Consider sharing the following tips with your clients:

- Prepare yourself for writing.
- Have a clear focus on the purpose for writing.
- Outline three main points you want to cover.
- Detail three brand attributes that set you apart from your competition that you want to be sure to cover.
- Remove emotionality from the words you choose. If you are married to a particular word, editing becomes more difficult.
- Chop words when you edit. Be on the lookout for redundant phrases, carefully examining the adjectives you choose.
- Copy your first draft into a new document before editing so that you can cut words out without worry.
- Avoid jargon, clichés, trendy words, or flowery language.
- Get to the point clearly, as opposed to saying things in a roundabout way.

- Keep shortening and clarifying: Check to make sure the flow of the writing makes sense. Rearrange sentences if things get jumbled or off-track. Rein yourself in!
- If descriptions become too long, refer the reader to another source for more information. A LinkedIn profile, professional blog post, or company website are great ways to elaborate on the brief information presented in a cover letter.
- Continue to ask yourself, "Does this strengthen my case for hire? Will readers really value this information? Is this in alignment with my most important brand attributes?"

To help myself write concisely, I follow the advice of pretending that I'm being charged money for every word I write. I also always have a second set of eyes review what I've written.

Learning to write shorter cover letters can mean the difference between a job seeker getting an interview or ending up in the reject pile. Using e-notes can give a candidate an even bigger leg up. There are several advantages to writing an e-note versus a traditional cover letter, one being that it forces the writer to be very clear and confident about the reasons why they should be considered. There is less room for rambling.

According to award-winning resume writer Gayle Howard of Top Margin, other advantages are that an e-note:

- Gives the impression of a more modern and tech-savvy candidate.
- Delivers a more considerate, to-the-point communication; says the writer values the reader's time and attention.
- Provides additional branding opportunities in the subject line and signature block.
- Allows for a higher likelihood that the message will at least receive a quick scan, since it is so brief and is visually segmented.
- Starts selling the job seeker quicker and more effectively than a lengthy letter.
- Permits the writer to bypass more acceptably a salutation to a specific person without appearing rude.

Most of the time, your job seekers will want to reap the advantages of using an e-note, especially when applying via job board, email, or company website. When they are communicating with someone they know doesn't usually read cover letters, or is particularly pressed for time, I highly recommend using an e-note.

However, clients may wonder what is appropriate for this newer type of communication.

Question #4: How different is an e-note, really? What does it consist of?

E-notes differ mostly in the length. E-notes also have shorter 2–3 line paragraphs and often a bulleted presentation style. When writing an e-note, extra attention is placed on direct, clear, extremely brief points that support a central strategy in conveying the case for hire. An e-note consists of

- Targeted subject line, ideally including the job title and branding statement.

Example: Subject: Business and Financial IT Director: Initiative-Driven Growth and Process Improvement

- Opening statement of one or two sentences where the candidate concisely spells out the obvious reason why she is writing. (Don't make a hiring manager guess.) Start the letter off strongly by giving a solid example or metric that illustrates how past accomplishments will be an asset to the hiring company in the future.

Example: Under my leadership, the IT department at XYZ Corp. delivered more than $2M in savings through technology upgrades and process improvements—at a cost of less than $20K. I am confident my proven leadership skills and technical expertise will be valuable as your next Business and Financial IT Director.

A word about name-dropping. If your client can mention a personal referral in the opening statement, he should do so! People hire people they know and like. Candidates increase their chance of gaining an interview if an internal contact or other trusted source will vouch for them.

- Bulleted body to substantiate the brand statement and garner interest.

Example: Further proof of my impact on operational efficiency and the corporate bottom line:

PROCESS IMPROVEMENTS—Slashed time to release new policies in half during first six months as VP of Operations.

TEAM ENGAGEMENT—Boosted attendance of operations center staff by 75 per cent in nine months through recognition and collaborative programs.

TECHNOLOGY IMPLEMENTATION—Improved production 40 per cent in billing department by modernizing technology and transitioning to paperless environment.

Conclusion:

In this section, the writer should be professionally assertive. This is the place to inform the reader, politely, that the cover letter and resume are not the final messages they'll receive from the candidate. In fact, the reader can expect a follow-up call next week.

Example: I welcome confidential discussions of how I may add additional value to MetLife. I will contact your executive assistant early next week to schedule a meeting. In the meantime, please see my enclosed resume.

- Closing: Signing off with "Sincerely," "Best Regards," or "Thank you for your consideration" is a courtesy not to be forgotten.
- Candidate's name: If the job seeker has a common name, she should consider adding her middle initial or credentials at the end of the name to prevent identity confusion when the employer searches online to learn more about her.
- Signature block: This is a must. The writer will want to provide contact information to make it easy for the hiring authority to contact him. The signature block should include a phone number, email, LinkedIn URL, and other social media information. She should also list any branding information, tagline, or website. Mentioning an award won or notable accomplishment is another opportunity to sell himself.
- Just use a dashed line or symbols to separate your signature from the e-note, as in these examples:

==============================

Jamie Johnson, MBA

Cell: 920-555-1212

Email: jjmba@gmail.com

LinkedIn: www.linkedin.com/jjmba

Twitter: @jjmba

++++++++++++++++++++++++++++

Eduardo C. Flores

Cell: 312-555-1212 ** Email: jcflores@gmail.com ** LinkedIn: Linkedin.com/jcflores

->->->->->->->->->->->->->->->-

Elena Kim

Voted "Best Realtor in Orange County 2013"

Cell: 405-555-1212

Email: realtor.elena@firstrealty.com

LinkedIn: linkedin.com/elenakim

An e-note is the perfect way to start the hiring conversation. Job seekers should be on the lookout for a response. They may be pleasantly surprised when the hiring manager writes back!

Question #5: When is a traditional, mailed cover letter still the way to go?

Candidates will want to mail a cover letter whenever that is requested. It's not uncommon for government positions, positions filled by a panel, or companies using a very formal hiring process. I've also heard anecdotal testimonies from colleagues in HR that they don't at all mind when a candidate follows up with a mailed letter after applying online. Although these anecdotes are not a formal survey, trying new things with a job search can sometimes produce positive results.

Question #6: Who do I address it to?

Remember the days when you had to send a cover letter To Whom It May Concern? The world has changed. Today, a hiring manager will appreciate a job seeker going the extra mile to use her name (and spell it correctly). Websites like jigsaw.com, Glassdoor.com, and LinkedIn can help in locating the decision maker.

If the applicant is not sure who to send the letter to even after searching online, he may try using informational interviewing techniques (blog post, 2013) to figure out a good contact. When addressing a cover letter to someone whose gender is uncertain, encourage him not to make any assumptions. A quick social media search often will show a profile picture to clear up the confusion. If all searches and strategies still lead nowhere, the Saddleback survey (2011) showed the following preferences for addressing a cover letter. Here is the breakdown for the question, "If candidates do not know who to send the cover letter to, how should they address it?"

40.5 per cent:	Dear Hiring Manager
27.4 per cent:	To Whom it May Concern
17.9 per cent:	Dear Sir/Madam
8.3 per cent:	Leave blank if don't know the name
6 per cent:	Dear Human Resource Director

Short of knowing a living, breathing human being to address it to, Dear Hiring Manager appears to be the next best option.

Question #7: What's the best way to send an e-note?

The cover letter should not be included as an attachment to an email. This approach asks the employer to take a few additional moments and hit a few additional keys to actually open the letter, and some employers will not be willing to do that. Instead, include the text of the cover letter in the email body itself.

Question #8: How do I write a strong, personalized cover letter—without sounding pompous?

After addressing the letter to the correct person and clearly stating the position being applied for, the candidate should quickly get to the heart of what she can contribute to the company. The best approach is to stick to the facts of relevant accomplishments, avoid jargon unless completely necessary, and use brief, readable language. It is possible to pack a lot of compelling information into a small space, as you can see in this example:

Advancing complex, multi-departmental operational projects to completion in higher education—with servant leadership strengths—is my specialty. Please consider allowing me to contribute my expertise to the University of Wisconsin—Madison for your Director of Customer Relationship Management position in the Department of Information Technology. I've excelled in this field by systematically analyzing policies, procedures, and team member dynamics, then applying relational leadership techniques to manage teams. My signature accomplishments:

Electronic Systems: Saved $1.4M in the first year of installing ATMs and executing Higher Pay, same-day electronic refunds for students—a dramatic improvement over prior 5–7 day wait time.

Electronic Storefronts: Implemented web system to take payment for courses, extra-curricular lessons, and donations to foundation, bolstering college revenue by $2.2M in first 6 months.

Automated Payments: Overhauled payment to third-party vendors from issuing paper checks to using Digitech ERP system, saving resources and overhead.

Steering change to attain initiative-driven staff development, operations process improvement, and technology modernization is the expertise I bring to the UW. I will follow up early next week to discuss how my success in financial and business management might add value to your organization.

Thank you for your consideration,

Evelyn Douglas

Attachment: Resume

Cell: (608) 555-1212 Email: Evelyn.Douglas@gmail.com

LinkedIn: linkedin.com/evelyndouglas Skype: @evdouglas

The content above shows the candidate's strengths without using "fluffy" wording that may be off-putting to a hiring manager.

Question #9: How do I avoid just regurgitating what's on my resume?

Most job seekers have heard that it's not good to be redundant in their cover letters. In that regard, they know what ***not*** to say. So, what ***to*** say? Again, they should simply state, right off the bat, what they contribute to solving the company's concerns. The cover letter is the place to provide additional information that will tie what is in the resume to the company's needs. Research can help job seekers figure out the company's challenges so that the accomplishments will resonate with them. Here are some things job seekers can do to get these insights:

- Read recent press releases on their website.
- Use Google, Yahoo! Finance, and Glassdoor.com to find out what insiders are saying about corporate culture.
- Check out what followers on social media are saying about the company and how the company handles those comments.
- Do informational interviews with connections in the company (or their competitors) to uncover issues that may not be public.
- Ask themselves, is the company growing? Or, going through reorganization and downsizing? What skills do I have that would contribute with regard to the issues they are experiencing?

In addition, job seekers may wish to add to their cover letter additional information that will help make their case. They can:

- Include clear statements that demonstrate how their unique value could provide benefits to the organization.
- State why the company is of interest, making the e-note more personal.
- Spell out exactly how the their skills, work style, or personality relates to what is known about the company.
- Paint a picture of future success to get the hiring manager thinking about how the candidate can fit in to their organization.
- Describe any professional or personal history with the company.

The cover letter is where the candidate truthfully explains why he wants to work specifically for that company. Pointing to aspects of the resume is acceptable, but expanding on key successes and making clear connections to the employer is key to getting the cover letter read.

Question #10: Do I have to write about how I lost my last job in my cover letter?

Although job seekers can expect to answer questions during an interview about why they are looking for a job, this fact doesn't necessarily need to be mentioned in a cover letter. It depends greatly on the person's situation. Of course, the purpose for communicating with an employer should be touched on. But if the details would hurt the job seeker and immediately rule her out of the interview process, it is vital to put a positive spin on the situation. Obviously, a letter stating, Since I was fired from my last job for stealing, I thought I'd apply with your company, would be a poor opening.

The applicant could instead write, I've always been skilled at recognizing and protecting process loopholes in your company's industry and was pleased when my colleague, Bob Smith, informed me of an opening in your auditing department.

In this opening, the sender is stating why he is writing: to apply for the position his friend told him about. No need to mention the incident that might hurt him if it were revealed too soon.

If it really is in the best interest of the candidate to give a specific reason, it's important that it's consistent with public record and social media content, concise, plausible, and ultimately, framed in a positive light.

Question #11: Do I have to give salary information in my cover letter?

This is a tricky question and requires a thoughtful strategy.

If the information is requested in the job posting, or by the recruiter for a position, a job seeker who fails to include it may be considered rude, lazy, or inattentive to detail. To avoid being disqualified, the issue will need to be addressed. But whether numbers are given is up for debate.

Donna Svei, Avid Careerist, recommends addressing any possible pay cut head-on (2013). Her client was looking for more rewarding work, not a large salary. Because the issue was addressed directly, it was not perceived negatively.

There are several options for dealing with a request for salary requirements. According to career expert Allison Doyle, of About.com, the candidate could:

Give a realistic range, based on industry research, My salary requirement is $90K–$100K.

State that she is flexible based on the total compensation and benefits package. If a salary history is required, it is critical to be honest. The employer may ask for proof of compensation later and the job seeker would not want to be caught in a lie.

Another recommendation is to not provide information that would be cause for an employer to eliminate the candidate outright. Instead, state that salary can be discussed at a later time once the applicant determines that the position would be a good fit. Ultimately, it is a touchy situation with no universal right or wrong answer but where career professionals can provide valuable guidance to job-seeking clients.

Cover Letter Recap

The bottom line for cover letters and e-notes is to write a clear and tight message, densely packed with accomplishments that will resonate with the hiring manager. It does take forethought and practice, but with one in five workers preparing to change jobs in 2014, according to a recent survey by Monster.com (2014), it makes sense for job seekers to make the best impression possible.

References

Brohaugh, William. *Write Tight: Say Exactly What You Mean With Precision and Power* (2007).

CareerBuilder. One in Five Workers Plan to Change Jobs in 2014, According to CareerBuilder Survey (2014). http://cb.com/1nmOQ3X

De Carlo, L. Global Hiring Trends 2012. Career Directors International. http://bit.ly/1fy3Wy4

Doyle, Allison. Disclosing Salary Requirements and Salary History. About.com. http://abt.cm/1fy3GPI

Enelow, Wendy & Louise Kursmark. Today's Modern Cover Letter: The E-Note (2013). Resume Writing Academy. http://www.resumewritingacademy.com/esummit-enote.php

Howard, Gayle. The Traditional Cover Letter. Is it Outdated? (2013). http://bit.ly/1icerJU

Johnson, Kristin. How to Ask for an Informational Interview (2013). http://bit.ly/1k9XwrU

Saddleback College Resume Survey (2011). http://bit.ly/1iMPJCs

Society for Human Resource Management. SHRM Cover Letters and Resumes Survey (2005). http://bit.ly/1cw6mi5

Society for Human Resource Management. SHRM Research Spotlight: Social Networking Websites and Online Search Engines (2011). http://bit.ly/1jLhmMA

Svei, Donna. Cover Letters: Taking a Pay Cut (2013). http://bit.ly/1b8QVbn

Cover Letter Sample and Checklist

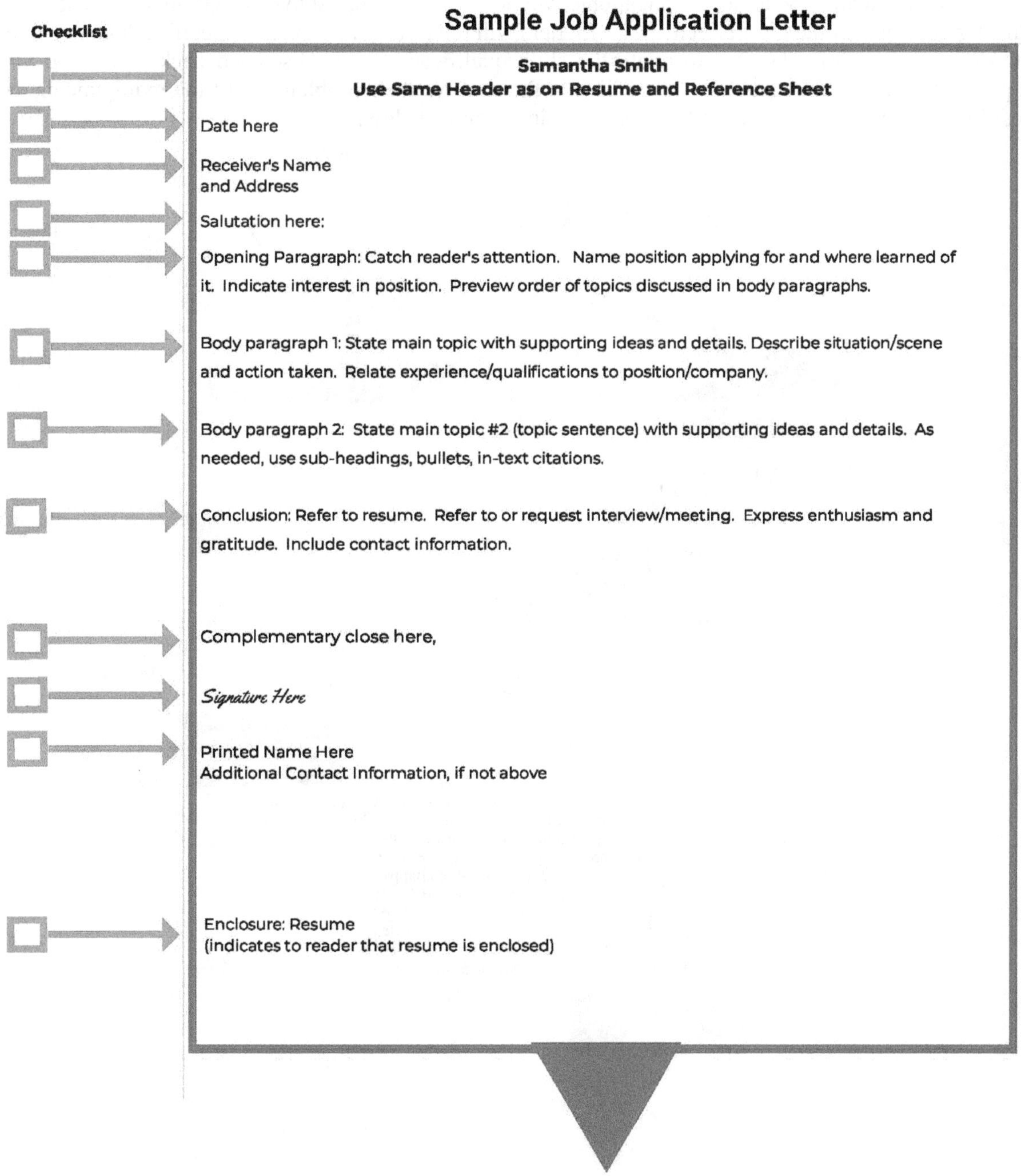

Checklist

Sample Job Application Letter

Samantha Smith
Use Same Header as on Resume and Reference Sheet

Date here

Receiver's Name
and Address

Salutation here:

Opening Paragraph: Catch reader's attention. Name position applying for and where learned of it. Indicate interest in position. Preview order of topics discussed in body paragraphs.

Body paragraph 1: State main topic with supporting ideas and details. Describe situation/scene and action taken. Relate experience/qualifications to position/company.

Body paragraph 2: State main topic #2 (topic sentence) with supporting ideas and details. As needed, use sub-headings, bullets, in-text citations.

Conclusion: Refer to resume. Refer to or request interview/meeting. Express enthusiasm and gratitude. Include contact information.

Complementary close here,

Signature Here

Printed Name Here
Additional Contact Information, if not above

Enclosure: Resume
(indicates to reader that resume is enclosed)

Figure 15.1. Sample Job Application Letter

Assignment: Write a Cover Letter

Using the principles discussed in this chapter, write a job application/cover letter. The letter should be targeted to a specific job advertisement. Use standard business letter format as discussed in Chapter 7.

When writing your job application/cover letter, recall the SOAR/STAR method discussed in Chapter 16. Some of the most effective cover letters will tell a story or explain a specific situation using the SOAR/STAR pattern. Then try to relate the skills/qualifications you discussed back to the job you're applying for. Tell the readers how you will help them, solve their problem, or fit the requirements of the position. See the "the Adapted STARR Method" infographic below.

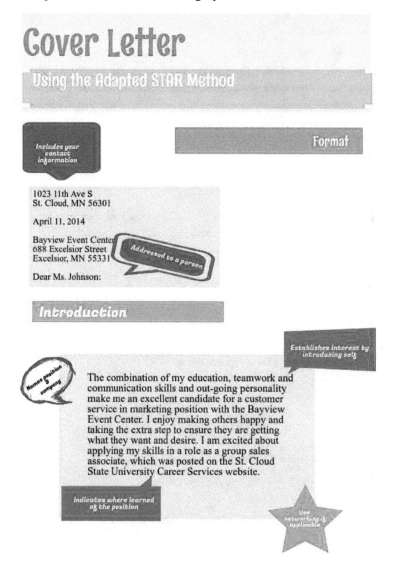

The Body

Follows order of Ideas

This fall I will graduate with a Bachelor's degree in marketing. Throughout my time at St. Cloud State University, I have learned about customer relations, professional selling and business management. My thorough education will allow me to immediately apply marketing skills as a sales associate with Bayview Event Center.

The most important skill I developed while in school is teamwork which I developed while playing for the St. Cloud State varsity basketball team. When I joined the team as a transfer student, I was immediately looked to as a leader by both coaches and teammates during the season's ups and downs. My longtime friend and starting point guard tore his MCLin his left knee with six games le in the regular season. I gathered the team and reinforced that if we played for our injured teammate and focused on every possession, we would continue to win. We overcame this difficult hurdle to end the season with only one loss and a trip to the conference championship. It is this determination, optimism and teamwork that I will bring to your team at Bayview.

Situation Action

Relates skills to position

The Adapted STAR Method

Situation: give an example of a situation in you were in that resulted in a positive outcome

Task: describe the tasks & challenges involved in the situation

Action: give an example of the actions you took

Results & Relate: describe the results and relate to the position

Show the interviewer how you fit the job

The Conclusion

After you review the attached resume for more information about my work and volunteer experience, please call me at (555) 555-5555 or email me at student@stcloudstate.edu so we may discuss how I can contribute to your company's needs. Thank you for your consideration and I look forward to speaking with you.

Include contact info & encourage action

Sincerely,

Name

Sign Name

Figure 15.2 STARR

Top 8 Cover Letter Mistakes

1. Including hyperlinks

2. Missing Salutation

3. Missing Introduction Information

4. Missing Topic Sentences and Details in Body Paragraphs

5. Missing Information in conclusion

6. Missing Signature

7. Missing Enclosure Notation

8. Lacking Proofreading and Formatting

1.   Hyperlinks

Explanation	Remove hyperlinks (the blue underline below emails and LinkedIn URLs)
Sample	student@gmail.com, https://www.linkedin.com/in/student
Revision	student@gmail.com, https://www.linkedin.com/in/student
Reason	Recruiters will not click through to your email or LinkedIn profile from a cover letter (or resume). Delete hyperlinks to show you know style conventions and pay attention to details.

2.   Missing Salutation and/or Punctuation

Explanation	A salutation should be format and be followed by a colon
Sample	Dear Smith,
Revision	Dear Mr. Smith:
Reason	The formal salutation indicates respect. The colon indicates you know proper business format and pay attention to detail.

3.   Missing or Unneeded Introduction Information

Explanation	Avoid starting with your name; provide a reason for the reader to keep reading. Mention position and where you learned about it.
Sample	My name is Mathais Naveen, and I am an accounting student. I read Acme Firm's posting for an an accounting internship.

Revision	As an accounting student at St. Cloud State University, I read Acme Firm's posting on Handshake for an accounting internship with interest. My variety of experiences prepares me to immediately contribute to Acme Firm.
Reason	Your name is clear in the header. Recruiters get hundreds of applications so stating which position you are applying for will help them position you. Indicating where you learned about the position, cues the recruiter to the posting.

4. Missing Topic Sentences & Details In Body Paragraphs

Explanation	Start with topic sentences. Provide details that aren't on your resume. Relate your skills to the position.
Sample	I will be entering my senior year at Brandeis at the end of this semester, and I will have completed the personal tax course. I have an extensive background in customer communication and service.
Revision	a. Topic sentence 1: "I am beginning my senior year at St. Cloud State University." b. Topic sentence 2: "I have an extensive background in customer communication and service." c. Details example 1: "I will complete the personal income tax course and volunteer with VITA this spring." d. Details example 2: "In my positions as a bank teller and paralegal, I effectively communicated with customers orally and in writing. These skills will allow me to provide effective customer service to Acme company customers."
Reason	Clear topic sentences allow readers to skip to topics that interest them. You can show your personality and explain your skills more in your resume by providing examples or personal details.

5.   Missing Information in Conclusion Paragraph

Explanation	Direct the reader to something specific on your resume. Include contact information in last paragraph. Express gratitude.
Sample	My resume is attached. I'll talk to you soon.
Revision	My attached resume includes details about my volunteer experience. Please contact me at the information above to discuss the position further. Thank you.
Reason	Complete information provides the recruiter with accurate information; missing information makes you look sloppy or as if you're trying to hide something.

6.   Missing Signature

Explanation	Need to sign the letter
Sample	No signature
Revision	Sincerely, *Mathais Naveen* Mathais Naveen
Reason	Use a different font to indicate you know you need to sign the letter, if you don't sign in ink.

7.   Missing Enclosure Notation

Explanation	Need enclosure notation
Sample	No notation
Revision	Below the signature block write: "Enc: Resume"
Reason	Using an enclosure notation tells the reader other documents are included with the letter and indicates you know business letter format.

8.   Lacking Proofreading & Formatting

Explanation	Too much blank space at bottom of letter. Errors in spelling, grammar etc.
Sample	Letter is too short; errors in spelling or grammar.
Revision	Add more content or increase spacing to fill empty space
Reason	Letter should include information that makes the reader want to know more about you. Any proofreading errors will eliminate you from consideration.

Applying This Skill: Peer Review Cover/Job Application Letter

Work with a peer. Trade rough drafts of your cover letters and follow the steps below to provide feedback and suggestions on each other's cover letters.

1. Circle all "I"s in the letter.

2. Underline all of the verbs (action words).

3. Suggest two alternative verbs.

4. Assess formatting:

   a. One page only

   b. Single spacing

   c. Left-justified text (no indentation)

   d. Blank line between paragraphs

   e. Short, unified paragraphs

   f. Margins: top, bottom, sides balanced

   g. Use header as in resume/sender address at top

   h. Date after sender address

   i. Receiver address after date

   j. Professional salutation (e.g., Ms., Dr., etc.)

   k. Colon after salutation

5. Introduction:

   a. States position applying for

      b.   Names source where found position

      c.   Mentions 2–3 qualifications (addressed in letter)

      d.   Uses networking (if applicable)

6. Body (2–3 Paragraphs):

      a.   In body paragraphs, in margins write:

      b.   "S" where writer describes situation

      c.   "TA" where writer describes tasks or action taken

      d.   "R" where writer discusses result

      e.   "RR" where writer related situation/skill to position applying for/how experience fits position/company

7. Closing

      a.   Refers to resume (w/ reason to look)

      b.   Provides info on how/when to contact

      c.   Refers to or requests interview (maybe state topics to discuss)

      d.   Expresses gratitude

Targeting Job Application Documents

Once you have a well-formatted reference sheet and resume and a well-written cover letter, what else can you to do make yourself stand out from the dozens or hundreds of other candidates for your ideal job? The best way to make sure your application is seen by the right people is to target your documents to the specific job and company you are applying to.

Companies, using either computer software (called Applicant Tracking Systems) or human resources staff, scan resumes and cover letters for keywords. Keywords are job qualifications, skills, or credentials needed in the position. Matching keywords or candidates allows companies to narrow the applicant pool quickly.

Using the right keywords in your job application documents may be the difference between your getting an interview or not. To identify the right keywords, read the job ad closely. Use the words in the ad in your resume and cover letter. If the ad says the job requires customer service skills, use the words "customer service skills," not "took care of customers." Common keywords include skills such as managing and leading, computer skills, titles of previous positions, licenses, or certifications. Incorporate as many relevant keywords as possible in your resume and cover letter.

Applying this Skill: Targeting Job Application Documents

Below, you will see a job advertisement and a sample resume. Fill in the bullet points on the resume so they are clearly related to the job advertisement.

THORNTON IMAGING STUDIO
We Need a Social Media Manager!

Passionate about working with social
media? Work with us!

SUBMIT YOUR APPLICATION TODAY!

Qualifications:
- Bachelor's degree from any 4-year course (Marketing preferred)
- Previous work experience in social media marketing or digital media
- Excellent communication skills
- Adept in different types of social media
-Customer oriented with good multitasking and organizational ability
-Excellent consulting, writing, and editing skills
-Strong attention to detail, accuracy and timeliness

Job Highlights

- Track and analyze analytics to gain insight on traffic, demographics and effectiveness
- Work with designers to ensure content is appealing
- Drive the day-to-day social media strategy
- Engage with audiences and promote company
- Work with team to create marketing plans
- Ability to work on multiple projects in fast-paced environment
- Facilitate planning and content execution for all social media
- Proactively partner with cross-functional teams to create content at vertical and campaign levels
- Manage timelines and deliverables

Submit application to HR@thorntonimaging.com
Created with Canva, Emily Carlson Goenner, 2022

Figure 15.3 Sample Job Ad

LinkedInEfakeStrong
EfakeStrong@gmail.com
555-555-5555

Enrique Strong
Internship Student

A passionate and self-motivated business student working towards a business degree at St. Paul University, seeking an opportunity for an internship position.

Education

Bachelor of Science, Marketing
St. Paul University, St. Paul, NE

Expected Graduation 2023

Relevant Experience

Business Development Intern, Mango and Spices   Jan-May 2020
-
-
-

Server, Hometown Restaurant   May 2019-Jan 2020
-
-

Sales Representative, Kohls   Aug 2018-April 2019
-

Fast Food Attendant, Burger Bugs   June 2017-Aug 2017
-
-

Volunteer Experience

Assistant Coach, Mighty Soccer   Summers 2018-2021
-
-
-

Volunteer, Adopt-a-Highway   2018-2019
-

Skills
-
-

Created with Canva, Emily Carlson Goenner 2022

Figure 15.4 Sample Resume

Figure 15. 5 Cover Letter and Resume Verbs.

Applying This Skill: Analyzing the Job Ad

Locate an ad for a job you would like to apply for when you graduate. Bring the ad to class. In class, you will complete the following:

1. Read the *entire* ad carefully.

2. Circle competencies/skills/qualifications listed in the ad that you already have.

3. Underline any qualifications/experiences/skills the ad mentions that you are lacking.

4. Fill in the columns below.

At the end of the exercise, you should see which qualifications you have that match the job ad. You will use those matches to enhance your job application. Use as many keywords as possible in your resume and cover letter. In your reference page, list people who will speak about qualifications the job requires. Use the situations/experiences you list to develop SOAR/STAR situations and stories you can use in your cover letter and interviews.

Qualifications I have	Situations/experiences that demonstrate
Ex: "Ability to build client relationships"	"I interned with Northwestern Mutual and worked with a staff member who showed me how to build a customer base. I developed my ability to contact customers by calling clients, setting up meetings, and following up on contacts. At the end of my internship, I had a client base of ten people."
Qualifications I'm lacking	How I might develop
Ex: "Experience with social media recruiting"	"Join AMA and work on social media; get an internship doing social media"

16

Interviewing Skills

Once your resume and cover letter have been reviewed and the company is interested in you, they will call you for an interview. Interviews may take place in an increasing variety of ways, including phone interviews, videoconference interviews, panel interviews, and more. No matter what type of interview you face, some basic skills are needed to succeed. In this chapter, you will learn about elevator speeches, behavioral interviewing questions, and informational interviewing. After completing this lesson, you will:

- Have a prepared and practiced elevator speech
- Be prepared to answer behavioral interviewing questions using the STAR/SOAR method

....

Reading 16.1

Ace the Interview

By Thea Kelley

The entire interviewing process boils down to one question, whether it is asked in so many words or not: "Why should we hire you (instead of one of our other candidates)?"

This chapter will help you answer that question clearly, credibly, and memorably—not just when it's specifically asked, but throughout your interview process, so that you stand out as "the one."

Relax and Be Confident

Almost everyone is nervous about job interviews. It's normal to have the jitters, or even to be downright scared. But it's not helpful when you're so anxious that you sweat heavily or your mind goes blank.

Relaxation exercises can help you stay calm before and during your interview. Search the Internet for "relaxation techniques Mayo Clinic" and you'll find several exercises you can use anytime, anywhere. Experiment with a few, choose the one you like best, and practice it frequently so it's ready when you need it.

As for confidence, that comes from being prepared. Put in some time and practice, and use everything you learn in this chapter to get thoroughly ready for successful job interviews. If you've been "winging it" until now, you may be amazed at how much more confident you'll feel when you're properly prepared.

Now let's think about the main messages you want to confidently communicate in your interviews.

Communicate Your Key Selling Points

There may be 50 reasons why a certain employer should hire you, but nobody can remember 50 reasons. So, narrow it down: What's the number one factor that is most likely to make them want to hire you? Now think of a few others that are almost as powerful. Those are your key selling points.

Ask yourself these questions to help you identify your key selling points:

- What qualifications do I have that are hard to find?
- What do I do better than my peers?
- What have my employers appreciated most about me?
- What are the most impressive accomplishments in my resume?

Once you have a short list, review it to make sure your key selling points are:

- **Relevant from the employer's point of view:** Although you might think the best reason to hire you is that you write very creatively, the employer may be more interested in your achievements in configuring databases.
- **Exceptional:** Presumably, all the candidates have the basic skills to do the job. What do you have that's above and beyond or hard to find?
- **Verifiable, not just an opinion:** If you have a professional certificate, that's a verifiable fact. Great communication skills are less concrete, so they may not be such a good key selling point unless you can offer some form of evidence, such as related experience in your resume, a writing sample, or a sound bite from a LinkedIn recommendation.

Prepare to communicate your key selling points memorably. Think about this: What do we remember?

- **We remember what comes first and last.** Emphasize your key selling points in your first interview answer—generally, your answer to "tell me about yourself"—and in your closing remarks.
- **We remember what is reinforced.** Make some reference to your key selling points in your follow-up messages.
- **We remember what is vivid**—what we can see in our mind's eye. Illustrate your key selling points with stories.

Tell a Story

Stories are to interviews what pictures are to a website. They illustrate the content and make it much more engaging. Stories are often required by the way an interview question is phrased. When you hear "tell me about a time when you (handled this or that)," you're being asked a behavioral interview question, which requires you to tell a story. Having plenty of stories ready is a must.

Even when a story isn't asked for, it can liven up your answer. A well-told story enables the interviewer to imagine you doing skillful work and achieving results. In her mind's eye she can actually see it—and seeing is believing.

You used stories earlier in the book to identify skills and craft accomplishment statements for your resume using the CAR format (challenge, action, result). You'll use these stories again in an interview, but you will add one more element to your story: the context or situation. We call it the SOAR technique because it includes the *situation* or context, an *obstacle* that required extra skills to overcome, the *actions* you took to solve the problem, and the *results* that benefited the organization.

So when interviewing, build your stories around SOAR: situation, obstacle, actions, and results.

Here's an example, told by a candidate for a sales manager job.

SOAR Story: Tripling Sales Leads

When I was sales manager at Terrific Technology, we had a third-party call center that was supposed to pass along leads to our inside sales team, but we were only getting about 10 leads a day. (The Situation)

So I decided to work closely with the call center reps. There was initially some resistance because they had their own methods. So I called their manager in Bangalore and got to know him, listened to his concerns, and collaborated with him to figure out how to make it work. We negotiated methods and schedules that worked for both of us. (Obstacle and Actions)

I then improved their scripts, provided a sales training webinar, and coached some of the reps one-on-one. (More Actions)

Within a month, the flow of leads went up to 30 a day, which increased revenue by at least $50,000 that year. (The Results)

How Does SOAR Help?

SOAR reminds you to organize your thoughts so that your stories are complete, compelling, and concise. SOAR also teaches you to make sure you include results. The most common mistake in interview storytelling is to shortchange the results. Many people telling this story would end with, "So I improved their scripts, provided a sales training via webinar, and coached some of the reps one-on-one."

"Hmm," thinks the interviewer, "So you spent a lot of time, but did it *work*?"

Be specific about results. Quantifying can really help: Say how fast, how much, or how many hours saved or dollars earned. If you don't have exact figures, estimate.

Develop Your Stories List

Start compiling a list of stories, especially stories that illustrate your key selling points. Having trouble remembering stories? Find lists of behavioral interview questions online, and they'll help jog your memory.

Try to build your list to at least a dozen stories, and preferably 20 or more. In today's lengthy interview processes, you may be asked dozens of questions. You don't want to have to tell the same handful of stories over and over.

Don't write your stories out as full scripts because that will make you sound over-rehearsed and result in a huge list that's hard to review quickly. Instead, for each story simply write down a title and a few points you might otherwise forget to mention.

Then list the skills and strengths the story demonstrates. Now, if an interviewer asks about a particular skill, you'll know which story to tell.

Use the template in Figure 16.1.1 to start your story list. This will be one of your most powerful job search tools.

> Title:
>
> Be sure to mention:
>
> Skills and strengths this story illustrates:

Figure 16.1.1 **SOAR Stories List Template.**

Tell Me About Yourself

Because it comes first, "would you tell me about yourself" may be the most important question in the whole interview. Build your answer around your key selling points, and you'll have an answer that shows you're the right person for the job.

For example, Claudia Candidate is interviewing for a job as an instructional designer. Following the instructions provided earlier in this chapter, she has identified the following as her key selling points:

- 10 years of progressively responsible training department experience leading up to her most recent role as a lead instructional designer.
- Strong accomplishments.
- Exceptional motivation to work for this company: She has been talking with people from this company and watching for openings for a year; working there is her dream.
- An MA in instructional design.
- Web design and graphic design skills above and beyond the requirements.

Her answer to "tell me about yourself" could sound something like this:

I'm really excited to be here because I use all your apps and I've been following Cool Company for a long time. I was thrilled to be referred to you by Shandra Smith.

As you can see in my resume, I've been working in training departments for 10 years, and I've progressed through various positions up to my recent role as lead instructional designer at XYZ company.

I've made a real difference there. For example, last year I led an overhaul of our sales training programs for 600 reps nationwide. Participant ratings went up from 7 to 9.5 out of 10, and the reps started performing better, which led to revenue growth.

Some of my other strengths include web design and graphic design skills and a master's in instructional design from QRS University, which gives me a solid grounding in [here she names a couple of hard-to-find skills relevant to the opening].

For me, the most motivating thing about designing training programs is finding out that people are actually doing their jobs better and enjoying them more because of what I created. That's always my goal.

Working here sounds like a perfect fit with what I'm looking for. I've talked to several people connected to the company, and I like what I've heard about the culture and where you're going.

Do you have any questions about what I've said so far?

Elements of a Good "Tell Me About Yourself" Answer

When crafting a good "tell me about yourself" answer, try to include most or all of these elements:

- an opening that gets the interviewer's interest
- focus on key selling points
- a very brief career summary
- an accomplishment example, demonstrating that you get results
- a little work-relevant insight into your motivations and personality
- a brief statement of your well-informed enthusiasm about the job
- a good question at the end (the one in the example is ideal—feel free to use it).

Then practice saying it. To make sure you don't sound robotic or over-rehearsed, don't memorize a script. Instead, create a simple outline or list of your key talking points (but don't write it out in full sentences).

Talk through your answer, referring to your outline, until you can say it from memory. Then practice with a partner, asking him to tell you what he liked best about your answer and what could be better. Keep working on it until you feel confident that your answer will leave employers with a clear sense of why they should hire you—and an interest in hearing more!

Prepare for Common Interview Questions

Plan your answers to common interview questions (which you can easily find online), as well as others you know they'll ask based on your resume, such as "How did you win this award?" or "Why is there a gap in your work history?" Create a list of typical questions and jot down a few notes under each as needed. As with your "tell me about yourself" outline, keep your notes brief. When you're preparing for a specific interview, you can look up the company on Glassdoor.com to see if past interviewees posted interview questions there.

Use every answer to market yourself for the job by keeping the focus on your key selling points. Every answer should show employers why they should hire you.

Sometimes it's not obvious what an interview question is really about, so you should get in the habit of asking yourself, "What are they really trying to find out here?"

Notice when the question requires a story. If it starts with a phrase such as "tell me about a time when" or "give me a specific example of," then a general answer isn't enough. Even if specific stories and examples are not asked for, use them frequently. SOAR stories will make your answers more believable *and* memorable.

Make sure you are authentic in your answers. Lies and exaggerations will probably come back to haunt you, and answers "borrowed" from websites can sound phony. Be strategic and be real.

One important question to prepare for is, "What are your salary expectations?" This is often asked in phone screenings, which can occur unexpectedly. In general, you should try to delay answering this question until later in the interview process. However, if pressed, it's best to provide a range that is based on your research of your market value. This issue is covered in detail in chapter 11, so review it for further guidance on handling salary questions. Plan and rehearse your answer carefully, because it can affect your earnings for years to come.

Once you're in the interview, listen carefully! Make sure you understand what the interviewer is asking. If you're not sure, ask a clarifying question. Don't repeat yourself. Once you've said what you need to say, stop. Table 16.1.1 addresses commonly asked interview questions and what the interviewer is looking for.

Table 16.1.1. Common Interview Questions and What They're Really About

The Question	What They're Looking For
"What's your story?"	• Why should we hire you? • Do you have the good judgment to handle this strange question and give me an answer that's relevant?
"Tell me about your current or past job."	• How did that job prepare you for this one?
"What's your biggest weakness?"	• Is it a weakness so serious it disqualifies you? • Are you transparent about areas in which you need to improve? • Do you strive for continuous improvement?
"Tell me about a time when you failed."	• Are you open and honest? • Do you learn from your failures? • Do you do everything you can to "save the day"?
"Tell me about your best boss ever."	• Do you value a boss who makes you stretch and grow, or one who's just easy? • Have you worked well with past managers?
"Tell me about a difficult person you had to work with."	• Are you able to work well with everyone? • Are you fair and nonjudgmental, or do you get caught up in complaining? • Can you answer this sensitive question discreetly, without damaging someone else's reputation (or your own)?
"Are you having other interviews?"	• Are you about to take another job? • Are we wasting our time interviewing you?
"Where do you see yourself in five years?"	• If we hire you, will you stay a reasonable amount of time? • Will you grow and take on more responsibility? • Are you realistic and patient about seeking advancement?

"Who are our competitors?"	• Do you understand our market position and our challenges? • Are you interested enough to try to find out?
"How would you describe the color yellow to a blind person?"	• Can you show us you're comfortable with ambiguity and unexpected challenges? • Can you demonstrate certain soft skills relevant to this job (e.g., creativity, intuition, and communication skills)?

Impress by Asking Good Questions

Acing an interview is not just about giving the right answers. Asking the right questions is crucial. Good questions show that you're seriously interested in the job, and that you're already thinking ahead about how to do it well. Failing to ask questions will make you seem uninterested.

It's important to prepare 10 or 12 questions for the end of the interview. You won't actually ask that many, but you need plenty because some may have already been answered by that point.

The end of the interview isn't the only time to ask questions. Asking questions early can arm you with information that helps you sell your skills, because the more you know about the employer's needs, goals, and activities, the better you can target your message.

Think about this. A good question:

- shows good communication skills and a sense of appropriateness
- focuses on the work, not the pay: until the company has made you an offer, never ask about compensation, benefits, flextime, or perks
- shows that you've done your homework: the best questions are grounded in the research you've done on the company. For example, "I've read articles about your company's new push for online self-service. How is that affecting this department?"

Any of the following questions could be customized and improved by referring to what you already know:

- What are the most important aspects of this role?
- Can you describe a typical day in this role?
- What are the goals and priorities for this role?
- Is this a new position?
- If not, what happened to the person who was previously in the job?
- What changes are ahead for this company in the coming year, and in the next few years?
- What are the greatest strengths and weaknesses of this company?
- What do you love about working here? Why have you stayed at this company?
- What do you find frustrating about working here?
- How would you describe the company culture, and how is it evolving?

These questions are good to ask a recruiter:

- What is the name and title of the person I would be reporting to in this role?

- What kind of person works best with him or her?
- What's the next step after our conversation today?

These questions are appropriate to ask the hiring manager (your prospective boss):

- What are your goals for this role? If I were successful, what would that look like?
- What are the top priorities for this role in the first 60 days?
- How does upper management view the role and the impact of this department?
- What training, development, and recognition have your reports received in the past year?
- What is your management style?

You could ask these questions to members of senior management:

- How does this department contribute to the growth of the company?
- How do you see this department's role changing as the company grows?
- How is this company looking to evolve so it continues to compete effectively?
- How could a person in this role support that evolution?

We've looked at how to answer questions and how to ask them, but only in terms of words. Now let's look at the important dimension beyond the verbal.

Nonverbal Communication and "Chemistry"

Employers don't make hiring decisions on a purely rational basis. A lot of it comes down to gut feelings, and nonverbal communication has a big influence. Some experts say two-thirds of communication is nonverbal. So, what do you need to do to make sure you're giving off the right vibes? Get feedback on your nonverbals.

Your first step is to look in a mirror or videotape yourself while you practice. This way you can see what you look like and gain some perspective. However you also need an outside perspective, so ask a friend or coach to do mock interviews with you. Ask for critique about not just what you said, but the overall impression you give. How was your handshake, smile and other facial expressions, eye contact, posture, movement, tone of voice, and appearance? What did you do well and what could use improvement?

Much has been written about body language—more than will fit into this chapter—so for now, let's look at some of the most important points.

First Things First

The interviewer's first in-person impression of you is likely to involve a smile, eye contact, and a handshake. When you are practicing, give special attention to these actions. Ask a friend for feedback.

Mind Your Posture

In most cases good posture means sitting up straight and leaning forward slightly, with both feet on the floor or with your legs crossed all the way; avoid resting your ankle on your knee, which looks too casual. Your hands can be in your lap, or sometimes gesturing. But don't cross your arms because it can make you seem standoffish; you want to look open and receptive.

Say the Interviewer's Name

Most people like to hear their own name, so use it when shaking hands at the beginning and end of the interview, and maybe once or twice in between.

Should you say "John" or "Mr. Jones"? The etiquette on this is changing, and not everyone agrees on it. One common view is that it's best to follow the interviewer's cues: If she calls you by your first name, reply in the same way. Other experts say it's better to address the interviewer formally until they specifically invite you to use their first name. Use the approach that seems to fit your particular situation.

Dress to Impress

What to wear depends on many factors—the role, the industry, and the company. As a general rule, dress one level higher than the way you would dress on the job.

If the workplace is casual (jeans, T-shirts, athletic shoes), come to the interview in business casual: dress slacks, a skirt or a dress, an open-collared shirt, semi-dress shoes, and maybe a blazer. If business casual is the standard workplace attire, wear a suit—preferably blue or gray, closed-toe dress shoes, and if you're a man put on a tie. If you'll be wearing a suit every day, you can't get much dressier than that. Wear a suit.

Etiquette

An interview is more formal than most day-to-day situations, so watch your manners even before you walk into the building and as you reach your car afterward. Here are some things you may not have thought of:

- Wait to be offered a seat before sitting down, or at least wait until the others have taken their seats.
- If offered a beverage other than water, it may best to politely decline. This is considerate to your host. Also, nervous people are more accident-prone, and you don't want to risk spilling coffee on yourself or your host's furniture! Water is simpler and safer.
- Don't place personal items—briefcase, water bottle, and so forth—on the interview table. Instead, put them under your chair or on an empty chair next to you. You may place a portfolio or notepad and pen on the table if you bring one.
- Don't just turn off your cell phone—put it out of sight.
- As of this writing, it is still inadvisable to take notes on an electronic device at an interview.
- When leaving the interview, if possible, stop in the outer office and thank the person who greeted you when you arrived.

Interview Formats: Know How to Ace Them All

Not every job interview is a one-on-one, question-and-answer session. There are many interview formats, and each has its own challenges and opportunities. Reduce the "surprise factor" by knowing how to succeed in any format.

Phone Screening

A phone screening can be a little like a "pop quiz"—it may arrive out of the blue. So as soon as you've sent in your resume, get ready. Keep all job announcements you've applied to readily available, along with your cover letters and resumes. When a recruiter calls and says he's calling about X company, you don't want to be struggling to remember, "Which job was that? What did I tell them about myself?" Having these materials handy helps keep you prepared.

The recruiter may subtly pressure you to "talk for a few minutes *right now*" even though it's not a good time for you. Asking to reschedule may put you at a disadvantage, because a busy recruiter may simply move on to other candidates. However, if it really is a bad time, it may be better to ask, "Is there another time we can talk today?" rather than do a poor interview because you're distracted.

In any phone interview, your tone of voice is crucial. Make a point of smiling, which can be heard in your voice, and stand up, which makes your voice sound more energetic.

One-on-One, Face-to-Face

This type of interview is familiar to most of us. Typically longer than a phone screening, an in-person interview may be a half hour, an hour, or longer. (A lengthy interview is often a good sign!)

Did you know that being more than 15 minutes early to an in-person interview can actually make a bad impression? It's smart to get to the interview location well in advance to ensure you won't be late, but wait in a coffee shop or in your car until 10 to 15 minutes before the scheduled time. Use this extra time to review your notes about the job, the people, and what you plan to say. You can also do your relaxation exercises and visualize a successful interview.

When you go inside, pay attention for clues about the company culture and what it's like working there. Be friendly, but not too chatty, with the receptionist and whoever else you encounter.

Panel Interview

Panel interviews are usually intended to standardize the interviewing process, so they are firmly structured. Often, several interviewers are lined up across from you, taking turns asking prepared questions. The situation may feel artificial and not very comfortable, but look at it this way: The interviewers probably don't enjoy it either. Let that thought give you a feeling of empathy toward them. Try to be gracious and put them at ease, and you may end up making yourself feel more relaxed as well.

As you answer the interview questions, include all the interviewers in your gaze and body language—not just the person who asked the question. And don't only focus on the friendly people; the grumpy one needs to be convinced, too.

If note taking is allowed, write down the name and role of each person present. Arrange the names on your notepad in the same way the people are arranged in the room—Kyle on the left, Lisa on the right—this will help you remember who is who. If possible, exchange business cards.

Group Interview

The term *group interview* can mean different things, but here we'll focus on a process in which multiple candidates interact together in a round-table discussion or small-group exercise. This format allows interviewers to observe interpersonal skills such as teamwork, leadership, and helping to facilitate the stated goals of the exercise.

It's a balancing act: Demonstrate your skills without taking over, and collaborate with people who may also be your competitors as you might do on the job if you were competing with teammates for a promotion while still working together for a common goal.

Behavioral Interview

Behavioral interview questions generally start with language such as "tell me about a time when" and require you to tell a specific story from your experience. Some interviewers rely heavily on such questions. The theory behind behavioral interviewing is that your behavior and performance in the past is the best predictor of how you'll perform if hired. So, as stated earlier in this chapter, it's important to develop a list of success stories that you can draw from to answer these questions.

Sequential or All-Day Interviews

It is increasingly common to have multiple interviews for a single position, and when they're crammed into one day it can be a bit mind-boggling. It is important to fight the fatigue! You may want to bring along a bottle of tea or a snack such as a protein bar.

In each interview, vary the stories and examples you tell because interviewers may compare notes later. If possible, take a few notes after each interview, before it all begins to blur together. This will help you write smart follow-up messages later.

Meal Interview

A meal with your prospective boss and teammates may not be called an interview, but it can have the same effect on your candidacy, so prepare. Plan your order in advance to save time. Order a very light meal so you can concentrate on communicating rather than eating. Avoid alcoholic beverages, even if the boss is drinking. Keep your phone off and out of sight. Be polite to restaurant staff.

Should you socialize or get down to business? Follow the lead of your host. One good conversation strategy is to ask the others what they enjoy most about their work and the company. Relax, but don't be caught off guard and be on your best behavior as to conversational topics and table manners—even if the boss is less correct!

Testing

Various types of tests may be given at interviews, including aptitude tests, which could involve anything from basic skills of reading, writing, or math to computer or technical skills, as well as behavioral or personality tests.

It's best to be honest in personality tests because they are designed to spot dishonesty. However, it may be helpful to take practice tests in advance. The Dummies website (www.dummies.com) is a great resource for practice personality tests. Chapter 10 covers preemployment testing in great detail, so review it for more guidance on this topic.

Case Interview

Case interviews are a specific type of testing. In a case interview, candidates are given a situation or problem similar to one they would face on the job and asked to resolve it. Many webpages and books have been written on this type of interview, and this chapter cannot begin to cover the subject.

If invited to this type of interview, plan to spend many hours preparing for it, over a period of many days if possible. You can read more about case interviews on websites such as www.LiveCareers.com and www.Vault.com.

Presentation-Facilitation Interview

You may be asked to develop and give a presentation, either on a topic of your choice or one selected by the interviewer. If your work involves training, you may be asked to facilitate a short workshop. Others within the company may join as an audience or active participants.

Of course you need to demonstrate your knowledge, but strive to make it enjoyable for others as well. Make it interesting and encourage comments and interaction. Use appropriate humor to put people at ease.

Video Interviews

Although many employers use video interviewing, few people really enjoy the process. Even the interviewers are likely to be uncomfortable. If you can make the experience feel more natural, engaging, and enjoyable for all concerned, you will stand out and make a good impression. Video interviews may be either two-way calls or asynchronous. Two-way calls happen in real time, typically through platforms such as Skype or Google Hangouts. In an asynchronous interview, you're not interacting with an interviewer in real time; instead, you are sent a list of questions and record your responses.

You should familiarize yourself with the technology. Test it out in advance if possible, and make sure you understand what to do before you start. It is also important to make sure your face is well lit. Look at yourself through your computer's Photo Booth or Crazy Cam application, through a camera, or even in a mirror, to see how your face is lit. Then adjust the lighting in the room as necessary.

Make sure you're looking directly into the camera because this creates the effect of eye contact. If the camera isn't at eye level, adjust its position. If you're using a laptop, put a box or books under it to raise it.

To really master digital interviewing, refer to Paul Bailo's book, *The Essential Digital Interview Handbook: Lights, Camera, Interview: Tips for Skype, Google Hangout, GoToMeeting, and More.*

"Wow Factor" Extras

Whatever type of interview you're participating in, consider demonstrating that you're the kind of employee who goes above and beyond by sharing something extra, such as a portfolio, PowerPoint presentation, or a 30-60-90-day plan showing how you will create value if hired.

Your portfolio could include work samples, summaries of projects, graphs and other visual aids, letters of recommendation, copies of certificates or recognitions, transcripts, or highly favorable performance evaluations, as well as your resume and references.

If you've prepared a presentation to show on a computer, make sure it can be simply and instantly displayed on your laptop or tablet without any need for additional equipment or setup.

If you bring a 30-60-90-day plan, make sure it is customized to the specific job and company, thoroughly researched, and brief—no more than four pages.

Know that some interviewers may not want to look at these extra items, so try to find out in advance whether they're welcome. Whatever you bring, choose the right moment to use it. A good time might be when the employer has asked a question related to the items you've brought.

Closing the Interview

You've marketed your skills impressively from the first handshake to the last question and the interviewer is wrapping it up. You're done, right? Not quite. Remember, you want to be remembered as the best person for the job—and in addition to first impressions, final impressions are memorable as well. So it is important to reiterate your key selling points and your interest in the job.

Remember Claudia, the instructional designer from earlier in this chapter? Here's what her closing statement sounded like:

> Thank you again for your time today. I'm even more excited than before. Your plan for the new training portal sounds exactly like the type of project where my web design and graphic skills can be a big asset. And overall, I've got the experience and education to lead your design team credibly and be a great resource. I think it's a great fit and I'd love to join your team!

Assuming they don't hire Claudia on the spot, she should then ask about next steps, including whether it would be okay to call on such-and-such day to follow up.

Follow Up Right—Not by Rote

Most candidates send a brief thank you note after an interview. But if you want to stand out, make sure your follow-up communications reinforce the reasons why you're the right person for the job. The purposes of the follow-up thank you note are to:

- Express appreciation.
- Reiterate your strong interest in the position.
- Remind the employer of your key selling points.
- Add a bit more information—another accomplishment, for example—or to correct a misimpression.

Should you send a handwritten note, an email, or a typed letter? Each has its advantages, and the impact depends on your industry. A handwritten note could seem old-fashioned in some industries, but could be a good way to stand out in others. Whatever form it takes, make sure your message arrives soon, preferably by the next business day.

Then stay on their radar screen. Additional written messages, or possibly a phone call, can help demonstrate that you're highly motivated and assertive. Take a helpful tone—"I wanted to see whether you need any additional information"—rather than asking whether they've made a decision.

Checklist: What to Bring to the Interview

As we approach the end of this chapter, you've probably noticed that there is a lot to remember about interviewing. Use this checklist to keep track of your logistics on the big day. Add or delete items to adapt the list to your own unique situation.

- Pen and notepad
- List of questions you want to ask
- Copies of your resume and cover letter
- Copies of up to three letters of recommendation
- Notes to review beforehand (for example, SOAR stories, talking points in response to common questions)

- Job posting, names of people you'll meet, any other details you have about the interview
- Master application to copy information from
- Carrying case (folder or briefcase)
- Address, directions (including an alternate route), and a map (paper or app)
- Cash for alternate transportation, just in case
- Plan B for wardrobe malfunction (spare tie, safety pin, spare nylons, makeup)
- Cell phone, off
- Optional: Portfolio, presentation, or 30-60-90-day plan.

Summary

Acing the interview is not simple; in any type of interview—from the shortest phone screening to an all-day interview on-site—there are many opportunities to answer the unspoken question, "Why should we hire you?"

You can demonstrate you're the one to hire by:

- initiating rapport with a firm handshake, eye contact, and a smile
- memorably communicating your key selling points right from the start
- effectively telling SOAR stories so the employer can easily visualize the skillful way you do your work
- nailing every detail, from appropriate clothing to what you brought (and didn't bring) with you
- marrying authenticity with strategy to sell your skills with every answer.

Successfully interviewing takes work. Reading this chapter was a great start, and now comes the most important part: Go through it again and act on every tip that applies to you. Plan and practice like the smart, hard-working professional you are! Because most candidates don't prepare enough, you will stand out and be remembered. Get ready for a job offer!

Reference

Sue Kaiden, "Ace the Interview," *Find Your Fit: A Practical Guide to Landing a Job You'll Love*, pp. 103–112. Copyright © 2016 by Association for Talent Development (ATD). Reprinted with permission.

Bailo, P.J. 2014. *The Essential Digital Interview Handbook: Lights, Camera, Interview: Tips for Skype, Google Hangout, GoToMeeting, and More.* Pompton Plains, NJ: Career Press.

Reading 16.2

Turning a Classic Networking Tactic Into a Job Lead

Young professionals looking for career development opportunities are reviving the informational interview, a classic networking tactic that fell out of favor with the rise of digital research tools.

By Sabine Vollmer

"Every time I made a career change, I would take as many people out to lunch as I could and pick their brains," says Mark Astrinos, CPA/PFS.

More than a decade after the convenience of online fact gathering caused the informational interview to fade, a new generation of job seekers is rediscovering the networking tactic.

Ethan Harkleroad, a recent accounting graduate of the University of San Diego, has used informational interviews to decide on a career, secure four internships, and establish contacts with mentors.

In their most basic form, informational interviews establish contacts to subject-matter experts such as CFOs, professors, or authors, and provide answers to career- or work-related questions. The interviewer seeks and arranges the contacts and comes up with and asks the questions out of curiosity, not to apply for a job. Informational interviews usually last 30–60 minutes.

Before digital search tools such as Glassdoor, Google, and LinkedIn, informational interviews were the best way for job seekers to get a taste of what it would be like to work for different accounting firms and industries, start a rapport with company executives, and build on contacts should a job opening come up.

Millennials are learning that informational interviews are still valuable in a digital world. Harkleroad said that the information he gets from those he talks to is more valuable than what he can find online.

"You learn about their experiences, their challenges, and what they would do differently," he said. "Every time I go to one of these interviews I get way more than I bargained for."

A Classic Networking Tactic With a Digital Twist

Harkleroad shares his penchant for informational interviews with other accounting graduates and, as research by accounting and finance staffing firm Accountemps suggests, other Millennials. Young professionals are resurrecting the networking technique with a digital-native twist. They research and connect with executives through, for example, LinkedIn, and may conduct the interview over Skype or FaceTime, said Bill Driscoll, Accountemps district president.

Thirty-six percent of the more than 2,200 CFOs Accountemps polled in large U.S. metropolitan areas said informational interviews are much more common today than 10 years ago. About one-third of the respondents said they get requests for informational interviews at least once per month.

Asking for and scheduling informational interviews makes a lot of sense for college students who, like Harkleroad, are at the beginning of their careers. But what about accountants who have worked in the profession for a while?

Informational Interviews Work for CPAs With Experience

Mark Astrinos, CPA/PFS, has worked as an accountant in the San Francisco area for about a decade, first in auditing and consulting, then in tax and compliance, and now as a financial planner for high-wealth individuals in Silicon Valley.

"Every time I made a career change, I would take as many people out to lunch as I could and pick their brains," he said. "It was scary to make these changes. The advice I received was very helpful."

"Every time I go to one of these interviews I get way more than I bargained for," says Ethan Harkleroad, a recent accounting graduate who has gained valuable career insights and opportunities from informational interviews.

"Every time I go to one of these interviews I get way more than I bargained for," says Ethan Harkleroad, a recent accounting graduate who has gained valuable career insights and opportunities from informational interviews.

People he asks to talk to are generally happy to spend a half-hour or an hour answering his questions, he said. Most recently he interviewed a financial planning expert, who's also an author and had written an intriguing article. To schedule an informational interview, Astrinos asked a friend to introduce him to somebody who worked at the same organization as the author. Within a week, the author emailed him to set up a time for a 20-minute phone call.

Informational interviews also remain a good way to impress an executive and develop a job lead, the survey found. Eighty-four percent of the CFOs Accountemps polled said they would probably alert someone who impressed them in an informational interview about a job opening.

5 Steps to Conduct Informational Interviews

Harkleroad and Astrinos follow processes that can be broken down into five steps:

1. To get started, Harkleroad turns to LinkedIn. It's an important tool for him to find and research people who are likely to answer his questions—for example, investment bankers in San Diego willing to talk to him about their day-to-day responsibilities, a local university professor who explained to him what an accounting major entailed, or a CFO who had started his career in public accounting and retraced the career steps that led to his being in charge of operations at a San Diego craft brewing company.

Astrinos uses LinkedIn and calls on high school and college alumni who are, or know, accountants in the Bay Area. He sometimes uses the contact information at the end of blogs or written articles to reach out to the authors, but he also networks at professional conferences and on Twitter.

2. Once he knows whom he wants to talk to, Harkleroad emails them or sends them messages through LinkedIn, asking for 20–30 minutes in person or over the phone. Occasionally, he asks a contact in his network to introduce him to the person he wants to interview.

"I've never received an email back that said no," Harkleroad said. He estimates he has an actual conversation with about two-thirds of the people he contacts.

3. He usually shows up at the informational interview with an agenda—questions he wants to ask that he has either memorized or written down. He has put the piece of paper with the questions on the table in front of him to look more serious and make sure he gets every question answered, Harkleroad said. A basic question about what the interviewee does usually opens the interview, he said, but the agenda frequently becomes secondary once an interesting conversation develops.

4. At the end of the conversation, Harkleroad thanks interviewees and asks them whether they know somebody he should also talk to. "You find the people you want to talk to, you reach out to them and then make contact with someone else," he said. (See the sidebar, "How to Mind Your Manners During Informational Interviews," for more advice.)

5. All of his contacts then end up in an Excel spreadsheet with notes and rankings to remind him when he last got in touch and what they talked about, and whom he should keep up with based on career goals.

Astrinos keeps his contacts on his cellphone and on LinkedIn.

In Brief

- An informational interview is a classic networking technique that fell out of favor with the rise of digital search tools. Young professionals are reviving the technique with a digital twist.
- Experienced accountants and recent college graduates have used informational interviews successfully.
- One young CPA explains, step by step, how to conduct an informational interview.

How to mind your manners during informational interviews

Professional recruiters, including Beth A. Berk, CPA, CGMA, and Accountemps, suggest keeping these five tips in mind as you set up and conduct an informational interview:

- **Pick the right person.** Research a few companies or industries in which you're interested and identify the right contact to talk to.
- **Be strategic about how you ask for an informational interview.** Ask a common contact for an introduction or send an email to start a conversation. If you use the phone, practice what you'll say ahead of time.
- **Come prepared.** Dress for a business meeting and come prepared with a list of questions to run the meeting, but don't oversell yourself.
- **Be patient and don't go into the interview expecting a job.** Landing a job interview can take time, but an informational interview that goes well can lead to referrals.
- **Show gratitude.** Send a handwritten thank-you note after the interview and keep your new contact updated on your job search and career progress.

The Elevator Speech

The term "elevator speech" refers to a hypothetical situation in which you enter an elevator and realize you're standing next to an executive who works for a prestigious company. In such a situation, you would only have 30–60 seconds to introduce yourself and make an impression. To do so, you need to deliver a concise yet detailed speech that explains who you are and what makes you unique, compared to your competition.

Although you won't often find yourself in that specific situation, you will have multiple opportunities to deliver an effective elevator speech, including at networking events and at interviews when a recruiter says, "Tell me about yourself."

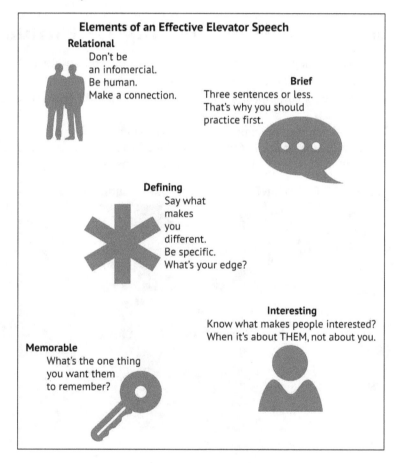

Figure 16.1 Elevator Speech Infographic

Assignment: Write an Elevator Speech

To prepare for interviews and networking events, draft your own elevator speech. Every elevator speech is unique to the individual delivering it, but here are some general principles that can help you write your speech:

Drafting Your Elevator Speech

1. Introduction
    a. Establish listener's attention (friendly feeling and curiosity)
2. Body
    a. Where you've been (past)
    b. Where you are now (present)
    c. Where you're going (goals for future)
3. Conclusion
    a. Call to action (e.g., goal, next steps, referral, appointment, etc.)

For this course, you will write and rehearse an elevator speech. You will want to practice your speech until you can deliver it smoothly. Then you will deliver your elevator speech in class as well as during your mock interview.

Behavioral Interviewing Questions

Most people are nervous when they go into an interview situation and so are often unable to present themselves in the best way possible. Practice is one of the most common suggestions for succeeding in interviews, and often, students who participate in many interviews testify to how much repetition improves their performance.

You probably know that most companies use "behavioral interview questions" to help determine if a candidate will be a good fit for the position. One way to shine in your interview (and reduce your nerves) is to prepare for the most common behavioral interviewing questions and practice answering them.

EFFECTIVE STORY TELLING: direct, logical, meaningful and personalized

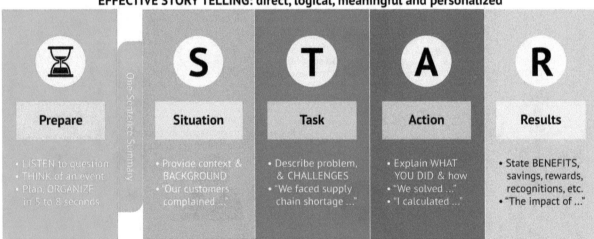

Do not think of new details as you answer. SAY what you had planned for & END

Figure 16.2 STAR Infographic

Interviewers are looking for specific elements in your responses to behavioral interviewing questions. Article 16.1 uses the acronym SOAR (situation, obstacle, actions, results) to define these steps; another common acronym is STAR (situation, task, action, result).

Interviewers who use behavioral interviewing questions typically ask questions about:

- Leadership
- Communication

- Teamwork or working with difficult people
- Conflict or solving problems
- Failure
- Overcoming adversity
- Stress/time management
- Greatest accomplishment
- Weakness

To prepare for a variety of questions using a variety of situations, complete the exercise below (Log of Accomplishments and Stories). Then you will have an opportunity to practice answering behavioral interview questions using the SOAR/STAR method.

Applying This Skill: Log of Accomplishments and Stories

Successful resumes, cover letters, and interviews will include details about specific situations. To prepare for the job search, develop a list of accomplishments and situations you might use to respond to interview questions. Mine the following settings for stories: work, education, volunteering, extracurricular activities, group memberships, and so on. For each of the topics listed below, write 1–2 ideas/specific situations. This will help you develop situations to use with the STAR interviewing method.

1. Ways you have worked effectively in a team

2. Problems or challenges you've overcome and how you overcame them

3. Accomplishments you are most proud of and why

4. Ways you've demonstrated leadership

5. What motivates you?

6. Failures and/or weaknesses and how you managed them

7. Communication and/or conflict resolution skills

8. Your greatest strengths

9. Honors, accomplishments, praise

10. Any other stories/situations that may be useful in answering interview questions

Applying This Skill: Peer Interview Practice

In this activity, you will pair with one or more of your peers to practice asking and answering behavioral interviewing questions. During one round, you will be the interviewee and practice answering questions based on the SOAR/STAR method and using the situations and stories you developed in the Log of Accomplishments and Stories activity.

During another round, you will be the interviewer. When you are the interviewer, please ask the following questions:

- Tell me a little about yourself (this is where the interviewee should use their elevator speech).
- What is your greatest weakness?
- What is your greatest strength?
- What motivates you?
- How do you define success?

Then ask about as many of the following as time allows. Ask follow-up questions as appropriate.

Tell me about a time when you demonstrated or dealt with:

- Leadership
- Communication
- Teamwork
- Working with difficult people
- Conflict or solving problems
- Failure
- Overcoming adversity
- Stress/time management
- Your greatest accomplishment
- Criticism

You may also ask some of the following common interview questions:

- Why should we hire you?
- Why are you a good fit for this company?
- What are your career goals? Where do you see yourself in ten years?
- Why did you leave your last employer?
- What do you know about the company?

- Do you have any questions for me?

Assignment: Mock Interview

As part of the job application preparation process, you will complete a mock (or a real) interview during the semester. This gives you practice with your elevator speech and behavioral interviewing questions practiced in class. In addition, it helps you make connections with recruiters. Every semester, students receive internship offers that start with the mock interview process.

You will schedule an interview through your school's career services center or find someone to interview you. If you are currently interviewing for jobs or internships, you may use that interview for this assignment.

To complete the mock interview assignment, you will write a memo (following business memo format) summarizing your preparation, the interview itself (including questions asked and how you answered), the lessons you learned, and the value of the experience to you. Specifics about content to include in the memo appear below.

Preparation and Notes

Before the interview, write at least one paragraph for each of the following:
- **Know yourself:** What are your interests, abilities, personality, and values? How do these fit the position that interests you? Be able to explain why you are interested in your career field of interest.
- **Research the organization.** Review the employer's website. Pay attention to their "about us" section. Look for their mission statement and news about the company. Who are they? What are their major products or services? Be able to discuss any of this with the interviewer.
- **Research a position on that company's website** and/or a position that you would be suited for as an internship opportunity and/or a first career position. Be able to name one position for which they hire new college graduates. Identify a few of the key qualifications for their position (or for the position you would like to obtain). Match your qualifications to the job position so you can speak to how you will add value to the company.
- **Prepare questions**, based on your research, that you will ask the interviewer.

Attend the Mock Interview

- Arrive a few minutes early.
- Dress professionally.
- Bring one to two copies of your resume.
- Act professionally; "no-shows" and late cancellations are unacceptable: They leave the employer with a negative impression of you, the business school, and the university. They also deny another student the opportunity of meeting with that employer.

Reflecting and Writing

Once you have completed your mock interview, write a memo describing your experience (up to 2 pages long); use appropriate *memo formatting* (see Chapter 5).
In your memo, include the following:

- Information about your *preparation,* including self-reflection, company research, and questions you prepared to ask during the interview.

- Name of the *company* and the individual (e.g., name and position, time with company, etc.) who conducted the interview. Indicate the date you completed the interview.
- *Summarize* the events that happened in the mock interview. In other words, what happened in the mock interview?

    o   Describe at least two questions you were asked and how you answered.
    o   Name a question you asked about the company and describe the answer.

- *Describe* the feedback you received (be specific). What did the interviewer think you did well? What could you improve? If you did not receive specific feedback, analyze your own performance based on the information learned in class. What do you think you did well? What would you improve for your next interview?
- *Analyze* how the interview went and *evaluate the value* of the information and the process of conducting a mock interview for you personally. Did the interview go well? Was it a useful experience for you?

Thank You Notes

Many people forget all about the old-fashioned thank you note, but this short message can have a huge impact on your career. In the job search process, thank you notes are a simple, easy way to show you are interested in a job and may boost your chances of getting a position. Even if the job isn't right for you, sending a thank you note with solidify your reputation as a considerate professional. In other business situations, thank you notes build goodwill and establish your presence as a thoughtful, considerate businessperson. Follow the easy steps below to write a thank you note to your interviewer.

Effective
Thank Yous

Anatomy of Stellar Gratitude Messages

More than half of job seekers never send thank you notes. More than half of hiring managers think less of candidates who don't send thank you notes. Enhance your chances at a job!

01 Greeting

A professional salutation is standard:
Dear Ms. Johnson,

Less formal may be appropriate:
Hi Andy,

02 Gratitude

Express appreciation for the time the interviewer took to meet with you.

03 Comment

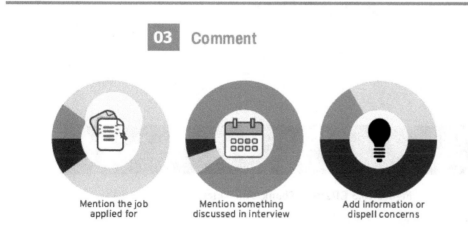

Mention the job applied for

Mention something discussed in interview

Add information or dispell concerns

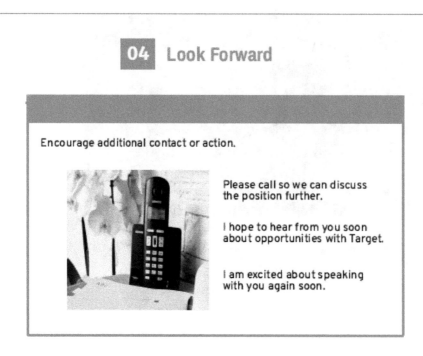

04 Look Forward

Encourage additional contact or action.

Please call so we can discuss the position further.

I hope to hear from you soon about opportunities with Target.

I am excited about speaking with you again soon.

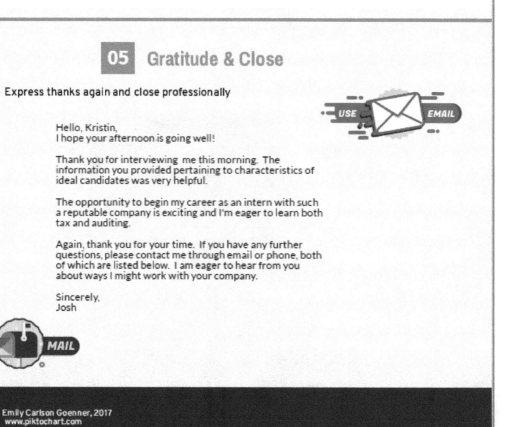

05 Gratitude & Close

Express thanks again and close professionally

USE EMAIL

Hello, Kristin,
I hope your afternoon is going well!

Thank you for interviewing me this morning. The information you provided pertaining to characteristics of ideal candidates was very helpful.

The opportunity to begin my career as an intern with such a reputable company is exciting and I'm eager to learn both tax and auditing.

Again, thank you for your time. If you have any further questions, please contact me through email or phone, both of which are listed below. I am eager to hear from you about ways I might work with your company.

Sincerely,
Josh

MAIL

Emily Carlson Goenner, 2017
www.piktochart.com

Figure 16.3 Effective Thank You Notes

Assignment: Interview with a Professional

In this course, we focus on skills you will need when you enter the workforce. We also focus on the job search. This assignment combines these two objectives by allowing you to network with a professional in your field and make connections between the information you are learning in this course and the way a professional sees communication in the "real world."

For this assignment, you will *identify* a person who is working in the field you want to enter. You will *interview* this industry professional and *report* on the information you learn as assigned by your instructor.

Interview Process

1. Identify a working professional to interview. For example, if you are an accounting major, try to find someone working in accounting. You may use your current network, LinkedIn, family, or other connections to identify a person to interview, but you may not interview a close family member (e.g., parent, sibling, etc.).

2. Set up the interview time/method. Conducting the interview in person is preferred, but you may schedule an interview over the phone, via Skype, or, as a last resort, using email. Give yourself plenty of time to set up the interview time. People are busy, and you need to allow time to schedule the process.

3. Prepare your questions, and bring writing materials to take notes. If you want to record the interview, ask permission prior to beginning. Don't be afraid to ask follow-up questions to clarify points or gather more information that interests you.

4. After the interview, you will present your findings to the class during one of the business meetings.

Interview Questions

You will ask the following nine questions. In addition, you may ask 2–3 additional questions of your choosing. Examples of additional questions appear below, or you may create your own.

1. On average, what percentage of your duties/work is spent on (and how do you use) each of the following:

    a. Writing?

    b. Reading?

    c. Listening?

    d. Speaking?

2. How are communication skills important in your career field?

3. In the past five years, has the amount/importance of communication increased, decreased, or remained the same for the following audiences:

    a. Internal audiences (coworkers, supervisors, board members, etc.)?

    b. External audiences (clients, business partners, community members, etc.)?

    c. International audiences (clients, partners, politicians, media, etc.)?

4. How have technological developments in the past 5–7 years revolutionized communication for you, your company, or your industry?

5. What are the top-three technology devices you use? Which of those devices would you be lost without (i.e., cannot go 24 hours without)?

6. Approximately how many email messages do you receive on a daily basis, and what advice do you have for managing the email demands of your job?

7. What are the top-three skills that entry-level employees *need* in order to succeed?

8. What are the top-three skills that entry-level employees *lack* or need to improve on?

9. If you were a student today, what would you do while in college to improve your chances of obtaining a job and succeeding in your first year of employment?

10. Create 2–3 additional questions:

Ideas for Additional Questions:

Present Job
- Describe how you occupy your time during a typical workweek.
- What skills or talents are most essential for effectiveness in this job?
  - What are the toughest problems you must deal with?
  - What do you find most rewarding about the work itself, apart from external motivators (e.g., salary, fringe benefits, travel, etc.)?

Preparation
- What credentials, educational degrees, licenses, and so on are required for entry into this kind of work? Required for advancement into this kind of work?
- What kinds of prior experience(s) are absolutely necessary?
- How did you prepare yourself for this work? What prepared you best for your position?

Lifestyle
- What obligations does your company/work place upon you, outside of the ordinary workweek? Do you enjoy these obligations?
- How much flexibility do you have in terms of dress, hours of work, vacation schedule, workplace flexibility (i.e., telecommuting)?
- Have you changed jobs due to lifestyle choices? Please explain.

Personal Advice
- How well suited is my background for this type of work?
- What do I need to do to become competitive?
- What educational preparation would be best?
- Are there certain majors, minors, or elective classes I can take to improve my chances?
- What kinds of experiences (paid employment or otherwise) would you most strongly recommend?

Summing Up Unit III: Preparing to Apply for a Job

Looking for a job can be a terrifying and daunting task. However, after completing Unit III, you should be well prepared, which will give you an advantage over many other job applicants. After completing Unit III, you should be able to:

- Share information, connect with people, and request and write recommendations on LinkedIn
- Create a professional reference sheet
- Create a professional resume
- Write a job application cover letter
- Prepare and give an elevator speech
- Answer behavioral interviewing questions using the SOAR/STAR method

- Conduct an informational interview

While completing this unit should give you job application documents you can use to find a job or internship right now, remember you need to update your documents for each application and continue to practice and prepare for interviews. Good luck with your job search!

Unit IV

Team Work and Presentations

- Chapter 17: Working in Teams
- Chapter 18: Giving Oral Presentations

While most people prefer to work alone, most companies and organizations use group or team work, at least part of the time. Working in groups and teams allows for successful completion of large projects because people bring different skills and talents to the group and the project may be divided into manageable pieces. Often, working together creates a synergistic energy that a single person just doesn't have; ideas may flow, skills are shared and developed, facts are checked, errors are minimized, productivity is increased, and deadlines are met. Knowing how to work successfully in teams and groups is a skill that will help you throughout your career. After completing Unit IV: Teamwork and Presentations, you will have a better understanding of how to work in a group or team and have experience doing so by completing two team projects.

Either in a team or alone, the majority of business people have to give presentations at some point in their careers, and some people do so frequently. Creating and delivering a presentation takes time and effort. After completing your this unit, you will understand how to create, prepare, and deliver an effective presentation. You will also complete one or more team projects that will help prepare you for tasks you may be asked to complete when you enter the workforce.

17

Working in Teams

Employers are always looking for people who work well in teams and work effectively as leaders. Some people are easy to work with, while others may be more challenging. Some people are natural leaders and assume that role easily, while others prefer to watch and play more supporting roles. All roles are important, and part of the purpose of this course is to allow you to practice different roles in the team. After completing this lesson, you will:

- Know your team members
- Understand your leadership role and how to work in your team

Working in Teams

The ability to work effectively in a team is one of the most highly sought after skills in the business world. According to a survey done by the Society for Human Resource Management, 83% of HR professionals rated teamwork as very or extremely important when considering an applicant (2016). Companies know that every great product, event, or project is created using a team-oriented approach. Successful companies know that projects and problems are usually too large and complex for one person to manage effectively, so gathering people with a variety of skills and talents helps create positive outcomes.

What exactly is a team? A team is a small group of people working together toward a common goal. Typically, a team is comprised of members who bring unique skill sets to the group. As a result, the team is stronger as a unit. The benefits of teamwork include:

- Greater productivity
- Increased efficiency
- Increased creativity, innovation, and cooperation
- Increased performance and success
- Greater job satisfaction
- Continued personal growth and professional development

While these benefits are many, groups may also struggle with a variety of issues, including struggles for leadership, the ability to give and take feedback, and effective communication.

In ineffective working groups, members may have differing goals, schedules, and work habits. Focusing on and developing a variety of communication skills will help improve members' ability to contribute to team success. To be effective team members, people need to:

- Listen carefully to others
- Contribute and explain their ideas and opinions
- Ask questions
- Participate in group discussions and communications (e.g., email, text, etc.)
- Support and respect other group members
- Know tasks and meet deadlines

- Participate in group decision making

The team projects in the course are designed to help students develop a variety of the skills needed to be effective team members. Groups will have time to develop and share ideas, make group decisions, develop tasks, and assign deadlines. The group projects involve individual and group contributions, focus on the process of project development and revision, and sharing of leadership roles. After completing the projects in this course, students should have developed some of the teamwork skills so highly desired by HR professionals.

Applying This Skill: Get to Know Your Team

After your new team members exchange names, make a list of 4–6 silly and unusual questions. The more unusual, the better. You may not ask the typical questions involving year in school, major, jobs, and so on. You don't need to answer the questions; just think of them and write them down.

Your instructor will inform you how to share the questions and when to respond to the get to know you questions. Online resource: Visit "Working in Teams" by Susan Oaks

....

Reading 17.1

Conflict Management Styles Assessment

Please **CIRCLE ONE** response that best describes you. Be honest, this survey is designed to help you learn about your conflict management style. There are no right or wrong answers!

Name _____   Date _____

	Rarely	Sometimes	Often	Always
1. I discuss issues with others to try to find solutions that meet everyone's needs.	1	2	3	4
2. I try to negotiate and use a give-and-take approach to problem situations.	1	2	3	4
3. I try to meet the expectations of others.	1	2	3	4
4. I would argue my case and insist on the advantages of my point of view.	1	2	3	4
5. When there is a disagreement, I gather as much information as I can and keep the lines of communication open.	1	2	3	4
6. When I find myself in an argument, I usually say very little and try to leave as soon as possible.	1	2	3	4
7. I try to see conflicts from both sides. What do I need? What does the other person need? What are the issues involved?	1	2	3	4
8. I prefer to compromise when solving problems and just move on.	1	2	3	4
9. I find conflicts exhilarating; I enjoy the battle of wits that usually follows.	1	2	3	4
10. Being in a disagreement with other people makes me feel uncomfortable and anxious.	1	2	3	4
11. I try to meet the wishes of my friends and family.	1	2	3	4
12. I can figure out what needs to be done and I am usually right.	1	2	3	4
13. To break deadlocks, I would meet people halfway.	1	2	3	4
14. I may not get what I want but it's a small price to pay for keeping the peace.	1	2	3	4
15. I avoid hard feelings by keeping my disagreements with others to myself.	1	2	3	4

Source: Reginald (Reg) Adkins, Ph.D., Elemental Truths. http://elementaltruths.blogspot.com/2006/11/conflict-management-quiz.html

Scoring the Conflict Management Styles Assessment

As stated, the 15 statements correspond to the five conflict management styles. To find your most preferred style, total the points for each style. The style with the highest score indicates your most commonly used strategy. The one with the lowest score indicates your least preferred strategy. However, all styles have pros and cons, so it's important that you can use the most appropriate style for each conflict situation.

Style Corresponding Statements: Total:

Collaborating (questions 1, 5, 7):   _____

Competing: (questions 4, 9, 12):   _____

Avoiding: (questions 6, 10, 15):   _____

Accommodating: (questions 3, 11, 14):   _____

Compromising: (questions 2, 8, 13)   _____

My preferred conflict management style is: _____

The conflict management style I would like to work on is: _____

How can I practice this conflict management style?

_____

_____

_____

_____

Brief Descriptions of the Five Conflict Management Styles

Keep in mind that one style of conflict management is not necessarily better than another; each style has pros and cons, and each can be useful depending on the situation. This assessment is intended to help you identify your typical response to conflict, with the goal that when you encounter future conflicts, you will be aware of not only your instinctive reaction, but also the pros and cons of that reaction for the specific situation. Furthermore, you will also be aware of the other styles of conflict management that you could draw on to resolve the situation, if one of the other styles is more appropriate for the current situation.

Owl: Collaborating

Owls highly value both their goals and their relationships. They view conflict as a problem to be solved and seek a solution that achieves both their goals and the goals of the other person. Owls see conflicts as a means of improving relationships by reducing tensions between two persons. They try to begin a discussion that identifies the conflict as a problem, and strive to resolve tensions and maintain the relationship by seeking solutions that satisfy both themselves and the other person.

Turtle: Avoiding

Turtles tend to value avoiding confrontation more than either their goals or relationships. They often find it easier to withdraw from a conflict than to face it. This might even include completely giving up relationships or goals that are associated with the conflict.

Shark: Competing

Sharks typically value their goals over relationships, meaning that if forced to choose, they would seek to achieve their goals even at the cost of the relationship involved. Sharks are typically more concerned with accomplishing their goals than with being liked by others. They might try to force opponents to accept their solution to the conflict by overpowering them.

Teddy Bear: Accommodating

Teddy Bears typically value relationships over their own goals; if forced to choose, Teddy Bears will often sacrifice their goals in order to maintain relationships. Teddy Bears generally want to be liked by others, and prefer to avoid conflict because they believe addressing it will damage relationships. Teddy Bears try to smooth over conflict to prevent damage to the relationship.

Fox: Compromising

Foxes are moderately concerned with both their goals and their relationships with others. Foxes typically seek a compromise; they give up part of their goals and persuade the other person in a conflict to give up part of their goals. They seek a conflict solution in which both sides gain something; the middle ground between two extreme positions. They are willing to sacrifice part of their goals in order to find agreement for the common good.

Reading 17.2

Conflict Management in Teams

By Kristin Behfar and Rebecca Goldberg

Successful teams have three things in common: (1) they meet their performance goals, (2) their members feel satisfied that they are learning/benefiting from being a part of the team, and (3) the process the team uses to collaborate sets it up for future success.[20] Recent research, however, suggests that in as little as five weeks of working together, only about 25% of teams meet these criteria.[21] The rest of the teams typically experience less-than-ideal processes and a decline in performance and/or satisfaction.

So what goes wrong? Most team members report that conflict among team members gets in the way of effective teamwork, and this conclusion is largely supported by academic research. The effect of conflict on teams is not always straightforward, however. Under the right conditions, for example, conflict can stimulate divergent thinking and lead to improved problem solving. On the other hand, it also tends to increase defensiveness, distract members from effective problem solving, and generate interpersonal animosity. So what determines whether a team can harness the benefits and limit the liabilities of conflict?

More than a decade of research provides a clear answer: how team conflict is managed. Because conflict happens in all teams (even the most effective ones), the presence of conflict has little bearing on whether one team is more successful than another. The factor most important to team success is how teams handle conflict when it does arise—and there are clear and reliable patterns associated with (in)effective conflict management. These patterns center on a critical tradeoff that teams implicitly or explicitly make when deciding how to deal with their conflict: the tradeoff between getting work done and making individual members happy.

The most effective teams create strategies to do both, but the majority of teams sacrifice one or the other. For example, conflict gets in the way of effective work if the team is unable or unwilling to address

[20] J. Richard Hackman and Charles G. Morris, "Group Tasks, Group Interaction Process, and Group Performance Effectiveness: A Review and Proposed Integration," in Leonard Berkowitz, ed., Advances in Experimental Social Psychology, vol. 8 (New York: Academic Press, 1975).

[21] This article is a summary of the research presented in: Kristin Behfar, Randall Peterson, Elizabeth Mannix, and William Trochim, "The Critical Role of Conflict Resolution in Teams: A Close Look at the Links Between Conflict Type, Conflict Management Strategies, and Team Outcomes," Journal of Applied Psychology 93, no. 1 (2008).

the root cause of the conflict. Low-performing teams typically struggle with this (usually because people did not speak their minds) or are unwilling to address the problem (e.g., when there were politics around taking sides or people are just too fed up to even try). This ultimately hurts performance because the inhibiting factors of the conflict are never managed—that is, removed from the team's process. In terms of individual satisfaction with the team, the distinguishing factor is how proactive versus reactive the team's approach is to conflict management. Teams that are proactive in identifying conflicts and addressing them before they escalate have more satisfied members. Teams that operate in reactive mode, wherein conflicts take them by surprise or keep the team in constant firefighting mode have less satisfied members. These tradeoffs around performance and satisfaction are summarized in Figure 17.1.1 below.

	High/Improving Performance Team is able and willing to identify and correct problems	**Low/Declining Performance** Team is unable or unwilling to identify and correct problems
High/Improving Satisfaction Proactive conflict-resolution strategies planned to preempt negative effects of conflict	Quadrant 1: The Ideal Team These teams create processes to foresee or anticipate conflict, allowing the team to either quickly resolve or prevent the conflict from escalating when it does occur. Example description: "We don't always agree, and if we don't, everyone understands why—and what their part might be in the problem. If someone is upset, we remind ourselves to focus on what (not who) might be causing the problem. We get the right person in the right role, and if someone is having trouble meeting a deadline, they let us know as soon as possible. We feel pretty good about helping one another out where needed."	Quadrant 2: Feeling Good, Doing Bad These teams create processes that are proactive about protecting relationships to the detriment of tackling the source of the problem. As a result, members feel valued and interactions tend to be pleasant, but the team is not willing to tackle difficult conflict in discussions and usually miss opportunities to leverage members' unique expertise or viewpoints. Example description: "Open disagreement is rare. We tend to incorporate everyone's viewpoint into our decisions. If we can't reach consensus, we just postpone the decision. This is not always the best, but everyone likes one another."
Low/Declining Satisfaction Reactive resolution strategies applied in reaction to existing problems	Quadrant 3: Recovering via Structure These teams create processes that reflect learning from their conflicts. Their strategies tend to rely on rules and structured agreements to prevent a similar problem from happening again. This makes team members more reliable (it acts as a substitute for	Quadrant 4: Minimize Misery/Avoidant These teams describe chaotic/trial-and-error processes that have no clear identification of the root cause of the conflict. Their overall orientation is typically to use strategies that move past (rather than address) the conflict. Example description:

	trust), but decreases satisfaction by constraining interactions. Example description: "Working in my team takes some effort. We have had some big differences. Now, when we have a problem, we force ourselves to stop and have these (sometimes time-consuming and uncomfortable) conversations about what each person can do so this won't happen again. We try to focus on the fact that we all want to do good work."	"When we have conflict, we get frustrated fast because big problems just never go away—they keep happening. Our conversations start tense and often escalate; people get upset and take sides. Many times we just give up and vote. The people who lose the vote just have to deal with it. We try to get most of our work done outside of our meetings and keep meetings short."

Figure 17.1.1. **Patterns in teams' outcomes according to the processes they create to manage conflict.**

Data source: Excerpted from Behfar et al.

It is probably safe to say that very few teams want to be in Quadrants 2 through 4. Teams land there because they do not successfully manage the tension between leveraging individuals' strengths and addressing their complaints. Put another way, in conflict situations, there are competing interests: what is good for the team is not always what each individual wants or is willing to do. In general, higher-performing teams create conflict-resolution strategies that make it clear how individuals need to contribute to the team and how that contribution aligns with their interests, whereas lower-performing teams focus more on appeasing individuals and addressing idiosyncrasies.

We will next discuss unique differences in how teams in the four quadrants manage conflict. It is important to note that people tend to use the same words (e.g., discussion, compromise, consensus) to describe conflict-resolution strategies, but research has demonstrated that those words represent strikingly different processes, as summarized in Figure 17.1.2.

	High/Improving Performance Conflict-resolution strategies focus on the group goal over specific individual complaints/quirks	**Low/Declining Performance** Conflict-resolution strategies focus on specific individuals' complaints over the group goal
High/Improving Satisfaction Proactive conflict-resolution strategies planned to preempt negative effects of conflict	Quadrant 1: The Ideal Team Resolution Focus: Equity Summary of strategies: • Work assignments based on skill and relevance to team performance • Forecasting scheduling and workload problems • Securing solid understanding behind compromises • Focusing on content over delivery style	**Quadrant 2: Feeling Good, Doing Bad** Resolution Focus: Equality Summary of strategies: • Work assignments based on individual interest and/or on who volunteers • In place of analysis, include all ideas • Strong focus on individuals goals, feelings, and needs versus how they can best

	The process behind the words: Discussion or Communicating: Evidence-driven exchange of conflicting views; members focus on evidence and analysis to make decisions Compromise: Each person understands how his/her interests align with the team goal—or what he/she is giving up and what he/she is getting back in return Consensus: All members are convinced they have compromised for good reasons	contribute to team performance The process behind the words: Discussion or Communicating: The topic has been raised and talked about (usually amicably) in a team meeting Compromise: The team has spent time trying to figure out how to make each person happy Consensus: All ideas have been incorporated (rather than debated to select the best one) and/or no one has voiced disagreement
Low/Declining Satisfaction Reactive resolution strategies applied in reaction to existing problems	**Quadrant 3: Recovering via Structure** Resolution Focus: Enforced Equity Summary of strategies: • Work assignments by assigned team role or convenience (due to others' uncompleted work) • Written or clearly articulated rules and consequences for not upholding expectations • Majority rule under time pressure • Putting disruptive members into a specific role The process behind the words: Discussion or Communicating: Members explicitly discuss conflicts and agree not to let differences get in the way of success Compromise: Members agree to follow team rules to prevent further disruption or to follow the majority opinion if under time constraints Consensus: Members share responsibility for correcting problems and agree to uphold team expectations	**Quadrant 4: Minimize Misery/Avoidant** Resolution Focus: Ad Hoc Summary of strategies: • Work assignments to divide and conquer; avoid meetings and one another • Frustrated members avoid debate and choose the path of least resistance or the easiest solution • Put conflicting viewpoints to a majority vote • Trial and error to correct process The process behind the words: Discussion or Communicating: Members openly air complaints and their (usually angry) expression is returned with an equally frustrated, in-kind reaction Compromise: Members agree to try a different method, assign a new person to a role, or one person has volunteered to do more work to avoid working with another member Consensus: Members have "given in" to a dominant member, they have agreed to

		disagree, and/or there has been a majority vote

Figure 17.1.2. **Summary of conflict-resolution strategies used by teams in each quadrant and examples of how the same words can represent different resolution processes.**

Data source: Excerpted from Behfar et al.

Quadrant 1: The Ideal Team

The teams in this quadrant orient themselves to resolve conflict using the principle of equity—each member is asked to contribute his or her fair share only in ways that serve the team. This means that not everyone equally gets what he or she wants, but members usually understand why team decisions are fair and equitable. The strategies unique to these teams include:

- Having explicit discussions about what members want to do versus what the team needs each person to do. Quadrant 1 teams are the only teams that actually divide work based on expertise rather than personal interests, convenience, or deadline emergencies. If one team member, for example, wants more client contact but other team members have better qualifications, these teams talk about how to balance individual needs for advancement with the team's need to best serve the client. These proactive discussions also allow them to avoid the critical mistake of debating the legitimacy of personal excuses (e.g., telling a member he or she is wrong to have personal priorities). By foreseeing where individual and team interests might conflict and allocating work accordingly, the likelihood of team members failing to meet expectations, exhibiting passive-aggressive behavior, and offering up excuses that irritate others diminishes.

- Proactively forecasting preventable problems. Most teams have busy people on them, which means (even with the best forecasting) they occasionally will miss a deadline or need help. Ideal teams are disciplined about foreseeing periods of work overload for each member and identifying workflow bottlenecks in advance. Being proactive about these issues prevents significant disruptions (e.g., from missed deadlines or delays), makes it easier for members to manage their time, and allows the team to agree on how to communicate about pending problems and change staffing arrangements or secure more resources if needed.

- Taking time to discuss individuals' compromises. The two practices above are often difficult because they require direct confrontation: telling a member he or she is not the best person for the job or selecting one person's idea over another's. The time spent to proactively discuss individual disappointments and to secure solid understanding behind compromises, pays off in the longer term because it is makes clear what each person is getting versus giving the team, that each person is valued (even if others consider him/her to be wrong), and why decisions benefit everyone in some way. This often includes the practice of debriefing previous decisions after getting feedback to confirm or disconfirm team wisdom.

- During conflict, focusing on content over delivery. When these teams have unanticipated conflicts, they "fight" by focusing on the content of the complaint—not the delivery. They do not react to demands and sarcastic or condescending tones, and instead focus on uncovering the underlying causes of the conflict.[22] One way they do this is to diffuse offensive behavior by naming it (e.g., "You are being way too aggressive right now, but I like what you are saying.") They also avoid the mistake of trying to change things about other members (e.g., a domineering member's personality) and instead find a way to get a disruptive member into a role that benefits the team. They might, for example, put an unbearably critical member in charge of reviewing all outgoing work in order to find errors.

---

[22] This is a similar practice that is described in negotiation as focusing on interests over positions (e.g., as described in Roger Fisher, William Ury, and Bruce Patton, Getting to Yes: Negotiating Agreement Without Giving In (New York: Penguin Group, 1981).

These teams are examples of textbook "ideal" collaboration, but that does not mean they do not experience difficult conflict. In fact, great teams typically have all of the same types and severity of conflict that other teams have. Where they are better able to contain any negative effects is by using equity as an underlying principle when managing conflict. Equitable resolution helps to maintain or restore a sense of fairness, ensure optimal resource allocation, and promote productivity and positive relationships between team members. The benefits of this orientation build over time. As each conflict is encountered and navigated successfully, team members bring these positive memories, behaviors, and expectations with them to the next conflict. Team members can be more willing to contribute and more willing to engage in the next conflict-resolution opportunity.

Not using these techniques, in contrast, can result in behavior that detracts from team performance and/or satisfaction, as seen in the other quadrants.

Quadrant 2: Feeling Good, Doing Bad

Teams in Quadrant 2 orient themselves to resolve conflict using the principle of equality—or giving equal weight to every individual and his/her interest. This focus on equality among individuals creates a team norm that values consensus and harmony at the cost of decision quality. For example, these teams consider themselves proactive because their discussions identify what it will take to keep each person positive and engaged in the team. This is indeed a good practice, but only when aligned with what the team is trying to achieve. When making decisions, these teams tend to find ways to equally include everyone's ideas rather than having evidence-driven, analytical discussions. These teams are not as common in organizations as (or are shorter-lived than) teams in the other quadrants because they do not perform. When they do occur, they often consist of members who have large status differences (and the lower-status members are afraid or unwilling to challenge higher-status members), or when there are other political reasons that silence members or make them unwilling to question the wisdom of team decisions.

Quadrant 3: Recovering via Structure

Teams in Quadrant 3 orient themselves to resolve conflict with enforced equity. Unlike the teams in Quadrant 1, which also use the principle of equity, Quadrant 3 teams are more reactive in dealing with conflicts that have escalated and disrupted team progress. These teams quickly learn from and address their conflicts, which is why they are able to prevent problems from reoccurring. Having to retroactively fix team problems tends to decrease satisfaction because it places team members in the position of having to do more for the team than expected—or having to play a role they would not otherwise have to if other members had upheld their responsibilities. These teams' strategies typically revolve around how to restore and enforce equity. For example, they often create rules, explicit agreements, and clear expectations about how to force members into playing an appropriate part. They consider these strategies ways to make members more reliable, and use them as substitutes for trusting one another to live up to their obligations. Examples of these agreements are picking up unfinished work, agreeing to vote when the team is out of time, or creating new roles that are better suited to each member and/or to isolate disruptive members. These strategies are similar to the ones employed in Quadrant 1, but they are put into place after there is a problem. This decreases satisfaction because the balance of individual versus team interests tips toward team interests. For example, members on the losing side of the vote tend to feel marginalized and do not fully understand why their ideas are compromised in favor of the winning course of action. These teams tend to work around conflicts and prioritize group output first, which has the effect of improving performance at the expense of individual needs.

Quadrant 4: Minimize Misery/Avoidant

Teams in this quadrant tend to have an unorganized or ad hoc approach to managing their conflict. They not only fail to balance individual versus team interests, they actually fail to address either one. Their strategies focus more on immediate complaints rather than underlying interests. For example, team members make the mistake of arguing about one another's intentions rather than figuring out how to leverage strengths, they openly tell disruptive members to change a trait or habit rather than figuring out how to minimize a disruptive member's effect on the team, and often get caught in a distracting negative spiral of interpersonal conflict rather than discussing how to accomplish the team goal. A history of unfocused and unsuccessful conflict attempts and an imbalance of individual and team interests generally limits the willingness and ability of members to engage in good-faith conflict resolution. In fact, when asked the question: What is going wrong in your team?, members often cannot pinpoint exactly what is wrong. Over time, a buildup of strong emotions and unsuccessful attempts at resolving conflict can cloud members' ability to recognize the cause of the problem, and therefore what they are reacting to may actually have nothing to do with what got the team off track initially.

When members do try to engage with one another, they often opt for Band-Aid strategies that do not address how the team is structured. For example, if they think their discussion lacks consideration of alternative viewpoints, they might try a formal brainstorming process. This solution can generate new alternatives, but does not contribute to decision quality because the team has a weak foundation for discussing and choosing a solution. As old conflict patterns escalate discussion, instead of employing evidence-driven analysis, these teams tend to organize in ways that minimize interaction (e.g., creating subgroups or becoming a de facto virtual team), they choose the easiest solution (e.g., giving in to the dominant voice), or to just rely on voting and majority rule. There is a tit-for-tat mentality rather than a process for sharing responsibilities, knowledge, and work; this leaves members guessing and reacting rather than collaborating and problem solving. These teams usually experience high turnover and require significant outside intervention to recover.

Sustaining a high-performing, highly satisfied team takes a great deal of maintenance and awareness. Over the lifespan of a team, it is highly likely that it will cycle through several or all the quadrants. Understanding the effect that different orientations toward conflict-management strategies have on a team's viability is important because it helps a team recognize where there are imbalances that create negative processes and interactions—and where to focus resources to prevent or reverse the negative effects.

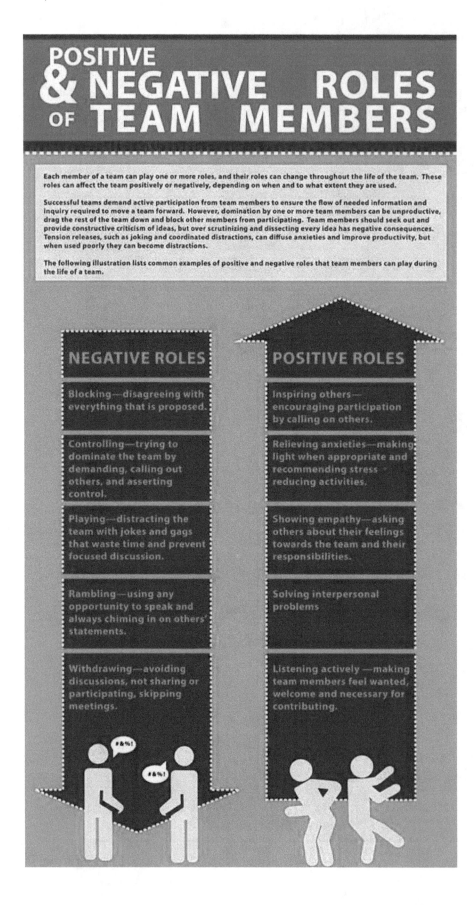

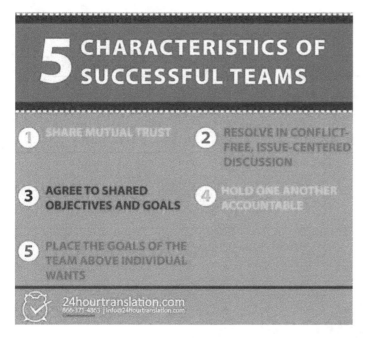

Figure 17.1 12 Rules for Multicultural teams.

Applying This Skill: Team Rules

One of the most common causes of frustration and failure in teams is lack of communication, and often the communication is about expectations. For example, suppose one team member doesn't respond to an email, because they assume no response is needed. Another team member is frustrated by the lack of communication. To help ease such communications, your team will create a list of five team rules. The rules may involve communication expectations, deadlines, workloads, ways of interacting with each other, and more. List your five team rules below.

1.

2.

3.

4.

5.

Assignment: Team Leadership Roles

In this course, each student will lead a major team assignment. Your job as leader will be to establish timelines, tasks, roles/responsibilities, quality standards, and more for your team. In addition, you will be responsible for compiling each person's portion of the team project, proofreading it, and submitting the team's assignment.

Each person will be a team leader at a different time during the semester. This allows people who tend to avoid leadership roles to practice that position and forces people who typically take charge to relinquish the roles to others. Both are important skills to have in the workforce.

Your instructor will explain the team leadership roles. Please identify the leaders and their roles below.

Leadership role	Student	Due date

Reference

SHRM/Mercer Survey Findings: Entry-Level Applicant Job Skills, SHRM 2016

https://www.shrm.org/hr-today/trends-and-forecasting/research-and-surveys/

18

Giving Oral Presentations

Team Oral Presentation

While most college students take a speech course at some point in their educational careers, many do not have instruction on giving business presentations, but over half of business graduates are presenting on a monthly to weekly basis. This course is designed to help you develop, plan, and deliver a presentation effectively. After completing this lesson, you will:

- Know how to plan an oral presentation using brainstorming and organizational planning
- Know how to prepare an oral presentation using audience analysis and purpose
- Learn and demonstrate best practices for use of visuals in presentations
- Create and edit visual presentations
- Practice research skills
- Identify and use credible business trade journals
- Summarize articles and present information concisely

Your instructor will assign you to a team. Your team will be required to research and give an oral presentation on a topic assigned by your instructor. Presentations should have an overall theme, introduction, and conclusion and should be developed considering your audience.

Each person will speak for 4–5 minutes. Dress is business professional or nice business casual.

Your team will prepare a visual presentation to accompany your oral presentation.

Completing the readings and exercises in this chapter and following the Steps to an Effective Presentation will help you prepare and present an effective team oral presentation.

···

Why Must I Give a Memorable Presentation?

Getting Started the Right Way

By Jason L. Snyder and Robert Forbus

Before you begin preparing your presentation ask yourself this simple question, what is my presentation about? If you answer that question with one or two words, then you skipped Chapter 3, where we talked about purpose statements. We won't force you to go back and read it now, but we do want you to understand one important point. World-class consultant and author Nancy Duarte reminds her followers that presentations are your opportunity to change your part of the world, even in business. Before you start putting together your presentation, you need to identify your "big idea": What idea are you selling to your audience and what are the stakes involved? You need to get out of the routine of saying, "my presentation is about increasing sales." Instead, get into the habit of expressing your big idea with the stakes involved. Try the following: "We need to adopt new sales strategies or we will be driven out of business."[1] Instead of thinking about topics you will discuss, think about how your big ideas will change your world.

Figure 18.1.1 summarizes a number of techniques you might use to energize the introduction to a presentation.

1. Ask a question	6. Make a startling statement
2. Tell a story	7. Tell a personal anecdote
3. Find a quotation	8. Use humor
4. Use a visual aid	9. Reference expert opinion
5. Cite a statistic	10. Tell a success story

Figure 18.1.1 Ten techniques for making a powerful introduction.

Supercharging Your Introduction

How many times have you witnessed someone who gets up before a group, gives his or her name, states the topic, and launches immediately into the material? Dozens? Hundreds? Thousands? For us, it's been in the high hundreds, for sure. By this point in our lives, the lazy introduction is the quickest way to make us grab our iPads and start updating our Facebook pages or checking our various email

accounts. We simply
believe if you do not care enough to make a compelling introduction that captures our attention, we
do not care enough to leave our iPads alone. The tips that follow, and in Figure 18.1.1, will help you
supercharge your introduction and capture your audience's attention.

Don't limit yourself to using only one of the tips. Many introductions will use more than one of
these tips:

Ask a Question

We like this approach least, because it's easy, but it is certainly better than no introduction at all. If
you take this approach, make your question rhetorical or provocative. Anticipate the response you
will get from the audience. We have seen too many presentations fall apart because the speaker asked
a question and the audience didn't provide a response.

Tell a Story

We find stories about something you've read or something you've seen or someone you've known
to be highly effective. Just make sure the story relates clearly to your topic. Stories not only engage
your audience, but you can leave them with a cliffhanger you will return to in the presentation's
conclusion.

Find a Quotation

We regularly thumb through online books of quotations when looking for ways to make compelling
points. We figure if someone else has said it, and it's good enough to be in a book of quotations, then
it's good enough for us. Plus, quotations make you look smart. Be sure to make the connection
between your quote and the presentation's topic for your audience. You can even share a quotation
and ask your audience questions about it if that works for you. We once delivered a presentation for
a client about strategic planning. In an earlier chapter, we shared the following quote that is attributed
to Dwight Eisenhower. We believe it is worth repeating: "Plans are nothing; planning is everything."
We asked our audience to tell us what that meant in relation to their organization's strategic planning.

Use a Visual Aid

One of us once saw a politician begin a speech by holding up a gigantic screw made of Styrofoam
and painted gold. It won't tax your imagination too much to learn that the politician was making a
speech about government waste and the need to reduce taxes.

Cite a Statistic

We like Mark Twain's famous statement, "There are three types of lies—lies, damned lies, and
statistics." Whether you agree with the author or not, a statistic can make a powerful point. Using
statistics can be difficult because the data must really have a "wow factor." It must be truly jaw-
dropping. The statistics also need to be relevant and accessible. In other words, people don't easily
grasp large numbers. What do "a million smokers" look like? How large is a stack of "a trillion
dollars?" It isn't really startling or dramatic if the statistic is not relevant and accessible.

Make a Startling Statement

We like these statements because they can be disruptive, provocative, or invoke laughter. There's hardly a better way to get someone's attention. Sarah Kay, the founder of Project V.O.I.C.E., delivered a now famous TED Talk. The presentation was about her work with Project V.O.I.C.E. teaching kids about the power of self-expression through spoken word poetry.[2] She said, "If I should have a daughter, instead of mom, she's gonna call me Point B, because that way she knows that no matter what happens, she can always find her way to me." These were the first words out of her mouth, and they had a profound impact on her audience. Watch her TED Talk here: http://www.ted.com/playlists/77/new_to_ted.html.

Tell a Personal Anecdote or Relay an Experience

We like these because stories are how people learn. It's the reason we've included so many in our book.

Use Humor

We like a good joke. But, we caution you to be very careful with humor. What one person laughs at, another finds incredibly offensive. Save your best retelling of Chris Rock jokes for your bar buddies.

Reference Expert Opinion

We like using expert opinions because it is a way to build credibility.

Tell a Success Story

We Americans love success, almost as much as we like to see successful people fail and come back from their failures. And remember, you can always use hypothetical stories, as long as that is clear with your audience.

Maximizing Your Impact

Having a supercharged introduction should get your audience engaged in your presentation. However, as we can tell you from years of experience in the classroom, getting an audience's attention and keeping it are two different things. As speakers, we need to work to keep our audience plugged in during the heart of the presentation as well. Figure 18.1.2 summarizes 11 ideas for keeping your audience engaged and maximizing your impact during a presentation.

1. Remember that you are the presentation	7. Do not memorize
2. Look your best	8. Demonstrate your magnetism
3. Put a smile on your face	9. Create potential
4. Demonstrate your passion	10. Empower your audience
5. Explain your purpose, then repeat and repeat again	11. Believe in yourself
6. Show your resilience	

Figure 18.1.2 Tips for maximizing your impact.

Consider how you can apply the 11 tips to improve your presentation impact:

- *Remember that YOU are the presentation.* Slides, handouts, leave-behinds, and other visual aids are awesome, but they aren't the presentation, YOU are.
- *Look your best—your very best.* People say don't judge a book by its cover, but we all do it to some degree. In fact, some research suggests that "humans can categorize others in less than 150 milliseconds."[3]
- *Put a smile on your face.* People who smile when they speak automatically "sound" more cheerful, warm, and approachable. Emotions, after all, are contagious.[4]
- *Demonstrate your passion.* If you don't show a metaphorical fire for your topic, your audience surely won't be inspired to listen and later recall your message.
- *Explain your purpose, then repeat and repeat again.* From the get-go, tell your audience what you want them to remember from your presentation. In your main points, reinforce what you want them to remember from your presentation. Then, when concluding, remind them again what you want them to remember.
- *Show your resilience.* Don't let interruptions such as questions from the audience rattle your nerves. Know your material well enough to answer questions. During a group presentation, be able to answer generally a question that might best be handled by someone else, and then hand off that question to the appropriate teammate for a more detailed response. Then, be prepared to pick back up where you left off.
- *Do NOT memorize.* Memorization prevents you from accomplishing number 6 above. Further, if you falter, it is very difficult to recover if you have memorized a presentation. Finally, if you memorize, you are less likely to sound conversational.
- *Demonstrate your magnetism.* The ability to attract money, people, and ideas is powerful, and it also helps your credibility.
- *Create potential.* Show your audience what is possible. They need to see the world you envision. Demonstrate the now versus the future.
- *Empower your audience.* Show your audience how their actions can have profoundly positive consequences. Give them the tools and guidance they need to carry out your ideas.
- *Believe in yourself.* Perfect practice makes perfect performance. Any athlete who is any good at his or her sport is an athlete who has done the same things over and over again, perhaps thousands of times. When you put that level of effort into your presentation, just like the athlete, you can't help but be confident.

Closing Well

You've heard them before: highly paid, very influential people ending a presentation or speech with "thank you" or "are there any questions" or, if he or she is a politician, "God bless America." Well, just because people use these closers doesn't mean these are good closing statements. It's just like when you were a child and you wanted to do something that your mother or father wouldn't allow. You might have whined, "But everyone else is doing it." And your parent(s) may have responded, "If everyone else were eating worms would you want them for dinner?" We hope you answered no. So if all these important people end their presentations with weak closing statements like the ones mentioned before, why do they do it? There are at least two reasons. First, it's not offensive. Second, it's easy.

By now, however, you've probably come to realize that we aren't big proponents of easy. This entire chapter attempts to persuade you to make a *memorable* presentation—one that the audience will recall and be influenced by well after you leave the stage, dais, or lectern. In our classes, we have adopted harsh penalties for student presentations that end in the expected way of "thank you" or "are there any questions." We encourage our students, and we encourage you, to push the limits of your comfort zone to develop memorable closing statements that summarize your major points (telling the audience what you've already told them) and reference the beginning of your presentation (tying the bow on top of the gift-wrapped box). The tips in Figure 18.1.3 are just a few of the many ways you can deliver a memorable closing.

---

1. If you told a story at the beginning of the presentation, return to that story and tie it to the major point(s) you want your audience to remember.

2. Find a short verse that refers to the beginning of your presentation and that gains the audience's attention through humor, empathy, sympathy, or inspiration.

3. Find a short quote from a famous person that reinforces the major points of your presentation.

4. Give a signal that you are closing. For example, "To recap the major points of my presentation, I ask you to remember …" or "In conclusion, please remember …"

5. Deliver a call to action. For example, "I challenge you to …" or "Join me in …" makes it easy for people to comply with your requests and ask them to respond quickly. The greater the distance between your request and the audience's action, the more likely they are to do nothing.

Figure 18.1.3 Tips for delivering a memorable closing.

Achieving Conversational Delivery Style

Search your memories for the most boring lecture, sermon, speech, or presentation you ever heard. We're willing to bet that one of the reasons you found it
boring was the speaker didn't present in a conversational style. Public speaking blogger Olivia Mitchell and researchers Mayer, Fennell, Farmer, and
Campbell (2004) agree that a conversational style, rather than a formal style, helps people learn better.[5] The late Steve Jobs, co-founder of Apple Computers, was very nearly a genius at presenting in a conversational style. We've considered the effectiveness of three additional individuals who are typically believed to have been great 20th and 21st century communicators and have gleaned tips from their style to share with you. Our tips are based on the speaking success of Jobs, the Rev. Billy Graham, President Barack Obama, and the late President Ronald Reagan. The lessons have been packaged into the six simple ideas in Figure 18.1.4 that anyone can use.

---

1. When writing your script, imagine you are writing to one person and one person only. When proofreading your script, put the words "Hey, Joe" or "Hey, Jane" before a sentence and read it aloud to yourself. Does it sound like you're speaking to a friend?

2. When rehearsing your delivery, imagine you are speaking directly to one person and one person only. Even if your audience has thousands of people in it, you still must reach one person at a time.

3. When presenting, avoid looking at your screen if you are using one for projecting images. Rather, look at one person at a time in your audience and speak directly to him or her. If you wish, glance at your screen or gesture to it, but never speak to it.

4. When writing, and later when presenting, seek ways to connect emotionally with your audience.

5. When rehearsing, imagine the one person in your audience who will be the most difficult to reach. Spend extra time figuring out how best to reach that one hard-to-reach person (in marketing terms, this person is your target).

6. When speaking, get out from behind the lectern. How many dinner conversations have you had from behind a lectern?

Figure 18.1.4 Tips for achieving conversational delivery style.

Designing Slides and Decks for Memorable Presentations

Please don't tell Bill Gates, but we really hate Microsoft's PowerPoint software. It isn't that the product is bad. It's that the product is awful. PowerPoint has allowed people with little or no graphic design taste to create slide presentations. These presentations are sometimes referred to as "decks." Many professors and other professionals rely entirely too much on slides. How so? They simply read what is on their slides (or decks). For these situations we borrow the term "death by PowerPoint," because it describes how these excruciatingly mundane presentations bore people to death. In this section, we will give you a few pieces of simple advice that will eliminate most of the errors that create "death by PowerPoint." For a detailed treatment of slide and deck design, we recommend the work of Garr Reynolds, who wrote *Presentation Zen*, which outlines an approach where less, much less, is more.[6] If you are a nondesigner like us, then you will also find Robin Williams' book, *The Non-Designer's Design Book*, to be useful.[7]

Consider the slide in Figure 18.1.5. It breaks the one rule you should always follow in slide design: You are the presentation! The slides should reinforce your message, not hijack it. If your audience can read your slides, then they have no use for you.

Who's Protecting the Children?

• Senator Charles Schumer of New York proposed banning the suspect baby bottles outright.

• Wal-Mart, Toys "R" Us, and CVS all announced plans to phase out polycarbonate bottles. Some companies have adopted BPA-free plastic.

• Yet most businesses stuck with BPA products—at least partly because they don't have a good substitute. Nearly all of the 130 billion food and beverage cans made in the United States each year are still lined with a BPA resin. The alternative called Oleoresin, is more expensive, has a shorter shelf life, and can't be used for acidic foods like tomatoes.

• Senator Frank Lautenberg of New Jersey has proposed an overhaul of the whole system. In May 2008, he introduced the Kid-Safe Chemical Act. The Act would reverse the burden of proof on chemicals, requiring manufacturers to demonstrate their safety in order to keep them in commerce. The E.U. passed a similar law in 2006, as did
Canada in 1999. (Canada has banned BPA in baby bottles.)

• The National Toxicology Program advised "concerned parents" to reduce their use of canned foods; use BPA-free baby bottles; and opt for glass, porcelain, or stainless-steel containers, particularly for hot foods and liquids.

Figure 18.1.5 Wordy slide.

Figure 18.1.6 Revised wordy slide.

How did the presenter end up with such a wordy slide? The main culprit is sloth. PowerPoint and similar programs are designed with default settings. When you open up a blank presentation and begin working with a slide, the bullet points are right there for you to use. How convenient. Are we wrong, or are we not sentient beings? Just because a program is set up with defaults, we are not compelled to use the defaults. Instead, we encourage you to figure out the point of each slide and to draw by hand—don't worry, we use stick figures—what you want the slide to look like. Alternatively, you can think about images that might evoke an emotional connection to the topic at hand. Once you're satisfied, open PowerPoint and try to force the program to recreate the drawing for you, or insert the image for you.

In Figure 18.1.6, we revised the slide from Figure 18.1.5. Less is more. The slide in Figure 18.1.6 would make an emotional connection with any audience. The audience would much rather look at a picture of an adorable baby and listen to you provide the details. What they would dislike is listening to you read the content from the slide in Figure 18.1.5.

Audiences don't just dislike wordy slides; they also dislike slides with tables and graphs that have too much information. The audience cannot reasonably process complex tables and graphs and listen to you. Again, if you remember that you are the message, you will limit your tables and graphs to images that can be processed quickly so your audience will focus on what you are saying. This approach to slide design requires you to be more thoughtful about your presentation materials, but with thoughtfulness and hard work, you won't victimize your audience.

Putting It All Together

We realized people would find it helpful if we could create a set of tips that help bring together the utmost important points regarding making memorable presentations. Consequently, we developed the tips below. Initially, we used these tips for a professional development activity we conducted three consecutive years for the *Travelers EDGE* program. We liked the tips so much that we now share them with all our students. Funny enough, we can always tell which students follow these tips, and which do not. Even more funny, the students are always astounded that we can tell the difference. Those wacky students.

Notes

1. Duarte (2012).
2. Project V.O.I.C.E. (2013).
3. Elsbach (2003).
4. Hatfield, Cacioppo, and Rapson (1993).
5. Mayer, Fennell, Farmer, and Campbell (2004).

6. Reynolds (2012).
7. Williams (2004).

References

Duarte, N. (2012). *Persuasive presentations: Inspire action, engage the audience, sell your ideas.* Cambridge, MA: Harvard Business Review Press.

Elsbach, K. D. (2003). How to pitch a brilliant idea. In *HBR's 10 must reads on communication.* Cambridge, MA: Harvard Business Review Press.

Hatfield, E., Cacioppo, J. T., & Rapson, R. L. (1993). Emotional contagion. *Current Directions in Psychological Science 2,* 96–99.

Mayer, R. E., Fennell, S., Farmer, L., & Campbell, J. (2004). A personalization effect in multimedia learning: Students learn better when words are in conversational style rather than formal style. *Journal of Educational Psychology 96,* 389–395.

Project V.O.I.C.E. (2013). Retrieved June 20, 2013, from http://www.project-voice.net/

Reynolds, G. (2012). *Presentation Zen: Simple ideas on presentation design and delivery.* Berkeley, CA: New Riders.

Williams, R. (2004). *The non-designer's presentation book.* Berkeley, CA: Peachpit Press.

Develop an Oral Presentation: Team Presentation Brainstorming

Brainstorming is a way to create and gather ideas for your team presentation. The idea is to come up with as many ideas, facts, and questions as possible. Later, you can narrow your ideas, focus them, and determine your purpose for the presentation. But now, be creative.

Nancy Duarte (2008), of Duarte Design, says your goal in a presentation is to create ideas (not slides) and move people. The first step is coming up with as many ideas as possible. Use a pencil and paper; computer programs were not designed to encourage creativity. List words, concepts, and ideas. Explore associations. Push ideas farther. Build off other people's ideas. Look at a topic from all sides. What can you discover? Go beyond the ordinary and expected. You may discover ideas or aspects of your topic that will inspire you and your audience.

You will be in a team based on a topic assigned by your instructor. In your team, write down anything you talk or think about. Be creative; go off topic, build on one another's ideas, laugh, have fun. Write each idea on a Post-it note—one idea per note. After 10–15 minutes, your team should have a poster piece of paper covered with a wide range of topics related to your team presentation.

The rules of brainstorming appear below.

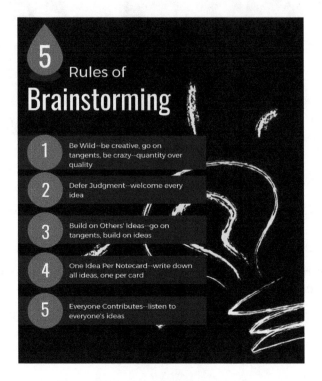

Figure 18.1 5 Rules of Brainstorming

Plan an Oral Presentation: Audience Analysis

Any effective business communication begins with considering the audience. What does the reader need or want to know? What does the audience care about? How can you connect with them?

Nancy Duarte defines the questions you should ask about your audience while preparing an oral presentation (see Figure 18.2).

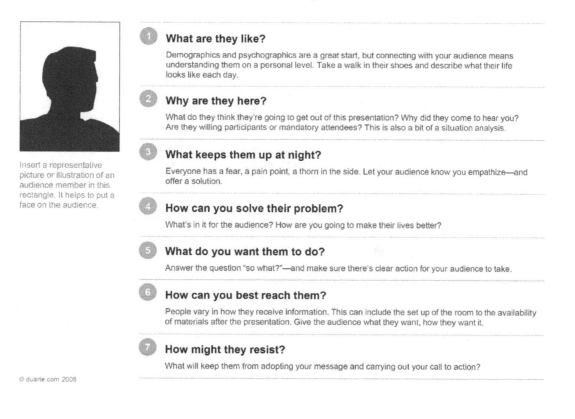

Figure 18.2 Duarte Audience Needs Map

Applying This Skill: Audience Analysis Exercise: "The Wreck"

To explore the idea of audience, in teams complete the activity below.

The Scenario: You are a sales representative for a midsized company. You've borrowed your boss's new car to take a potential client to dinner at a fancy restaurant. If the evening goes as you plan, you'll likely finalize a large contract that is important to your company.

You are anxious and excited about the dinner reservation, but you are late. On the way, you decide to take a residential street with little traffic. The borrowed car does not have great brakes, and you want to make up some time in an area with fewer cars. Light rain and darkness are falling. In a 35 mph zone, you're going almost 50 mph.

Approaching a stop sign, you don't stop quickly enough to halt at the sign. In fact, you travel about ten feet into the intersection. You think about putting the car into reverse and backing out of the intersection, but after a quick look to the left, you think you can proceed. Just then, on your right, a car approaches rapidly and hits the borrowed car on the passenger side, ruining the door and denting the car.

Now you're really late!

Your Task: As a team, prepare a short recounting of the incident for the audience assigned. You will retell the details to your assigned audience using any form you wish (e.g., phone call, in-person conversation, letter, memo, accident report, email, text, etc.). You may choose to emphasize some details while deemphasizing others. You may make logical inferences and add some detail, but do not substantially change the facts. Draft your message (written or script, if oral) and be prepared to share it with the class. Your instructor will assign one of the audiences below.

1. The client you were to meet for dinner, who has been in three accidents during the last year

2. A team leader for a cross-functional company project you're working on who thinks highly of you and trusts your opinion

3. A work associate who thinks you're always falling short and causing trouble (who is also a little jealous of your success but is liked and listened to by your boss)

4. Your boss, owner of the wrecked car

5. An insurance agent

6. A lawyer who will represent you and needs to know all the "facts"

7. A family member, friend, or spouse

Adapted from Karl Smart, "The Wreck: Meeting the Needs of the Audience," Business Communication Quarterly 63, no. 3 (September. 2000): 73–79.

Applying This Skill: Audience Analysis

Audience analysis may seem simple for your college class; most of your audience members are students like you. While that's true, you should still consider the following questions. Focus on what your audience knows about the topic and how they feel about it. If you're presenting information they know about, how can you make it more relevant or new? If you're presenting information they probably don't care about, how can you make it interesting to them?

- Who are the listeners?

- What is the audience size?

- What is the average age of the audience?

- What is the male–female ratio?

- How does the audience feel about this topic (attitude)?

- How much does the audience know about the topic? What do they know?

- What expectations does the audience have about your presentation/topic?

- How will you engage the audience?

Develop an Oral Presentation: Determining a Purpose

Every presentation should have a purpose, and the purpose should be more than "this is an assignment" or "to get a good grade." Those reasons will not be relevant when you have to give presentations in the workplace. In a professional setting, a presentation's purpose may be to sell an idea or product or convince people to agree with your plan or vision.

In this class, think of your presentation as a training session. You are the experts on a certain topic and need to deliver information to the rest of the class. What do they need to know about your topic? What do you want them to remember? Why is this important to them? Developing a clear purpose will help you plan and develop an effective presentation and will ensure your audience remembers you.

Applying This Skill: Determining a Purpose

1. What is the topic of your presentation? What are your main subtopics?

2. What is the goal of your presentation?

3. What are your three main points? How do they relate to the goal?

4. Why does your audience care about these main points/your goal?

Plan an Oral Presentation: Organization

Like any communication, presentations need a clear beginning, middle, and end and transitions between topics and presenters. Starting and ending your presentation well is essential to your success. If you start by saying, "Our presentation is about planning for retirement," your audience is not likely to be very excited or engaged. But if you start by saying, "What does this number mean?" and showing a slide with the number $1,060,751, you're more likely to get your audience's attention. In the conclusion, revisit that startling number to summarize all of your main points. Creating clear organization, effective introductions, transitions, and conclusions takes planning but will ensure an effective and memorable presentation.

Applying This Skill: Organization

1. Draft an outline of your presentation:

2. What is your attention-getting introduction?

3. What is your conclusion?

4. Where will you be presenting? What is the facility like? What are the visual aid/technology options?

5. How much time is allotted for your presentation?

6. Who speaks before/after you? How will you transition between speakers?

Plan an Oral Presentation: Do Your Research

When giving a business presentation, you need to provide your audience with credible, valuable information, so you need to do your research. In the future, you may need to read trade journals aimed at industry insiders, company reports, legal briefs or rulings, and industry analyses; you may need to interview experts or gather information from clients. Your audience expects you to be the expert on your topic. You need to provide them with the most relevant and reliable information possible.

Assignment: Write a Bibliography

Your team will research your assigned topic and create a bibliography of the sources. This is the basis for your oral presentation. The bibliography team member is responsible for coordinating this portion of the project, editing and submitting the bibliography.

Each team member needs to find at least three sources. All sources must be from academic or business trade journals. Points will be deducted for any citations from popular sources (e.g., *New York Times*, *HuffingtonPost*, etc.). Your team will select MLA or APA citation format and follow it correctly.

The final bibliography will include annotations for each source. The annotation for each source will include 5–8 sentences per source stating the following:

1. Brief summary of the article's information

2. What makes the article unique, compared with other articles

3. How the article will be used in your research project (remember to use concrete details)

Sample Annotation

The following citation is in MLA format:

Sandlin, Kathie. "The 7 Deadly Sins of Diversity Recruitment." *The 7 Deadly Sins of Diversity Recruitment*. The Multicultural Advantage, n.d. Web. 28 Feb. 2017.

> This article discusses issues a company may run into while creating a more diversified workplace. It describes a few common mistakes that companies should avoid. The author refers to these mistakes as the "seven deadly sins of diversity recruitment," and they include omission, limitation, imitation, and a few more. Each of these sins, whether they are consciously committed or not, ultimately creates a less diversified work environment. This article is unique because instead of discussing how to create an inclusive workplace, it talks about why a company may not be succeeding in building a diversified business. This article will be used to explain how companies are making efforts to diversify workspaces but are still failing.

Effective Visual Communication

Students are well versed in "death by PowerPoint" presentations. You have been victims and creators of such visual presentations, often since junior high school. With the influence of the popular TED Talks and industry experts such as Nancy Duarte and Garr Reynolds, visual communication is changing, and students need to learn effective ways to present information visually. Reading 18.1 provides useful information about creating effective visuals.

Applying This Skill: Drawing

In your team, select one student to be the "reader" for the next activity. The other students will be the artists. Your instructor will distribute paper and markers and the script. The reader will read a script aloud. The artists will draw the thing described in the script.

Assignment: Create a Visual Presentation

Your team will create presentation visuals to augment your oral presentation. You may use any presentation software of your choosing. The presentation visuals team member is responsible for coordinating this portion of the project, editing and submitting the visual portion of the presentation.

Each team member will create slides to accompany their portion of the oral presentation. In addition, the visuals should include:

- A title slide, including names of presenters (in order of presenting)
- Transition slides
- A conclusion slide

A printed copy of the visuals is due in class the day of your presentation. In addition, the presentation visuals team member will submit an electronic copy (attachment or link).

Applying This Skill: Rough Draft Visual Presentation Review

Part 1:

As instructed, develop slides to accompany your portion of the oral presentation. On the day assigned, bring that presentation and a laptop or tablet to class.

Part 2:

In your teams, you will review several slide decks via Slideshare.net (see "7 Tips to Create Visual Presentations" by Emiland and "Sample Slides" by Garr Reynolds about creating effective visual presentations). The slide decks are incredibly effective at demonstrating the key principles of effective slide design.

Working in teams, you will apply the principles discussed in the slide decks to your own presentation, discussing examples and ideas for changes to your presentation.

Applying This Skill: Rough Draft Visuals Checklist

Review the visual presentation team members have developed so far. Remember the concepts below. Follow the checklist to ensure the presentation is being developed following best practices.

Rough Draft Visuals Checklist

- Think Billboards—one idea per slide
- Images have Power—images have purpose & meaning
- Use Typography
- Use Symbols & Creative Data Presentation

Organization

- ☐ Includes title slide (w/ names) and outline slide
- ☐ Uses transition slides between topics/presenters (sign-posts)
- ☐ Cites sources for graphics/data (ethical use)

Background and Color

- ☐ Avoids busy patterns and backgrounds
- ☐ Color contrasts with text
- ☐ Simple and professional look
- ☐ Uses no more than three colors
- ☐ Uses color for accent/contrast
- ☐ Color use consistent with formality of presentation and topic
- ☐ Consistency between slides

Text

- ☐ Fonts clear and easy to read
- ☐ Text used as headlines (no more than 4 words)
  - o Short, easy to read phrases or single words
  - o Bullets (if used) use parallel construction
  - o Use only key words (remove articles, pronouns etc.)
- ☐ Appropriate font size used
  - o Easy to read (style & size)
  - o Capital letters used correctly
- ☐ Punctuation used correctly and consistently

Arrangement & Images

- ☐ Uses the following arrangement concepts effectively:
  - o Contrast
  - o Unity
  - o Proximity
  - o Hierarchy
  - o Space
  - o Flow
- ☐ Uses meaningful images (not clip art)

Table 18.1. Visuals checklist

Effective Delivery

As Reading 18.1 says, "*You* are the presentation." This means you need to prepare, plan, and practice your presentation delivery just as much as you prepare and plan your presentation's content. In the first activity below, you will identify traits and habits that make effective—and ineffective_presenters. Then your team will practice giving your oral presentation together.

Remember to prepare, practice, dress up, and smile!

1. Intonation and rhythm

2. Volume

3. Emphais

4. Clarify and enunciation

5. Pause

6. Pace

7. Emotion and Expression

Source: Activia Training, www.activia.co.uk

Figure 18.3 Tips on How to Use Your Voice Effectively in a Presentation

Applying This Skill: Identifying Delivery Elements

As a team, think about the professors you have that you like and dislike. What makes a professor effective? What makes a professor ineffective? What do you like when professors are teaching? What do you dislike? Make a list of recommendations for professors to increase effective delivery. Be prepared to share and discuss your list with the class.

Develop an Oral Presentation: Developing Effective Delivery

In the theater, movies, and TV, a table read is often the first time an entire cast meets with the director of the production. The cast reads through the script, which allows directors to hear the show out loud. It allows other actors in the show to hear each other, which is also important in group presentations.

As a presenter, you won't stop in the middle of the presentation to say, "That doesn't sound right." The table read gives you an opportunity to prepare in a variety of ways, including:

- Hearing the words you've written spoken out loud. The written and spoken word sound very different, so reading your words aloud is essential to creating an oral presentation that flows smoothly and easily.
- Identifying places where the presentation needs more or less information or clarification
- Determining the timing of the presentation: Is it too long? Too short?
- Identifying transitions (between slides and people)
- Seeing how team members (and their pieces of the presentation) work together

In addition, it's your team's first chance to discuss delivery. In an earlier exercise, you identified aspects of delivery that make presenters effective. Now, you can see how you and your teammates speak and sound. Pay attention to the following aspects of vocal variety:

- Tone: monotone, reading, rising and falling intonations
- Volume
- Filler words, such as "um," "ah," and "er"

- Enthusiasm
- Energy
- Smiles
- How all members of the presentation work together

Read the presentation a second time, paying more attention to delivery, including timing, tone, volume, pauses, emphasis, repetition, and rhythm. In your script/notes, indicate places where you want to pause or add emphasis.

Remember, your team succeeds or fails as a whole. You want to provide useful feedback and suggestions for improvement. Be kind, positive, and helpful when delivering your feedback.

A table read is best followed by a formal practice session, during which your team identifies where people will stand and how people will move during the presentation. Actors and professional presenters call the planning of movement and gestures during a presentation "blocking."

Your team will want to plan and practice your blocking as well as your delivery. Where will each of you stand when you are speaking and when others are talking? Avoid standing behind the podium, which acts as a barrier between you and the audience. In your practice session, consider how and where to move and stand; this helps avoid pacing and shifting weight, which distract the audience. Provide feedback about how people use their hands, how movement and gesture can add emphasis and impact, and how best to transition between speakers. Determine how the visual presentation will be advanced. Consider using a handheld clicker so the speaker can advance the slides, or develop a small cue. Avoid a presentation in which the speaker continually says, "Next slide" or turns to the person advancing the slides to indicate it's time to change slides.

Finally, discuss your wardrobe. In a business presentation, you are representing yourself, your company, and your brand, and you want to do so in a professional manner. Business professional attire shows respect for your audience, your topic, and your company. Follow suggestions for interview attire as well; avoid anything too tight, too loose, or too low-cut. Be well-groomed; iron your clothes. Wear closed-toed shoes, and polish them. Your appearance is the first thing people will notice, and you want to make a good first impression.

The more you and your team prepare and practice for your oral presentation, the better you will do. Practice on your own. Practice together. Practice often. Your time and effort will pay off in a polished, professional presentation.

Applying This Skill: Table Read

Your team will be given a portion of a class period to conduct a table read of your presentation. This will occur close to the date of the presentation but after you've had time to research and prepare your presentation.

For the table read, you will need to have the notes or script for your portion of the presentation. This requires you to have completed your research and prepared what you plan to say during the presentation. The slides for your portion of the visual presentation should also be nearly complete. Bring a laptop or tablet to make changes as needed.

Your team will sit in a circle. The person to begin the presentation will start. Read the presentation through, focusing on content and transitions. After your first read, discuss what worked well and what you think you can improve.

Assignment:
Show and Tell Mini Speech

Prepare a 2-3 minute speech about anything classroom appropriate.
Choose a topic you care about. You will deliver the mini speech in class.

Created using Venngage

Figure 18.4. Assignment: Show and Tell Mini-speech.

....

Reading 18.2

Speech Anxiety

By Jason Schmitt and Arthur Koch

Chapter Outline

- The Truth About Nervousness
- How to Develop Self-Confidence
- Food Feeds Your Confidence
- Stretch Your Comfort Zone
- Visual Imagery is a Powerful Tool
- Visualize for Confidence in Public Speaking
- A Script for Using Visual Imagery to Develop Confidence in Speaking
- Confidence is Key

Nervousness on your speech day is completely normal. It would be rather unique if you didn't feel any nerves prior to the speech. But nervousness isn't bad. It energizes us and excites us to do great things. In fact, nearly everything you do in life that is monumental you will do while being nervous. Our nervousness should help us realize we are doing something important.

When in a speech class there are things you can do to help reduce some nervous ness and center your mind and body for your speech. Exercising isometrically is one such way to help release some of your nervous energy. An isometric exercise is a procedure by which you contract a muscle for about 8–10 seconds against some immovable resistance, for example, a chair, table, or floor. Here are some isometric exercises you can try:

1. While sitting on a chair with your feet flat on the floor, grasp each side of the chair and attempt to lift yourself.

2. Sit on a chair with your feet flat on the floor. Put your hands on top of your knees while drawing in your abdominal muscles. Attempt to lift your heels off the floor.

3. While sitting on a chair, place the palms of your hands on the sides of the chair and press inward as hard as you can, with spread fingers.

Isometric exercise: A procedure of contracting muscles to reduce nervous ness.

A few minutes before it is your turn to speak, you should focus on your breathing. Deep breathing is a technique that is extremely important to relaxation and helps keep our emotions in check. Nearly every yoga course rooted in Eastern philosophy praises deep breathing. If you watch a new baby lie on a table, you will see that baby take deep belly breaths of air and fill their whole stomach, in and out. Inverse to that, if you look at your own breathing after a stressful day, you will notice your belly isn't regularly moving fully in and out as you breathe. Instead, you are taking shallow chest breaths. Chest breaths lead to feeling more stress. To center and relax, focus on taking breaths that move your belly in and out. This is especially important prior to delivering an important speech.

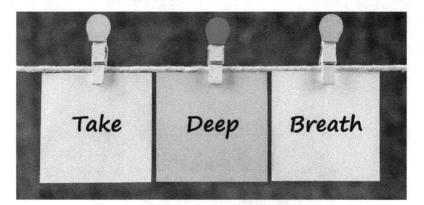

Figure 18.2.1 **It is very important as we get anxious to focus on taking deep breaths.**

Source: mozakim/Shutterstock.com

When it is your turn to speak, stand up and walk briskly and confidently up to the podium to deliver your speech. Try to be excited when you deliver your information to the audience. Focus your energy on the audience and not on yourself.

The Truth About Nervousness

Nervousness is learned behavior. Stage fright is the fear that you will not do as well in front of an audience as you would like to. The symptoms of stage fright might be any of the following: rapid pulse, dry mouth, difficulty swallowing, trembling, sweaty palms, or queasy stomach. The phrase "butterflies in the stomach" is often used in regard to stage fright. Most people have no difficulty when communicating to others in small groups or in one-on-one situations, but in larger groups this can often pose a problem.

Figure 18.2.2 **Nervousness is a completely normal feeling prior to speaking.**

Source: Rawpixel.com/Shutterstock.com

Stage fright: A fear that you will not do as well as you would like in front of an audience.

Public speaking is probably the class feared by more students than any other. Why? Because many see the situation as threatening. Emotions and nerves are hard to control. If you don't study for a chemistry exam and end up doing poorly on the exam, it is between you and the sheet of paper that is soon marked up with a lot of red ink. When in front of an audience, the rules of the game change. We are all biological beings. As such, some days we are on top of everything and all our tasks exceed our hopes. On other days, we may slack a little bit. We aren't as on top of the game. This is exactly the problem with the system that keeps our thoughts in order. It is beyond our complete control. And that is worrisome for a lot of people.

Figure 18.2.3 **The more success you have as a speaker, the less stage fright will play a factor in your speaking.**

Source: iQoncept/Shutterstock.com

Figure 18.2.4 **Confidence in front of an audience is a learned skill that is extremely valuable in life.**

Source: gpointstudio/Shutterstock.com

Some people fear that other classmates will be able to see their weaknesses and imperfections, and that is a scary proposition. Welcome to being a human—we all have those worries. However, worrying too much about what others will think about you is what causes stage fright and all the less than optimal feelings.

This particular fear usually diminishes after the confidence-building sequence of easy speaking activities in the early part of the semester. Positive feedback from classmates and from your own instructor is very powerful and, when supplemented with positive self-talk, can be very effective in replacing those fears. A more appropriate or rational nervousness is created because you care about what the audience thinks about you. Appropriate caring causes you to do all you can in order to do your best. It gives you the extra rush of energy that you need to be really alive and energized in front of an audience.

One really fascinating view of nervousness is that, on a physiological level, the physical signs of nervousness parallel the physical signs of excitement. That is to say that two people may experience the same symptoms, and one may name it nervousness, and the other may name it excitement. I urge every student to rename their nervous feelings genuinely as excitement and see how that changes their perception of their feelings.

Figure 18.2.5 As we develop more self-confidence, it helps us both in front of audiences and in our daily work lives.

Source: AJR_photo/Shutterstock.com

For several semesters, I had students rank themselves as speakers and had the audience rank the speaker in terms of how nervous they were. I used a scale of 0–20. It was quite consistent that the speaker perceived himself to be twice as nervous as the audience perceived him to be. That is, if a speaker said he was an 18 on the nervousness scale, the audience on average would perceive him to be closer to 9 on that same scale. It is reassuring to realize that, as a speaker, a person appears only half as nervous to the audience as they think they appear.

As the saying "Nothing succeeds like success" implies, the experience of doing well in the speech activities in class will go a long way toward helping you develop greater self-confidence. Self-confidence, or a feeling of trust in one's abilities, qualities, and judgment, is a vital skill for speaking. To this end, always talk about something you really know, prepare, and practice a lot. Be sincere and talk about things that really matter to you. Never try to "con" an audience into believing that you know something you do not. You cannot fool an audience. They can sniff out true passion. They can almost always tell exactly how much you do or do not know, how much time you have spent preparing, and, above all, how much time you spent rehearsing. Being both well prepared and well rehearsed creates almost certain success. This is what builds confidence.

Self-confidence: Feeling of trust in one's abilities, qualities, and judgment.

Let's go further into the importance of building confidence based upon the prior scenario. After you have prepared speeches and done well in a public speaking course, the better your confidence will be in job interviews. The better you do on job interviews, the greater the opportunities that will present themselves to you over the course of your life. The better the opportunities in life, the greater the impact you can make for the world, your family, and your general satisfaction. Based on this line of reasoning, the reasons to work hard in a subject such as public speaking go well beyond any grade or a classroom-exclusive goal. And to help you do well in the moment of stress, it is important to warm up prior to the important moment.

Warming up for an activity reduces stress and gets you ready for an upcoming task. Warm up for baseball by swinging the bat many times before taking the plate, or swing the golf club many times before stepping into the tee box. Likewise, it is important to warm up for a speech by giving several practice speeches prior to class. Another area where warming up is often forgotten about is warming up for a job interview. This means practicing interview questions many times before setting foot in a potential employer's office. Here are some regularly occurring job interview questions that can serve as a great warm-up tool to ease your nerves during an important interview.

Job Interview Questions

- Describe a situation in which you were able to use persuasion to successfully convince someone to see things your way.
- Describe a time when you were faced with a stressful situation that demonstrated your coping skills.
- Give me a specific example of a time when you used good judgment and logic in solving a problem.
- Give me an example of a time when you set a goal and were able to meet or achieve it.
- Tell me about a time when you had to use your presentation skills to influence someone's opinion.
- Give me a specific example of a time when you had to conform to a policy with which you did not agree.
- Please discuss an important written document you were required to complete.
- Tell me about a time when you had to go above and beyond the call of duty in order to get a job done.
- Tell me about a time when you had too many things to do and you were required to prioritize your tasks.
- Give me an example of a time when you had to make a split-second decision.
- What is your typical way of dealing with conflict? Give me an example.
- Tell me about a time you were able to successfully deal with another person even when that individual may not have personally liked you (or vice versa).
- Tell me about a difficult decision you've made in the last year.
- Give me an example of a time when something you tried to accomplish failed.
- Give me an example of when you showed initiative and took the lead.
- Tell me about a recent situation in which you had to deal with a very upset customer or coworker.
- Give me an example of a time when you motivated others.

Figure 18.2.6 The job interview, like public speaking, is another situation in life that often has nervousness associated with the pursuit.

Source: ESB Basic/Shutterstock.com

How to Develop Self-Confidence

Psychologically, there are several very important steps you can take to develop greater self-confidence. You can practice positive self-talk, repeatedly saying to yourself with as much conviction as you can muster, "I can do this," "I can take it one step at a time," "I can become an excellent speaker," "This class is getting easier every week," and "I really want to learn to be a powerful speaker!" A second physiological exercise is to diminish all talk of fear and nervousness. Substitute other less loaded words when you talk of your concerns. From now on, instead of "I'm really nervous," say "I'm really excited." If you are compelled to acknowledge your previous levels of nervousness, then say, "In the past, I have had some problems with nervousness, but it is getting better all the time." Renaming these things can be a powerful way to gain control over your psychological reactions. Constantly using "I am very excited" and eliminating the fear and nervousness talk form a powerful technique for changing your whole response pattern to the public speaking situation. In order for this to be effective in lessening nervousness, you do not have to believe strongly in your positive self-talk, but you do have to eliminate negative self-talk. Otherwise, the positive and negative statements will cancel each other out, leaving you to experience little growth in this area.

Another very powerful psychological idea is to change your focus from concern for yourself to concern for the audience. All too often, a speaker is so focused on the impression she is making that she forgets to be really focused on how well the audience is hearing, seeing, understanding, and so forth. When your attention is turned back on yourself, your mind will be filled with questions such as "Do I look scared?", "Do I sound stupid?", "What if I forget?", "Can they see my knees shaking?", and so on. The speaker who can forget herself and really be concerned whether the audience understands the very important ideas she is sharing will experience a genuine shift to a nurturing connection with the audience. This is the feeling that causes many speakers to get "hooked" on public speaking.

Figure 18.2.7 **Greater self-confidence is a learned behavior.**

Source: Sergey Nivens/Shutterstock.com

Ultimately, it is a very powerful feeling when you realize that you can share an idea that could change someone's life. This can only happen if you talk about things that are so very interesting and important to you that you truly want every person in the audience to understand. This means preparing well and working on that shift of focus. I have seen speakers experience this shift of focus and, when they have that experience, it eliminated most of their excessive nervousness nearly overnight.

Food Feeds Your Confidence

In addition to the previous well-proven methods for increasing your confidence, it is important to heed the advice of the old adage: "You are what you eat." Although drinking a Monster Energy drink might seem like a good idea right before your speech, you are already significantly altering your biology simply by speaking in public, and it is best to limit the other variables interacting in your ecosystem. During normal daily life, the result of drinking something sugar filled or caffeinated might be positive, but excess sugar or caffeine coupled with stress can often play havoc with the body of the speaker. Therefore, try to limit sugar consumption and caffeine prior to giving a big speech to an audience.

Another variable increasingly relevant to confidence is the recent movement to reduce or eliminate the consumption of wheat for many people. This diet, called gluten-free, has been proven to help a growing segment of people reduce cloudy thinking and excessive nervous ness, as well as many other physical ailments. In addition to wheat, many who show benefits of gluten-free eating also have positives associated with limiting the amount of dairy in their diet. All this can manifest in clearer thinking and fewer nerves during stressful situations.

Figure 18.2.8 Food plays an important role in keeping our body calm and focused under stress.

Source: Antonina Vlasova/Shutterstock.com

Stretch Your Comfort Zone

Your comfort zone is defined by your self-concept, your family culture, your community, national culture, and so on. As long as you are not violating any of the "rules" of any of these belief systems, you are in your comfort zone. Some of these rules are appropriate, but many are simply habits handed down that end up creating a big rut that controls the direction of our lives more than most of us realize. A more general approach to building confidence is to look constantly for opportunities to stretch your comfort zone in every area of life. If you are more comfortable waiting for someone else to speak first, push yourself to speak first as often as possible. Be on the lookout for little ways you can stretch that comfort zone. Push yourself in class. Keep more questions in store. Ask for information. Try dressing differently. Seek leadership roles. Volunteer at the library literacy program. Go to a town council meeting and ask a question. Take voice lessons. Take flying lessons. Go horseback riding. Drive somewhere you have never been. Challenge yourself to be aware and to act by choice, not by habit. Try out for a role in a community theater play.

Figure 18.2.9 Broadening your comfort zone increases your understanding and ability to relate to broader audiences in life.

Source: Olivier Le Moal/Shutterstock.com

Visual Imagery is a Powerful Tool

The next delivery topic is a visual imagery technique specifically for developing confidence in public speaking. Mental rehearsal is another name for visual imagery. This technique is a fascinating tool for changing behavior, and the same procedure presented on the next few pages can be adapted to create behavior change in any area of life. You could even use it to practice remembering more and scoring better on quizzes, or to stop procrastinating and complete paperwork and other preparations early. Be creative and see how many areas you can find to try the three-step method of visual imagery you are now going to learn.

Figure 18.2.10 **Visualizing success plays an important role in achieving our desired outcomes.**

Source: WAYHOME studio/Shutterstock.com

Visualize for Confidence in Public Speaking

Visual imagery for behavior change is a powerful technique. The legendary tennis coach Vic Braden was known for his quote, "Learn to think like a winner—think positive and visualize your strengths." Braden took this idea to the courts as he statistically counted how many first serves his students would get into the service box by just serving the ball without any prior thinking. Then, he coached his students to visualize, in their minds, their serve hit perfectly and going into the service box. After visualizing the serve, the students had a significantly improved percentage of actual serves that would go into the service box.

The subconscious mind does not seem to differentiate between actual physical rehearsal and mental rehearsal (visual imagery) when the mental rehearsal is done with the same concentration and vivid feelings associated with the actual physical rehearsal. The benefits from mental rehearsal done well are many. The rehearsal is completely under the control of the person doing the imagery; therefore, each rehearsal can be a positive, strengthening experience. The time involved is much less than actual practice requires, meaning more practice can be completed. The trouble some spots in an activity can be repeatedly practiced easily. The subconscious mind can build a storehouse of "success" feelings about an activity. These feelings then encourage continued successful performance, just as actual successful physical rehearsal would.

Figure 18.2.11 Athletes often visualize the perfect shot prior to the actual activity for an increased likelihood of success.

Source: nd3000/Shutterstock.com

The visual imagery pattern I recommend for speech students who want to experience more confidence and better speaking skills in front of an audience is a simple three-step pattern. It is suggested that you practice using this pattern (or your own personal version of it) at least three times a day. Each session should be brief (2–5 minutes), but as intensely vivid and "real" as you can create it. Do this brief visual imagery three or more times a day, for two to three weeks or longer, and you will find a tremendous development of skill and confidence as a result. Visual imagery can be done in any place where you can be uninterrupted for a few minutes. The very best schedule is morning, midday, and evening. Detailed instructions for using the visual imagery pattern follow.

A Script for Using Visual Imagery to Develop Confidence in Speaking

Step 1: Systematic Relaxation

Pay particular attention to shoulders, face, and stomach muscles. The purpose of Step 1 is to focus attention away from your outer environment onto your physical body, then relax your body sufficiently to avoid it becoming a distraction later in the process when you focus your attention within yourself. Sit with a centered posture—do not recline. Start with your toes and systematically relax every part of your body up to the very top of your head. Tensing and relaxing is good if, at first, your shoulders or other large muscle groups are very tense.

Step 2: Favorite Peaceful Place

Picture a vivid, sensory-rich scene in nature. You should use this same scene over and over, or, at least, until you change projects. I usually use the beach. Focus on all the sensory details possible: sky, water, waves, sunlight, the sun's warmth, sounds of birds and water, feel of sand underfoot, and so on. See yourself walking along the beach, experiencing the colors, sights, sounds, touches, and freedom of the beach as vividly as you can.

Figure 18.2.12 **Using visual imagery for confidence is a great tool for success.**

Source: Sangoiri/Shutterstock.com

Step 3: Rehearsing Your Desired Behavior

Picture yourself doing the behavior you desire to do just as perfectly as you hope to learn to do it—speaking with confidence and skill. The sequence I recommend is to see yourself sitting at your desk, aware that you are the next speaker. When it is your turn, you rise confidently and walk to the podium. You look confidently at individuals in the audience and, then, begin with a ringing, powerful opening statement. See yourself standing and speaking with real authority and clarity. You do not have to "hear" any actual words. Feel the energy and enthusiasm in your delivery. See people in the audience nodding their heads in agreement with your ideas. Feel your strong desire to communicate the interest and importance of the information you are sharing. See yourself finishing with a strong, dynamic ending statement. Hear the loud, spontaneous applause as your audience acknowledges your excellent speech. Notice how you really enjoy the feeling of having done a good job. Feel this enjoyment. This is a very important ingredient in the visualization—your enjoyment of your success. See yourself now returning to your seat with the same sincere and confident attitude. See yourself sitting with a big smile on your face—very pleased with yourself. Enjoy and strengthen this feeling for a few moments before you open your eyes and are finished with the session.

Confidence is Key

Keep in mind that, if you choose a topic from your own area of interest that you feel is worthwhile, prepare your speech carefully, with a clear purpose and your audience in mind, and regularly practice your delivery beforehand, you will project confidence when delivering your speech. You might feel anxious (or nervous) before and during the speech, but, unless you tell your audience that you are nervous, most likely they won't know.

Figure 18.2.13 **The more we engage in stressful situations, the more we are rewarded with increasing confidence and leadership traits.**

Source*: El Nariz/Shutterstock.com*

For years, I taught a course for business professionals. The course was designed to improve speaking ability, particularly in the area of delivery. Most of the students who took that course were successful executive types with high-level jobs who were highly motivated to improve their ability to communicate effectively. The course met for 3 hours once a week and, at every class meeting, the whole class delivered a speech. After the speeches were delivered, the class discussed the presentations they had just experienced. The students soon discovered that, although some felt nervous while delivering their speeches, this nervousness was not discernible to their audience. If someone said, "Boy, was I nervous," the response would invariably be, "You didn't look nervous." Once it became clear that their nervousness was not apparent to their classmates, the butterflies disappeared.

Another benefit of the course was that delivering a speech at every meeting gave each student important experience in speaking in front of a group. As everyone was in the same boat, the group was highly supportive. The more speeches those students gave, the better they got. There is nothing like success to boost your confidence.

On the positive side, being a bit nervous before giving a speech is an indication that you are "keyed up," which can be a desirable reaction. Have you ever watched a performer pace back and forth before going on stage, or an athlete bending, stretching, or just moving around before competing? They are keyed up and they are letting off a bit of the nervous energy or excitement that is building up for that moment on stage, on the field, in the ring, or wherever they are going to perform. This energy works to their advantage, and it can work to yours, too, when you let it help you deliver an enthusiastic speech.

* * *

Chapter Review

After reading this chapter, you should be able to:

- Define the symptoms of stage fright.
- Understand the steps you can take for greater self-confidence.
- Understand the relation between food and nervous energy.
- State why visual imagery is a strong tool for speech preparation.

Key Terms

- Isometric exercise
- Self-confidence
- Stage fright

Discussion Questions

1. Describe the difference between thoughts that make us confident and those that make us nervous.

2. Describe a moment in life where you did great at something stressful. What came from the experience?

3. Describe the relation between public speaking nerves and nerves we might experience at other critical moments in life. Similar? Different?

Exercises

1. Think of two or three situations beyond public speaking where you could try the visual imagery method. Describe each one, explaining what you would do in each step of the visual imagery technique.

2. Discuss the differences in delivering a speech and taking a paper exam regarding stress, our view of our self, and our confidence.

Source: *sculpies/Shutterstock.com*

Figure 18.5 Audience Behavior

How To Overcome the 10 Most Common Public Speaking

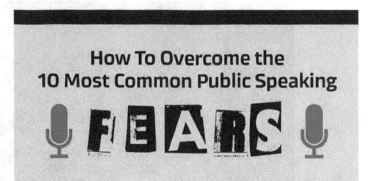

Formally addressing a group of people face-to-face on your own can be daunting. Public Speaking is an art, one of communicating with and effectively persuading your audience. More than 75% of people are anxious about talking in front of others.

This guide aims to reveal our worst fears, explain something of their history, and hopefully arm those fighting fears of speaking in public with some basic tools to overcome them.

What Causes the Fear?

The fear of speaking in public lies in our evolution as social animals. When faced with standing up in front of a group, we break into a sweat because we are afraid of:

⊖ Rejection

☺ Embarrassment

👎 Being Judged

We Fear Ostracism Even More Than Death, Because Not So Long Ago Being Kicked Out of the Group Really Was a Death Sentence.

There are 3 distinct causes of speech anxiety associated with different areas of the brain:

Hindbrain (Old Brain)
activates your survival system against a threat of speaking in public and being rejected by the group. It causes flight or freeze reactions.

Mid Brain
regulates emotions, and it will make you nervous when you're reminded of a previous nerve-wracking experience.

The New Brain (Forebrain)
is the conscious thinking part of your brain. Most of us have patterns of thinking that make us nervous.

Solution:
Accept the nervousness, don't fight it. Get used to the feeling by practicing a lot. You may be able to turn it to your advantage.

Solution:
Put it in perspective. How bad is speaking in public in comparison to losing a finger?

Solution:
Explore your patterns, what demands you have ("I must be interesting"). Analyse the truth and usefulness of these demands, and try to convert them into realistic goals.

"You've got to be able to communicate in life. It's enormously important. If you can't communicate and talk to other people and get across your ideas, you're giving up your potential." — Warren Buffet, the most successful investor of the 20th century

How to Overcome the 10 Most Common Public Speaking Fears

Fear	Cause	Step
Shaky Voice	"Fight or flight" response and anxiety.	**1** Focus on deepening and evening out your breath a few minutes before the speech. Being completely present will calm you down and improve confidence.
Speaking Too Fast/Too Slow	Too much content and/or lack of practice.	**2** Find your own unique rhythm by practicing in front of a mirror or camera in a way that meets your audience's need.
Self Doubt	Ego attack.	**3** Focus on serving the audience and giving them information. See the inner doubt as an opportunity to push your limits.
Brain Freeze	High stress interfering with brain activity.	**4** Practice as many times as it takes. Make the content "brain friendly": interesting approaches to explaining concepts and using visuals make your words memorable not just for you, but also your audience.
Technical Problems	Something we can't control.	**5** Always have a backup plan. Arrive early and test the equipment. In case of trouble, relax and laugh it off. Be prepared to continue without your visuals or Internet connection.
Bodily Issues	Excessive sweating, red face, body shaking caused by stress and anxiety.	**6** Observe and identify the biggest issue. Wear appropriate clothes. Practice responding to questions or situations that trigger the bodily reaction.
Cold Audience	Needs of the audience are not met properly.	**7** Prepare a speech that puts the audience first with interesting, memorable and useful content. Outline several questions to engage people into a discussion.
Confused Audience	You don't know the audience well enough.	**8** Run your presentation by someone close to the audience profile, share ideas and content to get valuable insights about how to improve it. While giving the speech make sure your audience is following, ask them directly, and shift the content appropriately.
Tough Questions	Lack of preparation. Projection of your worst fears onto the person asking the question.	**9** Prepare as much you can to answer any possible question out loud. Clarify what has been asked. If necessary, admit you are not sure, or engage the audience in the discussion.
Bad Reaction	Nasty comments and sour faces.	**10** Be open and try to understand the person making a comment, calmly talk it through, ask the audience for more input. Make contact with the sour face person in a friendly way, wonder what experience triggered such a reaction.

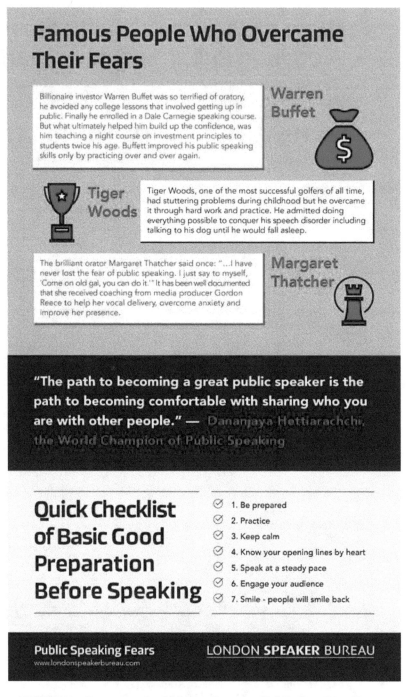

Figure 18.6 How to Overcome the 10 Most Common Public Speaking Fears

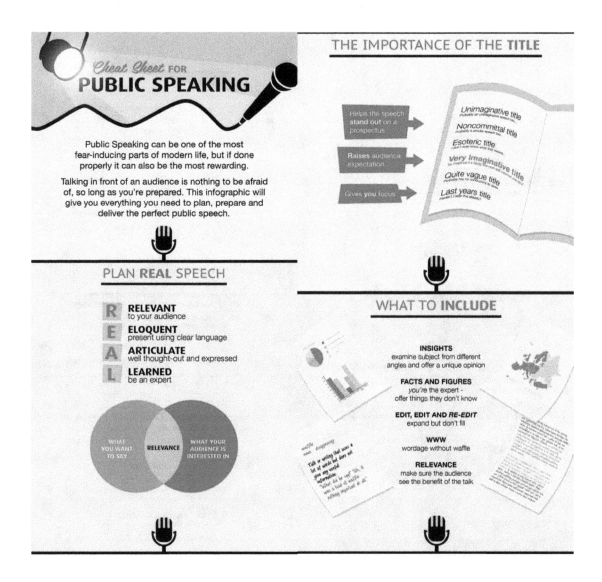

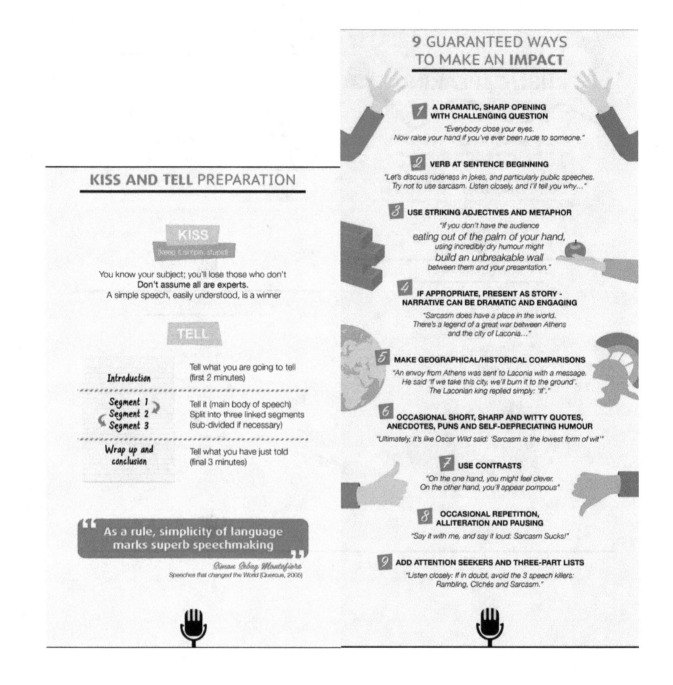

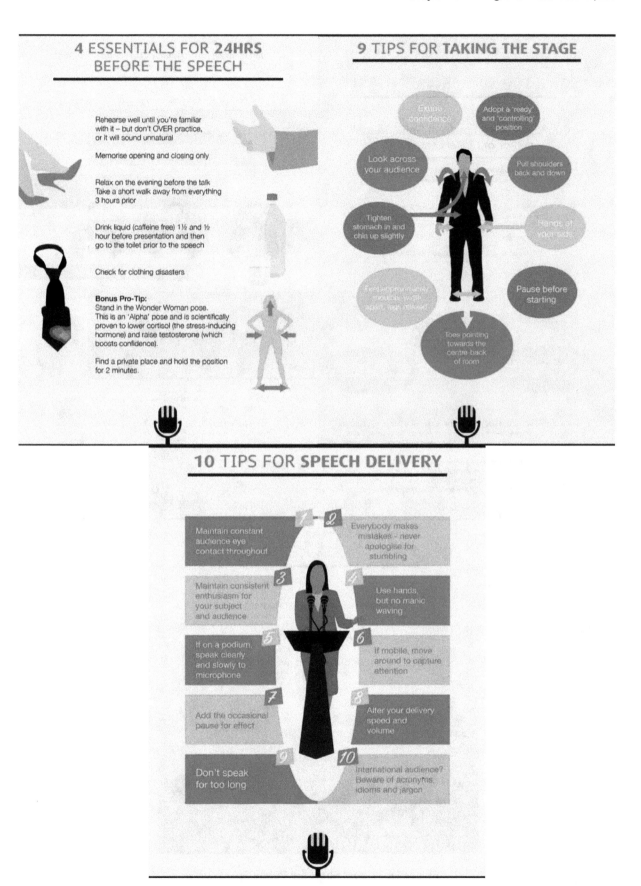

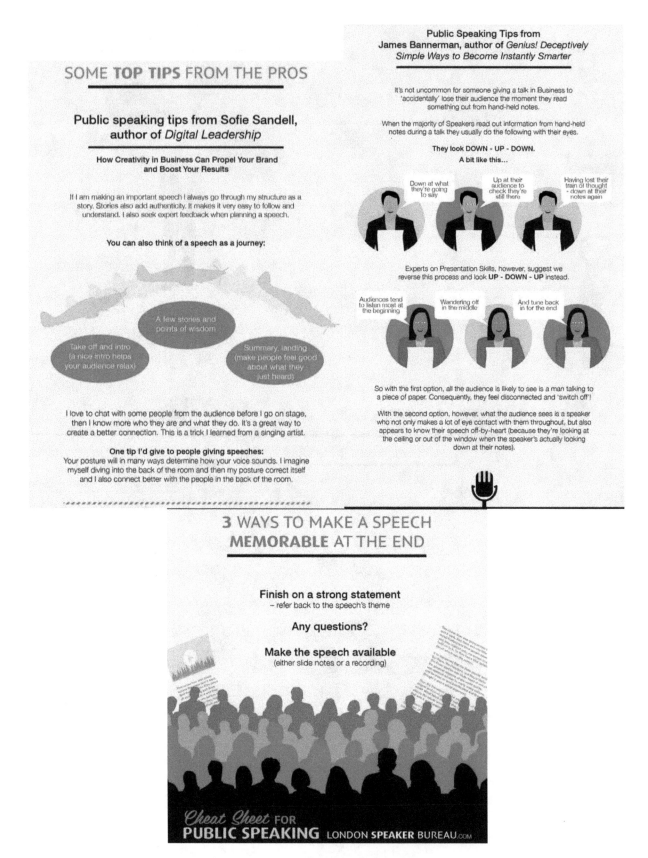

Figure 18.7 Cheat Sheet for Public Speaking.

Applying This Skill: Oral Presentation Review

After presenting and watching other teams present, reflect on how you did. Part of improving is identifying positive and negative aspects of our performance so we can repeat or change the behavior next time.

As a team, answer the following questions. Be prepared to share your answers with the class.

1. What do you think your team did well during the presentation? Why? What would you improve? How?

2. Think of the other team presentations. Which ones do you remember? Why?

3. Reflect on the presentations as a whole. Comment on good and bad aspects of the following: introductions, transitions, and conclusions; delivery, voice (tone, volume, inflection), body language, use of notes, and facing the audience; and visuals.

Reference

Duarte, Nancy. Slide ology. 2008; O'Reilly Media.

Credits

Fig. 1.1: Source: http://college.usatoday.com/2015/12/29/univ-of-s-d-on-billboard-typo-it-happens/.

Diane Huth, "Master the Secrets of Networking," *Brand You! To Land Your Dream Job: A Step-by-Step Guide To Find a Great Job, Get Hired and Jumpstart Your Career*, pp. 57-60. Copyright © 2017 by ISLA Publishing Group. Reprinted with permission.

Pamela Eyring, "Mind Your Business Manners," *Infoline*, vol. 25, no. 0811, pp. 1-12, 14. Copyright © 2008 by Association for Talent Development (ATD). Reprinted with permission.

Carol Fleming, "ARE: Anchor, Reveal, Encourage," *The Serious Business of Small Talk*, pp. 43-47. Copyright © 2018 by Berrett-Koehler Publishers. Reprinted with permission.

Fig. 2.1: "The Power of First Impressions," https://visual.ly/community/Infographics/other/power-first-impressions. Copyright © by Rockcontent.

Lynn Gaertner-Johnson, "Tips on Giving Constructive--Not Destructive--Feedback," *Complete Curriculum*. Copyright © 2013 by Syntax Training.

Jack E. Appleman, "Edit, Rewrite, and Refine," *10 Steps to Successful Business Writing*, pp. 123-128. Copyright © 2008 by Association for Talent Development (ATD). Reprinted with permission.

Mignon Fogarty, "The $10 Million Comma," QuickAndDirtyTips.com. Copyright © 2017 by Macmillan Holdings LLC. Reprinted with permission.

Kate Seamons, "How a Missing 'S' Killed a 134-Year-Old Company," *Newser*. Copyright © 2015 by Newser, LLC.

Janet Mizrahi, "Fundamentals of Professional Writing," *Writing for the Workplace: Business Communication for Professionals*, pp. 3-18. Copyright © 2015 by Business Expert Press. Reprinted with permission.

Josh Bernoff, "Bad Writing Costs Businesses Billions," *The Daily Beast*. Copyright © 2016 by Trans Lifeline.

Michael Edmondson, "Soft Skills," *Major in Happiness: Debunking the College Major Fallacies*, pp. 123-125. Copyright © 2015 by Business Expert Press. Reprinted with permission.

Elizabeth Dickinson, "Using Active Listening," *The Concise Coaching Handbook: How to Coach Yourself and Others to Get Business Results*, pp. 73-79. Copyright © 2018 by Business Expert Press. Reprinted with permission.

Beth Bratkovic, "Managing Conflict," *Government Finance Revie*, vol. 26, no. 3, pp. 51-53. Copyright © 2010 by Government Finance Officers Association. Reprinted with permission. Provided by ProQuest LLC. All rights reserved.

Golnaz Sadri, "Improving Emotional Intelligence," *Industrial Management*, vol. 55, no. 1, pp. 18-22. Copyright © 2013 by Institute of Industrial and Systems Engineers. Reprinted with permission. Provided by ProQuest LLC. All rights reserved.

Fig. 6.1: Emily Goenner, "5 Steps of Ethical Decision Making Progress." Copyright © 2022 by Venngage Inc. Reprinted with permission.

Paul Falcone, "The Real-World Impact of Workplace Ethics," shrm.org. Copyright © 2022 by SHRM (Society for Human Resource Management). Reprinted with permission.

David C. Thomas and Kerr C. Inkson, "Conclusion: The Essentials of Cultural Intelligence," *Cultural Intelligence: Surviving and Thriving in the Global Village*, pp. 159-163. Copyright © 2017 by Berrett-Koehler Publishers. Reprinted with permission.

Fig. 6.2: CDC.gov, "Disability Impacts all of us," https://www.cdc.gov/ncbddd/disabilityandhealth/infographic-disability-impacts-all.html, Centers for Disease Control and Prevention.

Fig. 6.3: TollFreeForwarding.com, "Body Language Around the World." Copyright © by TollFreeForwarding.com.

Fig. II.1b: Source: https://cdn.pixabay.com/photo/2013/07/13/11/36/documents-158461__340.png.

Everett Chasen and Bob Putnam, "Write Effective Letters and Memorandums," *The Manager's Communication Toolbox*, pp. 24-30. Copyright © 2012 by Association for Talent Development (ATD). Reprinted with permission.

Janet Mizrahi, "Basics of Document Design," *Writing for the Workplace: Business Communication for Professionals*, pp. 19-23, 141. Copyright © 2015 by Business Expert Press. Reprinted with permission.

Jack E. Appleman, "Master Emails and Electronic Communication," *10 Steps to Successful Business Writing*, pp. 139-156, 213-214. Copyright © 2018 by Association for Talent Development (ATD). Reprinted with permission.

Janet Mizrahi, "Persuasive and Bad News Messages," *Writing for the Workplace: Business Communication for Professionals*, pp. 52-54, 141, 143-144. Copyright © 2015 by Business Expert Press. Reprinted with permission.

Debbie DuFrene and Carol Lehman, "Productive Virtual Team Meetings," *Managing Virtual Teams*, pp. 49-60, 65, 67-71. Copyright © 2015 by Business Expert Press. Reprinted with permission.

Jack Appleman, "Applying Writing Skills to Social Media Copy," *10 Steps to Successful Business Writing*, pp. 157-163, 213-214. Copyright © 2018 by Association for Talent Development (ATD). Reprinted with permission.

Fig. 11.1a: Copyright © 2015 Depositphotos/HonzaHruby.

Fig. 11.1b: Copyright © 2014 Depositphotos/Rawpixel.

Fig. 11.3: Nielsen, "F-Shaped Reading Pattern" Copyright © 2006 by Nielsen.

Fig. 11.8: https://uxmag.com/articles/content-as-conversation. Copyright © by UX Magazine.

Fig. 11.11: Website screenshot: © DBA Products.

Fig. 11.12: Source: https://bench.li/images/5845.

Fig. 12.1b: Source: https://www.iconsdb.com/black-icons/mind-map-icon.html.

Samantha White, "Write a LinkedIn Profile that Draws in Recruiters," *Journal of Accountancy*, vol. 223, no. 2, pp. 20-21. Copyright © 2017 by ProQuest LLC. Reprinted with permission.